Anglo-Catholic

SMARROR.
1991

From Canon Slade
School
Sixth Formers'
Conference.

Easter 1991.

Anglo-Catholicism
A study in religious ambiguity

W. S. F. Pickering

First published in 1989 by Routledge
11 New Fetter Lane, London EC4P 4EE
and 29 West 35th Street, New York, NY 10001

This edition published in Great Britain 1991
by SPCK, Holy Trinity Church, Marylebone Road,
London NW1 4DU

British Library Cataloguing in Publication Data

Pickering, W. S. F. (William Stuart Frederick),
   1922–
   Anglo-Catholicism.
   1. Church of England. Anglo-Catholicism
   I. Title
   283′.42

ISBN 0 281 04517 8

Printed and bound in Great Britain by
Biddles Ltd, Guildford and King's Lynn

To the memory of my mother, Ruby Emily Pickering (1900–86), whose strong, simple Christian faith so much influenced me as a child.

Contents

Contents

Contents

Contents

Preface

For some people writing a book is the source of much pleasure. They are enthusiastic to proclaim a message, reveal a discovery, create profound characters, unearth an exciting plot. The finished work gives satisfaction in having created something worth while which can be made widely known. For me this book has not had that effect. Before undertaking the task I felt an initial enthusiasm roused by trying to write an objective assessment of Anglo-Catholicism. I thought there would be satisfaction in expounding the achievements of the movement and in seeing the interrelation of its ideas. As I began to undertake the research, to recall old times, and to evolve a theoretical framework, potential gladness began to fall away and turned into heaviness. I had to accept the facts, see what they added up to, and seek an explanation. But why should the task have turned out to be so displeasing when other books I have written have given me gratification?

The short answer is that when I was a young boy I was in part religiously nurtured in Anglo-Catholicism and visited many of the churches influenced by the movement in and around London. My religious convictions were unquestionably strengthened, as, through friends and reading books, I became more and more attracted to ritualistic services which were so much more exciting and absorbing than those of the parish church which I attended from time to time with my parents. I was proud to be a server, to talk to Anglo-Catholic priests, and to boast of my knowledge of the peculiar niceties of ritual. This early affectionate attitude towards Anglo-Catholicism has never left me, but, during the Second World War and subsequently at a theological college, I found myself distanced from my early love. And so after over forty years of absence I was back in it once more. But with a difference. The emotional piety was replaced by the sharp tools of sociology. It is this which has proved to be so painful. As is so often the case, however, with pain there is purification. The writing of this book may have been one such occasion. Critical analysis inevitably leads to a search for basic positions and the raising of fundamental issues. These are evident in the introduction and the concluding chapters and I trust that in them my own position with regard to Anglo-Catholicism is plain for all to see.

Preface to the SPCK Edition

This book first appeared in May 1989. Nothing has occurred, in the way of criticisms or events, which has vitiated any of its observations or generalizations. Indeed, the conclusions with regard to the present situation have been strengthened by the continuing turmoil within Anglo-Catholicism and the Church of England as a whole.

While Anglo-Catholicism in its various forms and shades continues to appeal to many people, myself included, its splintered and bewildered position becomes increasingly obvious. The seemingly petty splintering, representing a totally un-Catholic sectarian ideal, and centred on clerical in-fighting, has been accelerated in the past year by the emergence of a movement within a movement. 'Affirming Catholicism' is led by two prominent clerics, Richard Holloway, bishop of Edinburgh, and Rowan Williams, the Lady Margaret Professor of Divinity in the University of Oxford. It wishes to be liberated from much of the traditional Anglo-Catholic position epitomised by the Church Union. Here is an attempt to rally the more liberal, and perhaps the more intellectual, Anglo-Catholics who, basically, do not want to leave the Church of England through the exit offered by the ordination of women to the priesthood. 'Affirming Catholicism' supports such ordinations. But beyond accepting what is virtually a heresy in the eyes of many, the new movement, admittedly still in its early days, has not spelt out in detail what it wants to affirm.

The issue of the ordination of women, involving, as it now does, blatant power struggles with all their political debasement and recriminations in the General Synod, was not considered in detail in this book – for the simple reason that the book is primarily a sociological study and not one committed to a theological point of view. The priesting of women, which extremists argue would negate the Catholic structure of the Church of England, has become the litmus test of their spiritual integrity. The issue may well bring about the *coup de grâce* to Anglo-Catholicism as we have defined it. We have suggested that there is a much larger issue at stake. This is to define categorically and with as little ambiguity as possible what is meant by the Catholic nature of the Church of England and how it manifests itself in church order and liturgy. The litmus test of women's ordination to the priesthood is clearly of secondary importance, for it is a test that Anglo-Catholics themselves have determined, and is not one agreed on by 'Catholics at large'. The old question remains: Who is a Catholic? Is the answer to be found in a self-definition or a local definition? What authoritative body can provide the answer? In *whose* eyes is the Church of England Catholic? Such questions are acute for churches of the Anglican Communion. It is not so for bodies such as the Old Catholics or the Polish National Catholics which claim to be Catholic, at least by the consensus of those churches themselves. To call oneself a Catholic in a social group which does not acknowledge its Catholic coherence and is not based on an affirmation of consensus is to face serious problems of definition.

Nor have Anglo-Catholics addressed themselves to the crucial issue of deciding, amongst themselves, at least, the means by which legitimate changes can be made in matters of faith, morals and church order. This is a problem for all established religious bodies. But it is particularly acute for Anglo-Catholics since they owe allegiance to no body whose authority they accept. For the extreme-minded perhaps the only body to be recognised is the Roman Catholic Church, of which they are not members. The only legitimate candidate would be the General Synod of the Church of England, together with its canon law. To the decisions of this body in weighty matters they will not commit themselves. Nor would they be prepared to abide by the voice of their bishops, individually or collectively, without some let-out proviso.

In the meantime discontented Anglo-Catholics continue to take the road to Rome, because, I would argue, they are unable to accept and contain the ambiguities of their position. In the new wave of conversions, both unknown parish priests and more prominent leaders, such as the principal of the theological college of the Community of the Resurrection, are to be found. Anglo-Catholicism can ill afford such serious losses.

And such losses are all the more crucial as the forces of secularization, affecting nearly all churches, continue to hit Anglo-Catholicism particularly hard. One statistic much quoted is that in the predominantly Anglo-Catholic diocese of London church membership according to electoral rolls in 1990 was 47,000, which represents 1.5 per cent of the population of the diocese (*The Times*, 11.8.90). Further, the number of young men training as *bona fide* Anglo-Catholic priests is relatively small.

Anglo-Catholicism as a whole remains without strong or charismatic leadership. A likely candidate was Graham Leonard, bishop of London, but at retiring age he is not to the fore and after a brief spell of prominence is no longer trusted by the rank and file. While it is true that the movement has seldom had outstanding leaders, there have always been a number of very competent clergy associated with it – men with organizing ability. That there are clergy today of such ability is evident in the tussles of the General Synod and in the Cost of Conscience movement, which has rallied some Anglo-Catholics in trying to decide what path they should follow if women's ordination were accepted by the Synod. Some movements do not have and do not need dynamic leaders. But such movements are as a rule unified in terms of goals and means of achieving the goals. Anglo-Catholicism today is precisely the opposite and desperately needs someone who can pull it together if it is to persist.

But over and above these social and practical issues, one relating to the subject of the book itself has been raised by critics. Aspects of a more liberal, Prayer-Book Catholicism did not receive enough attention, said some. In defence, it should be pointed out that difficult problems confront a sociologist in defining objectively a movement such as Anglo-Catholicism which has no clear boundaries. Having shown the problems, it was suggested that what was meant by Anglo-Catholicism was clearly seen in practice in the inter-war period in the great Anglo-Catholic congresses (see chapter 1). This is no occasion to rehearse or amplify the arguments. It is true that in general the focus has been on the more extreme position because it revealed the ambiguities of the movement and it was extremism which brought such hostile criticism against Anglo-Catholicism as a whole. Furthermore, as is well known, there are analytical and didactical advantages in examining extreme or 'pure' models.

Finally, as one reviewer rightly observed, the way that Anglo-Catholicism has been sociologically analysed in terms of its inherent ambiguities, is also applicable to the larger body of which it is a part – the Church of England and its sister churches around the world. Different factors are of course at work, but many of the issues raised in this study can be directly extended to a church which in a general way stands between Roman Catholicism and traditional Protestant churches – a point hinted at in the introductory remarks.

W. S. F. P.
January 1990

Acknowledgements

I wish to thank those who have read all or parts of the manuscript and who have offered comments and criticisms. I must take the consequences of not having accepted every piece of advice I was offered. In particular I should like to mention F. W. Dillistone, Peter Dunleavy, Donald Gray, Mark Hodge, and Randolph Wise. I also appreciate the many comments which have been made about some of the chapters of the book which have been given as seminar papers in various universities.

Of those whose assistance was more demanding in the matter of time, I should thank the typists of the manuscript, Mies Rule and my wife, Carol. Trite phrases apart, my wife has been a constant source of encouragement and of helpful criticism. Without her vigilance and prompting this book would never have come to fruition.

Introduction

What is written in the pages ahead is a sociological exploration of Anglo-Catholicism. But it is not sociological in the popular sense of concentrating entirely on the contemporary situation through the use of surveys or face-to-face interviews. Such methods and techniques frequently employed by sociologists have considerable merit. They have not, however, been adopted here. The reason is simply that resources necessary to utilize them in terms of time, money, and manpower have not been available. It is hoped that in the future researchers and others will have opportunities to use such methods to examine Anglo-Catholicism.

In this book another sociological method has been employed, in which historical data have been obtained from books, newspapers, and other records. In fact there was little alternative but to adopt such a method, which is at least relatively manageable by someone working alone. The book is, thus, not only a sociological study, it also reveals something of the past in order to try to understand the present.

But immediately a paradox emerges. There is a dearth of historical studies of Anglo-Catholicism. It is quite remarkable that no definitive book has ever been written on the subject: as John Kent says, nothing serious has been published for the period after 1845 – the year of Newman's conversion to Roman Catholicism (Kent 1987:90). It is remarkable because the movement has exerted no mean influence, not only on the Church of England but also on churches separated from it. Despite deep-seated controversies, court cases, mob violence, reprimands and hostility from bishops, Anglo-Catholic clergy have brought about radical changes in the ethos of worship in parish churches from say the 1870s onwards. W. N. Yates has written: 'Anglo-Catholicism was a subject that produced violent public reaction, both for and against, even to the extent of being a major issue in some parliamentary constituencies at election time . . . in setting up a Royal Commission on Ecclesiastical

1

Discipline' (Yates 1983:122). No movement within the Church of England has so changed its overall ethos. A virtual metamorphosis it certainly was but documentation of it has remained extremely limited. True, there have been articles and chapters in books on English church history but none of them of sufficient scope and thoroughness to make further work superfluous. Of course, on the Oxford movement, which gave birth to Anglo-Catholicism, there has been a plethora of historical studies, although most of them have centred upon the great personalities of the movement, on the triumvirate of Keble, Newman, and Pusey. And there have also been studies of the less well known figures, such as H. Froude, W. G. Ward, F. W. Faber, J. Neale, and so on. Research on such people never seems to end. But when the movement becomes diffused and extended, and when it begins to grow at the grass roots, the interest of academics appears to wane. And much of the published material about Anglo-Catholicism in later years, apart from theological apologetics, has centred on the lives of its heroes. In this case they have not been great national figures but parish priests working valiantly, one is encouraged to believe, in the slums of London and other industrial cities. Both movements have this much in common: what is known about them comes not from their history in general but from a knowledge of the lives of their leaders.

This short study of Anglo-Catholicism can make no claim to meet the need for a comprehensive book on the development of Anglo-Catholicism written by a professional historian. And a professional historian the present writer certainly is not. Nevertheless, as was mentioned earlier on, it is necessary to turn to historical sources in order to look at Anglo-Catholicism in a sociological mode and one hopes that the way such material is used will not go against the canons of historical scholarship.

But where is the focal point to be? Today, the movement is a shadow of its former self. There is not only great merit in studying but almost a necessity to study Anglo-Catholicism at its peak, that is, roughly in the period between the wars. It is precisely here that one sees its ideals, its practices, and its influence most clearly exhibited.

In the light of the limitations set by the study it has been possible to do little more than raise questions and suggest hypotheses. It is hoped that, where sufficient material has not been available to support a hypothesis, other scholars will find evidence to substantiate or to negate the ideas suggested, as we hinted above. Let it never be forgotten that to pose questions is the beginning of all intellectual enquiry, indeed the beginning of science itself.

Sociologists inevitably asks questions which cannot always be answered, or at least cannot be answered immediately without a great deal of research. They feel impelled, however, to ask questions which they hope will lead to generalizations or which will be helpful in the understanding of the phenomenon which confronts them. 'Why' questions are very much their stock-in-trade which they try to answer by relating the phenomenon to other types of social phenomena. This, sociologists like to think, differentiates them in at least one way from historians.

It is not surprising, therefore, that there is little here which focuses on personalities – on famous priests or little heard of eccentrics who were particularly rife in the movement. Rather, the concern is for ideas, policies, practices, rituals, modes of propagation, and so forth. Of course, quotations from clergy and references to them will be made in abundance and much will be said about churches which were the bastions of Anglo-Catholic ritual and influence. Hagiography is important, as are particular shrines and 'temples' for Anglo-Catholicism. But references to people and places are by way of illustration. Those who delight in a biographical approach to the movement will have to turn elsewhere and their attention is drawn to items which appear in the bibliography.

No one should pretend that the task of analysis or explanation is approached without any presuppositions or with a completely open mind. Inevitably assumptions have to be made at the outset and these may be sufficiently coherent to form some kind of framework or theoretical basis. What they are in this study of Anglo-Catholicism, a religious phenomenon of much complexity, we must now declare.

As conventionally defined, a religion spans two orders of reality: one relates to the here-and-now; the other is seen to be totally removed from it, for it stands far outside it. This other order of reality – this other world – is often referred to as the divine, the transcendental, for in it are located God, gods, spirits, mysterious and unknown forces. They are in an order of existence which is seen to stand over against the mundane, the ordinary, the worldly, the everyday. The two orders of reality are extended in dichotomous terms to body/soul, flesh/spirit, earth/heaven, man/God, death/life, profane/sacred, time/timelessness, to give but a few examples. Such dichotomies are found in all religions. No religion is free from them. Without them, religion as such would disappear.

Ontologically the existence of two totally opposite ultimate

3

principles does not in itself create a mental problem. The dualism raises serious intellectual questions when the two principles or orders of reality are related one to the other and influence each other, and when their relationship may imply a hierarchy, some ultimate principle. But left entirely by themselves, as it were, they are not necessarily intellectually disturbing. However, it must also be said that if they were entirely static, entirely isolated, then religion itself would be static. But religion implies action. Some movement is necessary for spiritual force, grace, power, spiritual liberation, and eternal life to occur. It occurs in communication between the two realities and, if there is no communication, there is no religion. Thus, interconnection between the two is necessary in order to release the spiritual energy which is generally made available to the believer, the practitioner, or the group.

It is precisely here that the problem enters. When religion is made to 'work' – to be religion in fact – the two opposite poles in coming together are forced to intermingle (see Durkheim's position in Pickering 1984:147ff.). In this interaction ambiguity inevitably emerges. It emerges because the human mind finds it difficult to grasp how two opposites can intermingle and not lose their identity or be in some way compromised. The result is neither one thing nor the other. How can two 'others' meet, release energy, and not lose their unique and separate characteristics? The nature of one or both is inevitably partially or totally negated.

The position taken here is that all religions contain elements of ambiguity, either in statements of ambiguity or in actions which contain ambiguity. From them no religion is free. And no religion is free from them because no religion can be totally rational, totally obvious, totally natural, totally 'scientific'. Every religion contains ambiguities which logicians find impossible to accept and which are not in keeping with the precise mathematical language which scientists strive after, even though they may not always achieve it.

Controversial questions immediately arise out of stressing, albeit briefly, these characteristics of religion, which are of crucial importance when one tries to understand it. The first, and perhaps most important, is whether the word ambiguity is the correct one to describe what has been singled out and the second is whether such an analysis depends on a particular definition of religion.

By ambiguity is meant that 'which is open to more than one interpretation; equivocal' (*Shorter Oxford English Dictionary*).

Ambiguity occurs in a statement or around an object where the meaning is not clear, but also where the individual components of the statement or object are clear in themselves, but are in some measure contradictory when related. Thus, the components are unequivocal but what leads to ambiguity is that they are both equally appropriate to the statement or object. That which is ambiguous has two or more significations, either of which can be accepted (see 'equivocal' in the *SOED*).

Some might argue that a better word for what is being described would be paradox. A paradox is that which is contradictory or absurd, and may refer to any statement or object which contains elements of conflict or elements which seem totally opposed to one another. In common parlance ambiguity and paradox are very near to one another but ambiguity is preferred to paradox in this case since paradox implies absurdity whereas ambiguity, at least initially, does not. Further, a paradox immediately conjures up the unlikelihood of resolution, but this is not necessarily so for ambiguity where in practical terms some sort of compromise may be reached. The compromise, for example, may be obtained in an interpretation of the ambiguity when one of the components is accepted in all its fullness and the other played down or even disregarded. Perhaps the point of difference can be pressed too far but paradox suggests a hiddenness – something which is not immediately clear. Ambiguity is a more neutral term without the emotional accompaniment which is often associated with paradox. Again, paradox often implies a conflict between two opposing elements; in ambiguity there may not necessarily be such a reaction between the two elements although they stand over against one another. Further, it might be argued that truth is by nature paradoxical but those who take such an approach would never say that truth is by nature ambiguous. Ambiguity, therefore, stands for something slightly different from paradox, something of 'a lower order' of thinking, as it were.

The word dialectic might be put forward as another candidate. But on account of the subject matter dealt with here it is to be rejected by reason of its Hegelian implications. Dialectic stands for a process in which two opposing elements are, or have to be, resolved in the formation of a synthesis. Ambiguity does not involve the notion of automatic resolution, as in the idea of the emergence of a third force or entity. In ambiguity there may or there may not be an acceptable outcome. Sometimes ambiguity has to be accepted in all its starkness.

Ambiguity is the best word for the purpose on hand because it is applicable not only to propositions of belief but to social action as well, and it is precisely the latter which is as relevant to religion as belief statements. Indeed, what is of concern is not so much statements which are to be philosophically analysed as to their precise meaning but social actions and entities which might be described as ambiguous. Ambiguous situations, rather than paradoxical ones, exist where components of actions are at variance with one another or where actions would appear to contradict beliefs. In strengthening the selection of the concept of ambiguity, it should be mentioned that symbols, which are employed so much in religion, are generally referred to as being ambiguous rather than paradoxical. Indeed, if a symbol ceases to present ambiguous possibilities, it becomes a sign, for example, a road sign. Ambiguity must never exist in such a form of communication.

What has been put forward might be seen to apply only to certain kinds of religions or to religion defined in a specific way. It is true that initially when calling to mind inherent ambiguities in religion, a fairly conventional definition of religion is assumed. So viewed, a religion is a system of beliefs and practices centred on a god, spirit, or some transcendental being or force. However, a definition more in keeping with the thought of the French sociologist, Emile Durkheim (1858–1917), would be just as applicable. He defined religion in terms of the sacred and wrote:

> A religion is a unified system of beliefs and practices relative to
> sacred things, that is to say things set apart and forbidden,
> beliefs and practices which unite into one single moral
> community, called a church, for those who adhere to them.
> (quoted in Pickering 1984:178)

Durkheim contrasted the sacred with the profane, the profane being that which threatens to denigrate or annihilate the sacred. Such a dichotomy, held to be at the heart of religion, is readily extendable to other dichotomies such as body/soul and spiritual/temporal (Pickering 1984:120). As we have already suggested, where dichotomies exist ambiguity nearly always arises in the attempt to resolve them. So, whether the substantive component in a definition of religion is a transcendental being or a wider, impersonal notion of the sacred, the characteristic of ambiguity in religion remains.

An extension of Durkheim's definition focuses on beliefs and practices which an individual or society sees to be of the highest order – what, in the long run, is of greatest importance to living. As with Durkheim's definition, this allows for the inclusion of non-traditional religions and non-institutional attitudes of a religious kind. Immediately there come to mind such phenomena as humanism, civil or national religion, communism, and common religion. This wider approach is consonant with Max Weber's concept of religion as man's search for ultimate meaning in an ultimately meaningless universe. Such an approach does not logically exclude the characteristic of ambiguity. For Weber the attempt to find meaning where no meaning is apparent inevitably leads to irrationality and, by extension, to ambiguity. Neither humanism nor nationalism is completely free from ambiguity. But one can go further. Indeed, as soon as a contrast is made between the ideal and the real in terms of human behaviour, the same issue of ambiguity arises. Man creates ideals which are never realizable. He therefore has to find some reason why the ideal is beyond his grasp.

So ambiguity is not confined to a particular religion or type of religion, nor are ethical systems free from it. It applies to them all. But does it apply in the same way and to the same degree? Before an attempt to answer this question, it might be helpful to offer more examples of ambiguity. To do so we look at a traditional religion, Christianity, not least because Anglo-Catholicism stands within that tradition.

First we turn to ambiguities in religious texts and beliefs. Not only in the Old Testament but also, and particularly, in the New, paradoxes and ambiguities abound. Take, for example, such texts as: 'Whoever loses his life for my sake shall find it' (Matt. 16:25), or 'So the last will be first, and the first last' (Matt. 20:16). Again, 'Therefore let anyone who thinks that he stands take heed lest he fall' (1 Cor. 10:12) (How can anyone live in perpetual uncertainty? A person has to be sure of something.) Probably no doctrine or religious idea has aroused more controversy than that relating to the Kingdom of God. Christ's teachings suggest that the Kingdom has already been brought into existence: yet it is to come. It exists but it has to be brought into existence. It is similar to the ambiguity surrounding predestination. Certain people are saved and predestined to eternal life yet preaching has to go on to the saved and to the unsaved alike. If one contrasts sets of ideas within the New Testament, not surprisingly there is much ambiguity. Man is saved by faith in Christ: yet each is to work out his own salvation. Faith is a gift of God: yet Christians are urged to have faith. And what of the observation based on New Testament teaching that Christians have to be in the world and yet not of it? The notion of a miracle is also riddled with ambiguity. God intervenes over and above natural laws, thus contradicting the general procedures of working in the world he has created. Is He subject to so-called natural laws, or not? The resurrection of Christ is indeed a miracle, involving the denial of the ordinary and the natural by a peculiar resolution of the meeting of categories which initially stand opposed to one another. It is little wonder that today Bishop David Jenkins of Durham wants to get round some of the problems of the resurrection in an attempt to make it more 'rational' and to overcome ambiguity by denying the factual truth of the bodily resurrection of Jesus Christ.

Within traditional Christianity there is the allied problem surrounding the birth and person of Christ. To be born of a virgin seems absurd, since if a virgin bears a child the normal biological processes are transcended. And Christ as a person is seen to be ambiguous in himself for he is both God and man, thus containing within one human life two ultimate principles. Is he man or God? Again, for many believers the eucharist is thought of as being akin to issues surrounding the person of Christ, in so far as in the celebration of the mass there is both real bread and wine, and the presence of Christ himself. The two coexist in an incomprehensible and ambiguous way in the liturgy itself or in the Elements. To some this is best left as an insoluble mystery. To others the problem is dealt with by positing the doctrine of transubstantiation, itself not without ambiguities. To others again, the problem may not be so acute since they do not believe that Christ is specially present in the Elements and the whole act is for them symbolic and nothing more. But let it not be forgotten, as we have said, that symbols themselves are ambiguous modes of communication.

These few examples of ambiguity which stand at the heart of Christian faith and practice have been taken at random. The number could be multiplied several times over but to no point for the present argument.

Another issue has to be considered. If all religions or religious systems are incapable of being logically coherent, are some more ambiguous than others? The answer must surely be both yes and no – an ambiguous answer in itself! The quantification of ambiguity is impossible. How does one measure ambiguities? To assume that within a system they can be added up and given some kind of overall total is absurd. All religious systems are different and some cover wider areas of social and personal life than others. Yet, in the eyes of many, certain religions are more ambiguous than other religions. Compared with the great religions of the world, those labelled primitive are precisely that. Why? Because the major religions, Christianity, Islam, Hinduism, and so on, have over the centuries been more systematic and re-flective than most primitive religions. They have had theologians who have attempted to produce coherent doctrinal systems. Thus, it might be said that at a purely doctrinal level traditional religions are more 'rational' than those of preliterate peoples. They have a distinctive philosophical basis and appeal to the thinking mind. On the whole, they are less given to fetishism and to superstition and magic. Modern anthropologists might disagree strongly and maintain that both traditional and primitive religions are just as coherent and rational as the great religions of the world; or, at least, that they are no more ambiguous or irrational. Everything turns on the nature of rationality and whether it is something essentially western. This much debated subject is too large to be considered here.

But, against the idea that all religions are much the same in the matter of ambiguity, it might be argued that some religions can deal more coherently with certain human predicaments than others. Suffering is the most obvious issue. Nearly all religions claim to deal with suffering which may affect an individual or groups of individuals. There are those who would postulate that Hinduism, given its basic doctrines associated with karma, has a logic about it that is not found in the religions of Judaism, Christianity, and Islam. Indeed, the problem of suffering is acute in such religions. In Christianity, in particular, human suffering is incomprehensible in the face of the doctrine of an all-powerful creator God, who is at the same time the essence of goodness and love. Why should man suffer the way he does, given the fact that he is created by God out of an act of love? Why should man suffer physical and mental agonies, often to an excruciating degree? This problem, which is at the heart of theodicy, is intellectually without resolution. It can be personally resolved by devotional means, by the individual allying his sufferings with the sufferings of Christ (see Pickering 1980).

Since our interests are within Christianity, or more specifically within one small section of it, can it be said with any justification that one particular form of Christianity is more or less ambiguous than another? Max Weber made the point that Protestantism, especially strict forms of Calvinism and the Baptist sects, was more rational than Catholicism (see Weber 1930:147). What he meant by this was that Protestantism, or radical forms of it, devalued the sacraments and was therefore less ritualistic, less superstitious, using fewer symbols than Catholicism. Again, it could be argued that he saw in Calvinism a concern for the serious side of life to which all human beings should aspire. In practical terms this meant fewer religious holidays and the notion of personal asceticism, which, incidentally, helped to create economic wealth. But, leaving aside the problem which Max Weber tried to account for, namely the rise of bourgeois capitalism at the time of the Reformation, could it not be argued that both Calvinism and Roman Catholicism, with its Thomist theology, developed systems of thought which attempted to minimize ambiguity? By contrast, Anglicanism and Lutheranism never evolved comparable theological systems. Followers of a *via media* position would thus appear to live with a higher level of ambiguity than Catholics and Calvinists. This would seem to be very much in line with Weber's thought, for no matter how the rational might be defined – and it is a problem with Weber – it is certainly superior to ambiguity. Neither the Church of England nor the Lutheran churches have produced systematic thinkers. With few exceptions no great theological names appear in Anglicanism, except perhaps some of the Caroline divines, and there are those who would argue that Martin Luther was more a biblical exegete whose interest was in religious experience rather than in creating a systematic theology. At least potentially and within limitations, Roman Catholicism and Calvinism do not contain the ambiguities that may be found in the other forms of Christianity just mentioned. And this is quite apart from the fact that they all possess those ambiguities which are to be found in what might be called basic Christianity. It might well be argued that of all the major Christian denominations the Church of England is the most ambiguous, for reasons which will become apparent in this book.

Of course, the firm believer often assumes that she or he is relatively free from ambiguity in matters of faith and practice: it is others who are 'illogical'. Thus, the 'rationally' inclined Hensley Henson was convinced that both the high church and low church parties of the Church of England in the later nineteenth century did not 'exhibit a very coherent or logical faith in their respective principles. Both profess principles they cannot apply in practice, and which they would not if they could' (Henson 1898:5). He clearly implied that his own position was far less ambiguous than others. Maybe he was right but that did not mean his own religious stand was without ambiguity.

Over and above the fundamental ambiguities in Anglicanism, Anglo-Catholicism has had more than its full share. The reason, as this book sets out to show, is that Anglo-Catholicism, as it emerged in the second half of the nineteenth century, attempted to impose a Catholic ethos of worship and religious life on a church which for three hundred years had been perhaps the chief bastion against Roman Catholicism. England was a Reformation country and had been particularly effective in attacking the authority of the pope and in eliminating within itself the alleged abuses and superstitions of medieval Catholicism. England was an island, able to defend itself successfully against Catholic invasion. It was an impregnable fortress flying the Protestant flag. In the religious wars of the sixteenth and seventeenth centuries and later, the religious and political goals of England were always to support the Protestant cause, never the Catholic. Anglo-Catholics attempted to reverse this general attitude and to show that in theory and practice the Anglican Church was essentially Catholic and should not be seen as part of the Protestant world. Admittedly this occurred long after religious wars had ceased, but what Anglo-Catholics wanted was that the Church of England should stand shoulder to shoulder with the Roman Catholic Church rather than link arms with Protestants. Inevitably, such a policy caught Anglo-Catholics in a web of ambiguities which heretofore had not existed in the Church of England. In trying to combine the ideals of Catholicism, often directly borrowed from the Roman Catholic Church of the day, with a religious body whose whole history was closely identified with what the official Roman Catholic Church saw as a heresy, Anglo-Catholics found themselves in what to many outsiders seemed an impossible position. The question which arises, and which is the subject of much that follows, is whether Anglo-Catholics were aware of their position and how far they attempted to deal rationally with the ambiguities they had created for themselves.

The task of the church leader, but above all the theologian, is to consider the ambiguities contained in the religion with which he is identified. The theologian has to come to grips with and to make rational and understandable non-rational assertions and practices. Much of his work is to try to show how a particular ambiguity has arisen, perhaps on account of historical events or through new philosophical ideas. Assuming that theology is an attempt to understand religious phenomena rationally, theologians must come to terms with ambiguity. Of course, some theologians may see that there is no alternative but to explicate the ambiguity and admit its insolubility. In some respects that might be seen to be an intellectual defeat so that the perennial search is an attempt to make sense of what is initially nonsense. The theologian's work, therefore, is always one of interpretation. Interpretation is necessary just because of the existence of paradox and ambiguity, which give rise to intellectual tension.

The predicaments which faced Anglo-Catholics obviously needed the help of theologians and there was indeed a great deal of theological activity when the movement began through the thinking and action of the Oxford Fathers (see ch. 1). However, Anglo-Catholicism did not produce prominent theologians who contributed to the discipline at an international level (see ch. 5.2). Anglo-Catholics appeared to remain content with the position in which they found themselves.

There are many ways open to the theologian for dealing with ambiguity. They are of no concern to us here since theology as a discipline is not the subject under discussion. What is more relevant sociologically is to raise the question of why people stay in systems which, to the outsider at least, are riddled with ambiguity. Obviously a convert does not see the newly embraced religion in such terms. But those who leave are aware of ambiguity and this will be considered later on when some attempt is made to account for the large number of conversions from the ranks of Anglo-Catholicism to the Church of Rome (see ch. 9). But most people remain with the system, no matter how many the ambiguities. Why they stay where they are, we shall raise at the end (see ch. 10).

Given the fact, therefore, that there are various individual responses to the presence of ambiguity in a religious system, the sociologist finds it well within his province to study and analyse the nature of the alternative courses of action. Anglo-Catholicism is a particularly interesting case for such an exercise.

I
The phenomenon of
Anglo-Catholicism

Chapter 1

What is Anglo-Catholicism?

1 Introduction

What would have immediately struck someone entering a generally recognized Anglo-Catholic church just after the Second World War, say in the mid-1950s? To anyone with a very limited knowledge of the Church of England, it would have seemed just like going into a Roman Catholic church of the day, Religious pictures would be on the walls or over the altar. There would be several statues, one or two of which might have been clothed, and in front of them, a cluster of candles would perhaps be burning. A crucifix would be found above the pulpit. There might also have been one over a prayer desk, which would have acted as a confessional, if there were not an actual confessional, Roman Catholic style. There would be Stations of the Cross around the walls. And the focal point of the church would have been the high altar, decked with many candles, behind which there might have been a giant reredos with statues of saints. Around the church there would be carefully tended side-altars. A lamp might be burning in one of them; those with special knowledge would be aware that it was the place where the Blessed Sacrament was reserved. And a smell of incense may have pervaded the whole building, especially if the main Sunday service had just taken place.

At a quick glance around the church, all this and more would have immediately struck the visitor. And should he or she have been present at the most popular Sunday service, the conviction of being in a Roman Catholic church would have been even stronger as doubtless there would be three priests conducting the service, attired in richly coloured eucharistic vestments, accompanied by numerous servers. And, apart from the incense, there would much bowing and genuflecting, and perhaps the music would be plainsong. The epistle and gospel would not be read but sung accordingly. There would, however, be hymns that were unmistakably Anglican. If the service started about 11 o'clock it might be concluded with the angelus, which consists of prayers said in honour of and to the Blessed Virgin Mary. And should the observer attend church in the evening, instead of evensong there would be the service of benediction and a public recitation of the rosary. There would be daily services, held early in the morning. On one day of the year, Corpus Christi, the Blessed Sacrament would perhaps be carried around the church, the floor strewn with flowers.

Such would have been a typical Anglo-Catholic church about thirty years ago and what the observer would have seen would have been fairly uniform amongst all Anglo-Catholic churches. Today, the position is both different and more complex. One can still find many Anglo-Catholic churches of the genre just described – churches which inside look like Roman Catholic churches of that period and where services held are also like those of the Roman Church of that period. But there are now probably more Anglo-Catholic churches which have modified their furnishings and, especially, their services to coincide once again with those of the Roman Catholic Church. The changes occurred after the Vatican Council of the 1960s and were in many cases towards simplicity of ritual and the clearing out of what was seen to be much decadent ecclesiastical furniture. Services veered towards what might simply be called a more Protestant position (see ch. 11.8). Many Anglo-Catholic clergy felt they must do likewise and this has led to much diversity of practice. Consequently today it has become far less easy to pick out Anglo-Catholic churches than once it used to be.

In terms of elaborate rituals it is often said that some Anglo-Catholic churches are more Roman than Rome – what goes on is a veritable paradise for ecclesiastical scene-shifters, Roman pattern! But, no matter the point of comparison, there would appear to be little difference between Anglo-Catholic and Roman Catholic places of worship and services, either at present or in the recent past, and this is precisely how some Anglo-Catholics want it, for it is the image they strive to create. So difficult has it been to distinguish between the churches that at various times Roman Catholic priests have had to instruct their more ignorant followers that they must not confuse the two and so find themselves worshipping in what is nothing more than an Anglican church. Some Anglo-Catholic churches have co-operated in this and placed on their notice-boards such words as 'This is not a Roman Catholic church.' Let it not be forgotten that Anglo-Catholic churches can be found up and down the English countryside, in villages as well as in towns and cities, and, despite their internal appearance and the ritual of their services, they stand as an integral part of the parochial system of the Church of England.

2 A confusion of terms

Anglo-Catholicism has been traditionally associated with other names such as ritualism, the high church, the Oxford movement, and Tractarianism. It is necessary to see precisely what is being discussed and to differentiate the terms.

There is little difficulty in understanding what is meant by the Oxford movement. The movement is generally reckoned to have begun as a result of John Keble's famous assize sermon of 14 July 1833, in Oxford, when he called on the Established Church to assert its autonomy and to reject encroachments from the State by firmly opposing what might loosely be called Erastianism. The result was the immediate emergence of a group of academics and academically minded people, mainly based in Oxford, who set in motion an extraordinary revival in the Church of England. As it crystallized, it loudly proclaimed that the Church of England had a Catholic heritage and was therefore Catholic in essence. The revival rested on the fact that the Church of England was not just a Protestant church which had emerged at the time of the Reformation but was basically Catholic – part of the Catholic church – and had not cut itself off from its progenitor. It had reformed itself but had not radically changed its nature during those turbulent times. The early Fathers of the movement, John Keble himself (1792–1866), John Henry Newman (1801–90), and Edward Bouverie Pusey (1800–82), constituted the initial triumvirate; in the early days, there were also secondary but prominent figures such as F. W. Faber (1814–63), R. H. Froude (1803–36), Charles Marriott (1811–58), and Isaac Williams (1802–65).

The immediate task which engulfed the Oxford Fathers was nothing more than an intellectual one, that of propagating and reasserting doctrines relating to the foundation and origins of the Ecclesia Anglicana. Keble's sermon had been prompted by Parliament's threat to close certain Anglican bishoprics in Ireland. The battle immediately became one of ideas. It had very little to do with ritual or worship. Theology, and in particular the theology of the church, was of prime importance. Once that battle was won, practical consequences in the matter of worship would follow. Although such externalities were not the immediate concern of the Fathers, in various small ways what was said anticipated them. The early days of the Oxford movement were like a spring of water, which may have had various sources but which eventually gave rise to a mighty river. It brought life to a church that had lost its vitality and was sterile and moribund. When the revival came, it was from a most unexpected quarter, for, unlike the Methodist and Evangelical revivals, it sprang from theological reflection. The emphasis of the Oxford Fathers on theology was apparent, not least in the publication of the *Tracts for the Times*. They began to appear in 1833 and came to an end in 1845. In all they numbered ninety. Far from being penny tracts they were weighty and scholarly essays covering such subjects as apostolic succession, fasting, the work of the clergy, and the Thirty-nine Articles. It was the logic of the final tract, written by Newman himself, which made him see that he had no alternative but to withdraw from the Church of England. *Tract XC* was condemned by the university of Oxford, which challenged it and decided against the possibility of a Catholic interpretation of the Thirty-nine Articles (Knox 1933:363). At the very outset the *Tracts* created a great deal of opposition on account of their Catholic leanings. Critics saw that their fears were justified when Newman was received into the Church of Rome. For obvious reasons the name Tractarian applied to all those who accepted the doctrines of the *Tracts*.

But, if the followers of the Oxford movement were called Tractarians on account of the *Tracts*, is it correct to refer to them as being high church? The answer is both in the affirmative and in the negative. They were generally labelled high church and often thought of themselves as such. Anyone who attempts to show historically or theologically that the Church of England has a historical lineage which connects it directly with the Catholic church (and perhaps the Roman Catholic Church) can as a rule be called high church. Also, those who support ritualistic services are said to be high or high church. The problem, however, is that the term is not applied only to the Oxford movement and all that it stood for: its context is somewhat wider. This is because it has been used to describe certain theologians such as Richard Hooker (1554–1645) and Richard Bancroft (1544–1610) of the Elizabethan period, and the Caroline divines, such as William Laud (1573–1645) and Lancelot Andrewes (1555–1626). These bishops and theologians were strongly opposed to the Puritan Reformers and their followers. They subscribed to a high doctrine of the church, seeing it as a divine institution, governed by an episcopate and being a true dispenser of those sacraments found in the early church. The Caroline divines also stressed the

Divine Right of Kings and under the reign of William III became known as 'non-jurors'. Thomas Ken (1637–1711), bishop of Bath and Wells, is often seen as a true forerunner of Anglo-Catholicism (see Kaye-Smith 1925, chapter 7, and, for a more detailed study, Legg 1914). Both the early high church Anglicans and the Tractarians were nicknamed high and dry: doctrine was what mattered above all else (see Crowther 1970:23ff.).

There can be no doubt that there is a connecting link between these old high church theologians and the Oxford Fathers, who looked upon them as being the true Anglican thinkers who stressed the Catholic nature of the Church of England. At the same time they did not support them on every issue. Compared with high-churchmen 'of the old sort', the Oxford Fathers were hesitant to accept, for example, the doctrine of the Divine Right of Kings. But, theologically, the basis of Anglican Catholicity is to be found amongst the Caroline divines, as one may see in the writings of the Oxford Fathers. In them may be seen the true heart of Anglicanism, if that is in part expressed as a form of church order in a Catholic mould.

One term associated with the Oxford movement from its early days was ritualism. It was often employed in a derogatory way. No one can deny that some early Tractarians soon became interested in ritual and hoped to introduce ceremonies and rites which up until then had been totally absent in the Church of England, or were to be found in the Prayer Book but which needed to be restored. It is not correct, however, to equate ritualism with Tractarianism, or to say that every ritualist would call himself high church, or vice versa. The position is not as simple as that. The founding Fathers were above all cautious in the matter of ritual, for fear of losing ground over secondary issues. Being rationally minded they wanted first and foremost to outline careful, well-argued, unassailable theological positions. They fully realized that with a deep concern for the sacraments, baptism, confession, and the eucharist they would have to deal with liturgical and ritual matters. But in the early days the Fathers demanded little more than that public worship should be conducted reverently and in complete compliance with the rubrics of the 1662 Prayer Book. They were careful to observe the rule of law and were opposed to anything which indicated liturgical disorder or chaos, for clearly such states were contrary to the concept of Catholicism. Being by training and background intellectuals, and having varying degrees of aesthetic sensitivity, they wished to see the establishment of the beauty of worship within Anglican churches (which some cynics might suggest is the worship of beauty). They visualized the parish church as a holy temple, not a common-or-garden meeting-house. As a result of many decades of neglect there had to be a great deal of tidying up of church buildings and an attitude of dignity and reverence inculcated in priests and people alike. In this way congregations could be made aware that they were worshipping in the House of God, a building set apart and held to be sacred.

Many changes did in fact take place in parish churches and in college chapels. Clergy started to wear cassocks and surplices; the latter were directed in the rubrics of the Prayer Book. Indeed, what the Tractarians wanted above all else was to restore the Prayer Book and all its rubrics and instructions, which had been greatly overlooked. One example was the saying of matins and evensong daily by the clergy. Another outcome was that tidiness and cleanliness began to make their presence felt and much rubbishy furniture was thrown out. Box pews were changed for seats or lower backed pews facing the altar. Such changes were intended to allow the worshipper to see what was going on in the chancel and at the altar. The altar itself was given prominence: it was not just a domestic table which happened to be used occasionally for religious purposes. Music was introduced or improved. Hymns were sung. Gradually candles were introduced. Religious pictures were put on the walls. Even a cross was placed on the altar.

Clergy who tended to move in this direction were frequently called ritualists. Not surprisingly, amongst the population at large, and indeed amongst other clergy, it was changes in ceremonial rather than a renewal of doctrinal assertions that drew criticism and hostility, as well as enthusiasm. As the changes became rather more obvious, as ceremonial appeared to be increasing, fears arose about the Church of England being led towards the terrible Roman Catholic Church and about certain clergy being traitors within, who would deliver their church into the hands of the pope. From the 1870s up until the time of the First World War, and indeed at odd times after it, court cases emerged, some of them brought by Protestant groups within the Church of England and some by bishops, in which clergy were accused of ecclesiastical offences. The accused were castigated as ritualists and the term applied not only to those who were looked upon as being extreme but also to others who in a quiet and inoffensive way tried to make worship more reverent, more beautiful, and richer in symbolic content. There can be no doubt that such changes in worship had their origin in the Oxford movement (see pp. 25–30). As Judith Pinnington has correctly said:

'Ritualism may not have been the logical, or even originally the consciously intended, outcome of Tractarianism, but it was both spiritually and sociologically inevitable' (Pinnington 1983:97).

The movement towards more solemn and dignified forms of worship spread quickly. This affected the services of morning and evening prayer – the main services of the Church of England at the time – and holy communion, which was usually celebrated only a few times a year. Some clergy were keen to make changes in the services but did not necessarily accept all or many of the doctrines, such as apostolic succession, which were propagated by the Oxford Fathers. Thus, ritualism strictly referred to a wider movement than that contained within the Oxford movement and did not necessarily involve those who wanted to be identified with it. Nevertheless, the influence of the ritualistic component of the Oxford movement has been enormous in bringing about a revolutionary change in the practical conduct of worship in the Church of England (see ch. 5.3). In the end virtually every parish church in the land was influenced by ritualism. However, it must not be forgotten that the word ritualist was frequently used to describe Tractarians, and more particularly Anglo-Catholics, especially in the second half of the nineteenth century and up until the time of the First World War. Anglo-Catholics did not use the word to describe themselves: it was a term of reproach employed by others.

The term sacramentalist was also used in connection with the Oxford movement in its early days. Quite simply it meant someone who emphasized the sacraments of the church. In practice it was a synonym for Tractarian or ritualist but was not much used after the turn of the century.

Anglo-Catholics certainly, and doubtless Tractarians as well, did not like to be called ritualists because the term implied that all they were interested in was ritual itself. Most Anglo-Catholic priests felt that they were being maligned when the term was applied to them. They were not concerned with ritual for its own sake but with ritual as the action component of the Catholic faith. On the contrary, they felt that it was wishy-washy, middle-of-the-road Anglicans who introduced ceremonies and rituals just for the sake of them – to make their churches 'pretty', colourful, or more interesting. That was mere idolatry! Ritual is of no value and a vain thing if it is not based upon sound doctrine. What must always come first – what has always been the essence of Catholicism – is truth, truth about God, Jesus Christ, and the church. Once these intellectual propositions, enshrined in the creeds, are accepted, then Catholic rituals will have their true place and meaning. Such a rational approach, it might be argued, was not accepted by all Anglo-Catholics and many of the laity and clergy showed themselves in fact to be more interested in expressions of ritual than in the expositions of their faith beyond simplistic statements (but see ch. 3).

Anglo-Catholic is a term usually associated with the Oxford movement. For some people the two names are interchangeable. But to make them so is inaccurate. What is implied by Anglo-Catholicism is not the same as what is meant by the Oxford movement or Tractarianism. For example, there have been and still are those who would call themselves followers of the Oxford movement but who would repudiate the suggestion that they were Anglo-Catholics. Anglo-Catholic, however, was a name which was quickly applied to the Oxford movement for a number of reasons. For one thing the Oxford Fathers began the publication the *Library of Anglo-Catholic Theology*, which appeared in 1841 as a series of theological works written by seventeenth-century Anglican divines, including those whose names were mentioned earlier. The term was also given to devotees of the Oxford movement a little earlier, in 1838. The Latin term, *Anglo-Catholicus*, is said to have been used on one or two occasions in the seventeenth century (*Oxford Dictionary of the Christian Church*). Certain ideas and ideals began to emerge in the Oxford movement which were scarcely perceptible when it began. Some of these were labelled extreme, in that they approximated to corresponding components of the Roman Catholic Church. Those who held such views began to be known as Anglo-Catholics. Anglo-Catholicism thus became a movement within a movement, or a more extreme wing of a movement, advocating advanced or Catholic practices and ideas which many thought were quite alien to the tradition of the Ecclesia Anglicana. It can be argued that Anglo-Catholics wanted to take the Oxford movement into fields which the Fathers were reluctant to enter, either because of a principle or because, on grounds of expediency, it was felt that the time was not ripe. Anglo-Catholics never repudiated any of the positions adopted by the Tractarians but they felt that the Fathers had not developed their initial theological advance. It is not surprising, therefore, that some have called Anglo-Catholicism 'the second stage' of the Catholic revival or the Oxford movement. If Tractarians were lambasted by Protestants for being Romanizers, then Anglo-Catholics were Romanizers *par excellence*.

E. A. Knox clearly differentiated Tractarianism from Anglo-Catholicism. As a firm upholder of the Protestant ethos of the

Church of England, he staunchly rejected ritualism and ceremonialism. He wrote: 'we acknowledge unhesitatingly that the
Tractarian Revival was no mere re-awakening of ceremonialism,
but entirely alien in its intention to the ceremonial development
which claims parentage from it' (Knox 1933:377). The relation
between the Oxford movement and Anglo-Catholicism might be
seen to be that of mother and daughter. The daughter saw herself
as originating from her mother yet having a distinct personality of
her own. The mother realized that the daughter was in some
measure an extension of herself. Because of the closeness of the
bond, each was loyal to the other. The daughter fully realized
and never repudiated the debt she owed to her mother: the
mother was always loyal to the daughter and ready to protect her
in the face of criticism and hostility. Despite disagreement
between mother and daughter, external threats quickly brought
about a closing of ranks.

Useful though such an analogy is, it is nevertheless not easy to
differentiate Anglo-Catholicism clearly from the Oxford movement; and there are a number of reasons for this. As has just
been said, neither the Oxford movement nor Anglo-Catholicism
has ever been anything more than a movement within a church,
and an Established Church at that. Membership of the movements
has been by way of personal loyalty and identity, by self-declared
allegiance. There has never been an official organization which
has embraced entirely either or both movements. Membership
cards are completely unknown and indeed are held to be
undesirable. In this respect a contrast might be made with
membership of a trade union or the Methodist Church; it is well
known that the organization of the first was to a large extent
based on that of the second. Generally speaking, one is a
member of such groups or one is not, and, while even in these
cases the boundaries may at times be fuzzy, they are relatively
clear-cut compared with those which might be used to designate
followers of the Oxford movement and Anglo-Catholicism.

Another problem is to differentiate Tractarians from Anglo-
Catholics within the general high-church movement. The reason
is quite simply that the boundaries between the two groups are
extraordinarily vague. They are really best seen as resting on a
continuum along which it is very difficult to draw a line, on one
side of which is Tractarianism and on the other Anglo-
Catholicism. To put it crudely, Anglo-Catholics are one degree
further on than Tractarians. But precisely what that one degree
consists of is not in itself very clear. What is meant by Anglo-
Catholic has to be deduced from the general usage of the term.

Probably it is best to point to certain groups or societies which are generally known to be Anglo-Catholic, so that at least there is some point of identification. To be specific one could refer to the Guild of the Servants of the Sanctuary, the Federation of Catholic Priests, the Society of Mary, the Church Union, Ecclesia, the Catholic League, and so on. These societies, which exist today, have been created for particular ends but they are all seen to be definitely 'Catholic'. No one organization completely covers Anglo-Catholicism in its entirety but membership of these and similar groups and societies immediately identifies followers as being Anglo-Catholic. And what of those who do not belong to such associations and yet claim to be Anglo-Catholic? As we have said, only a personal response to the question will provide the answer. The notion of a movement within a movement is essentially associated with diffusion and confusion. This does not mean that one should not try to penetrate the haze and see objectively what Anglo-Catholicism is and how it is different from related movements. An answer to this problem can be found in viewing the problem from a slightly different angle.

3 The task of Anglo-Catholicism

One approach to the problem of identifying Anglo-Catholicism is to ask the question: what have Anglo-Catholics seen to be their task? The answer is simple enough: to catholicize the Church of England. One prominent priest of the 1920s, Fr Atlay, said that the work of Anglo-Catholic priests was 'to convince their people, by all their teaching and example, that Catholicism in its fullness belongs by inheritance to their own Church of England' (in ACPC 1921:190). At the 1923 Anglo-Catholic congress it was stated that the aim of the movement was 'to extend the knowledge of the Catholic faith and practice at home and abroad and by this means to bring men and women to an acknowledge-ment of our Lord Jesus Christ as their personal Saviour and King' (quoted in Kaye-Smith 1925:197). In one respect the work of catholicization was not necessary, since Anglo-Catholics, along with supporters of the Oxford movement, held that the Church of England was inherently Catholic. They accepted the basic premise that no one can suddenly create a 'Catholic church'. The Catholic church is one: it has a historical point of origin and a historical continuity. It cannot therefore suddenly emerge at a later point. The Church of England is not a Protestant church, such as the Church of Scotland, which is Presbyterian and which came into existence at the time of the Reformation. It is at heart

Catholic – possessing a continuity with the Catholic church, not least as it existed in the middle ages in England. Therefore, there was no question of turning a Protestant church, the Church of England in this case, into a Catholic church, for that is like squaring a circle. What was required in the English situation was to make bishops, clergy, and laity conscious of their heritage and to propagate vigorously what might be called Catholic faith and practice. It was argued that during the eighteenth century and the early part of the nineteenth century, if not before, the Church of England had theologically and liturgically forgotten its essentially Catholic nature, which is enshrined in its Prayer Books of 1549 and 1662. What was hidden and forgotten had to be publically proclaimed and made manifest for all to see. As G. W. E. Russell said at the turn of the century to a meeting of the Confraternity of the Blessed Sacrament:

> The work of the Oxford leaders was not to introduce the
> Catholic religion into a Church which was ignorant of it – not
> even to bring it back into a Church which had once possessed it
> and then lost it – but to drag it out of obscurity into the light of
> day, to call public attention to it, to defend it, and glorify it.
> The leaders fanned the embers till they burst into a flame.
>
> (Russell 1902:330–1)

Such a statement of intent and achievement was common to Tractarians and Anglo-Catholics alike. The main point of difference between the two was the way in which and the speed at which the embellishment or catholicization should proceed. Without adding anything to the ecclesiology of the Oxford movement, Anglo-Catholics wanted to express the Catholic heritage by radically changing the ethos of parish life as it existed in the nineteenth century. Here they disagreed with their mother in so far as they aimed to bring about far-reaching changes at a much faster pace than she did.

The problem which faced all those who wished to see the Catholic tradition of the Established Church restored in a church which seemed so fundamentally Protestant was that of knowing precisely what had to be reintroduced in the matter of worship and what had to be emphasized in the matter of doctrine. It was the former which was the main concern of Anglo-Catholics. They wanted to transform the religious ethos so that it was distinctly and unmistakably Catholic. But how was that to be worked out? What norms should be applied? What ideals should be projected? Very shortly after the emergence of the Oxford movement, as theologians and clergy began to think about the application of the principles which had been established, there appeared to be three possibilities for the restoration of a Catholic way of life:

1 Introduce practices used by the primitive or early church.
2 Restore the practice and cult, with some modification, which existed in England in the high middle ages.
3 Copy, with perhaps some modification, current practices in the Roman Catholic Church, especially those found in northern Europe.

The first solution was that advocated by most of the Oxford Fathers: Pusey himself held that the catholicization of the Church of England was to proceed along such lines. There were, however, a number of problems connected with the policy. Some wanted to make the norms of doctrine and liturgy those of what were called the undivided church, that is, the church until the schism of 1054, when the eastern and western churches went their separate ways. This was held to be the period of the one church (see Kaye-Smith 1925:174ff.). Such a position has direct affinities with the branch theory of the church (see ch. 6.2). If exclusive emphasis were to be placed on the early church, it would by no means be easy to determine precisely, in the mid-nineteenth century, what the liturgical practice of the church was. Very few firsthand accounts had been handed down. Scholars saw that it would take considerable time to examine the necessary early documents. Moreover, there was no guarantee that at the end of a prolonged academic venture a clear picture would emerge. Some saw the urgent need for immediate change in the Established Church. It could not be delayed by twenty or thirty years until the appearance of learned publications which, in the end, might not add up to very much. Again, a serious lapse of time might also mean the loss of the initiative which had arisen as a result of Keble's 1833 sermon. Yet another argument against this solution came from those who held that in the course of its development Catholicism had been transformed, from its early days when it was little more than a sect to the time, some thousand or more years later, when it was a universal church. The social and religious ethos had completely changed with the passing of years. Could it be said that what was the norm in the year AD 200, 500, or 1000 should be the norm in the nineteenth century?

The second possibility mentioned above would at least overcome some of the criticisms levelled against those who wished to restore the liturgies and practices of the early church. Scholars knew much more about church life in the middle ages than they did about it in the first and second centuries. For example, there was to hand the Sarum rite which had been used by the Reformers in the compilation of the 1549 Prayer Book. This rite, used in Salisbury cathedral in the middle ages, was held to be more 'Catholic' than the 1662 Prayer Book, although it had been subject to changes and reforms. Not surprisingly, historical and liturgical research was still necessary if this solution of using patterns of worship established in England in the middle ages was to be adopted as the norm for the Church of England in the nineteenth century. Nevertheless, the Sarum rite was seen to be an excellent foundation on which to build. Through the influence of the Oxford movement and certain Catholic-minded scholars who advocated it, English cathedrals in particular, but also some parish churches, began to use ceremonial based on the Sarum rite. Its most ardent advocate, not least for parish churches, was Percy Dearmer (1867–1936), who put forward his ideas in a well-known book on the subject, *The Parson's Handbook* (1899). It went through twelve editions. Those who adopted the policy, both in cathedrals and parish churches, were said to be followers of the pure form of Gothic liturgy (see Anson 1960:306ff.). Not surprisingly the movement was closely tied in with the imitation of Gothic architecture and, in a somewhat removed way, with what is generally called the Romantic movement. Indeed, one of the criticisms levelled against those who devotedly attempted to transplant medieval services and practices to the Church of England was that they introduced an ethos which was not only Romantic but also ludicrous in nineteenth-century industrial Britain. Again, the Sarum rite was considered to be less practical than the Roman rite, although the reasons were never very clear, for the Roman rite was hardly any more suitable on rational grounds for a modern industrial society. Those who followed the Sarum usage were often castigated as being followers of the 'British Museum religion'. Indeed, the work of scholars which entailed a careful examination of what went on in the past, was often parodied as being liturgical archaeology (for further analysis of this position, see Hughes 1961, chapter 5, and Maughan 1916 and 1922:v).

The third answer seemed the most sensible. It was a quick, almost instant solution to the issue of the catholicization of the Church. Why not adopt one, with perhaps a few alterations, from a system that was seen to be working well in modern society? Why not live in the present? The Roman Catholic system was certainly Catholic and was immediately available. What could be wrong in copying it?

Convinced, therefore, that this was the obvious and most sensible solution to the catholicization of the Church of England, a number of clergy influenced by the Oxford movement went to France and Italy and brought back with them statues, pictures, vestments, confessional boxes, candlesticks, and so on. Such an activity began in the middle of the nineteenth century and continued right up until the time of the First World War and indeed beyond. These early Anglo-Catholics saw with their own eyes, though they seldom looked behind the scene, how well Roman Catholicism worked. Not only did they introduce ecclesiastical furniture and furnishings from the Continent, they also imported rituals associated with the mass, as well as extra-liturgical services such as benediction, exposition of the Blessed Sacrament, the saying of the rosary, and various litanies of the saints, especially that of the Blessed Virgin Mary. These were introduced wholesale to various parish churches, sometimes discreetly, sometimes with an arrogant openness. Clearly, the Oxford Fathers never anticipated such innovations, which took place under their very noses, and for which they might be considered in some way responsible.

All those who chose to implement the third policy, both in the past and the present, can indeed be labelled Anglo-Catholic. Their identity is beyond question and the adjective extremist was and still is justified. They have been called Romanizers and, not infrequently, Anglo-Papalists. Their form of Catholicism was sometimes called baroque or rococo. Quite simply, Anglo-Catholics were more Catholic and less Anglican than the Tractarians. Further, as they grew in numbers, such was their enthusiasm for what they saw in Catholic churches on the Continent that some became experts on the subject of liturgy and, as we have said, were dubbed, more Roman than Rome. One or two priests have been known to boast that some Roman Catholic clerics have come to see them celebrate mass in order to learn how to do it properly!

There have been some Anglo-Catholic priests who have rationalized their position by arguing that to adopt Roman practices and habits would hasten the reunification of the two churches, which has always been a fond hope of Anglo-Catholics (see ch. 7.4). Darwell Stone, perhaps the most learned of all Anglo-Catholic theologians in the 1920s and 1930s, whilst he did not accept Roman Catholic doctrine lock, stock, and barrel, advocated adopting Roman ceremonial. The English Catholic, he said, 'values more than he can easily express anything which can be rightly adopted in the Church of England, which may lessen

differences from and promote similarities to the Church of Rome'
(Stone 1926, quoted in Clarke 1932:273).

One of the relatively early agencies for propagating Roman
practices and ideas was the Society of Saint Peter and Saint
Paul, which was founded in 1911 and which was a publishing
house and shop in the West End of London. It was strongly
supported by Denys Prideaux, Maurice Child, N. P. Williams,
and Ronald Knox. It had little about it which was Anglican. At
one time it called itself 'Catholic Publishers to the Church of
England', modifying a phrase found at that time in the English
Roman Catholic world. It had an imprint like the papal arms.
Since it was non-profit making it was able to produce cheap
literature amd tracts, usually adorned with rococo patterns.
Attacks were launched against the Sarum rite and Percy
Dearmer. It had a sarcastic and provocative air about it which
greatly irritated bishops. Although its influence began to wane
after the First World War with Ronald Knox's conversion to
Roman Catholicism, it was very much behind the Anglo-Catholic
congresses and published the reports. (For more details on this,
the most Anglo-Papalist of societies, see Kemp 1954:33ff.;
Waugh 1959:114ff.; Knox:1918; Anson 1960, chapter 30 – which
covers the details of the baroque church furnishings.)

St Bartholomew's, Brighton, was, from the late nineteenth
century, one of the leading Anglo-Papalist churches (see ch. 4.5).
Within the great building, with its rich furnishings and elaborate
music, mass was sung very much in keeping with a Roman
Catholic mass of the day. In 1904 an observer described the
climax of the service as follows:

> The voice of the celebrant was not heard from the *Sanctus* until
> the post-Communion Lord's Prayer. If the Prayer of Humble
> Access and the Prayer of Consecration were said at all, they
> were inaudible, and the manual acts concealed. The only
> evidence that the consecration had taken place was the ringing
> of bells, the burning incense, the elevation of the Host and
> chalice.

> (Bowen 1904:68)

What better reason than that revealed in this account is needed
for the nickname 'smells and bells' given to Anglo-Catholic
practices?

A church of the same period was the completely romanized
St Saviour's, Hoxton, which had as its vicar the popular and
saintly Fr E. E. Kilburn. Its ethos around 1910 has been
described in this way:

Perpetual Reservation on the High Altar, Benediction, the Rosary, Shrines of the Sacred Heart, of Our Lady of Victories and of St. Joseph, Corpus Christi processions through the streets, the complete disuse of the English language, the regular use of the Latin Missal, Rituale, Vesperale, Ritus Servandus, and for the people the 'Simple Prayer Book' of the Catholic Truth Society and the Westminster Hymn Book gradually became the order.

(Carpenter 1949:171; see the following pages for the way the bishop of London attempted to deal with the incumbent)

Another example of extreme Anglo-Catholicism at a slightly later date is to be found in the the Catholic League. The League was started in 1930, largely through the efforts of Fr Fynes-Clinton, who for many years was rector of the Wren church of St Magnus-the-Martyr in the city of London, and who remained there until his death in 1959. The aim of the society was to foster fellowship amongst Catholics in communion with the see of Canterbury. Its treasured hope was the reunion of the Anglican Church with the Roman Catholic Church. The League attempted to promote 'Christian living in the Church of England in strict conformity with the teaching of the Church of Rome (as promulgated at the Council of Trent)' (Lunn and Haselock 1983:6). In the matter of liturgy the Roman missal, breviary, and devotional practices were used by priest members of the society and the laity were encouraged to adopt a spirituality and discipline similar to that found on the Continent (Lunn and Haselock 1983:6). Members of this Anglo-Papalist group have played an important role in Anglo-Catholicism. The aims of the Anglo-Papalists may be seen in the following quotation: 'The true nature of the English Church could only be recognized when she was once again united with the rock from which she was hewn' (Lunn and Haselock 1983:12). They and many Anglo-Catholics wanted to declare symbolically their adulation of the Roman Church by all that they did and in the clothes they wore in and out of their churches. In recent times a subtle change has occurred, however, due to what has happened in the Roman Catholic Church over the last twenty years or so. Now, members of the League 'must be instructed and practising Catholics accepting the faith of the Church as defined by all the councils up to and including Vatican II' (*The Messenger*, January 1986, p. 13). So Anglo-Papalists have to change accordingly.

Not all Anglo-Papalists have been happy with the label, although they may accept the truth implied in it. Thus, Dom

Anselm Hughes, an Anglican Benedictine, has stated:

> We are those who, as the nickname is meant to imply, believe
> that the natural and lawful visible head of the Catholic Church
> on this earth is or should be the Pope; that it is most
> unfortunate that we are separated from him . . . and that we
> most earnestly desire that this separation should come to an
> end.
>
> (Hughes 1961:148)

Of course he sees that Anglo-Papalists and Roman Catholics are
not the same and wishes that if a name has to be given to him and
his co-religionists it should be the word 'papistical' (Hughes
1961:149). No matter what precisely is meant by it, he would
settle for any word which is derived from the word pope. It is a
fact that, especially today, some Anglo-Catholics, perhaps a good
many, are unhappy about the term with which they are generally
associated. The two words, Anglo- and Catholic, do give rise to
ambiguity (see ch. 6.2). Nor does papalist or papistical command
much popular following. Some now prefer 'Anglican Catholics'
or 'Catholic Anglicans', depending on where they wish to place
the emphasis. Once again, the names do not seem to have caught
on. For our purposes Anglo-Catholic and Anglo-Papalist are the
most useful terms.

4 Popular identity

The agent for any liturgical changes in a parish was, and still is,
the incumbent. As the person directly responsible for the well-
being of the parish, the vicar, the rector, or the priest in charge is
the one who has the ultimate authority for the conduct of services.
He is, therefore, in a legal sense entitled to introduce ritualistic
or Anglo-Catholic practices. Whether or not such practices are
legal in themselves is beside the point. Precisely through these
means, individual churches have become famous for the richness
of their ceremonial. By a strange combination of the policy of the
patron and the appointment of a suitable priest, Anglo-Catholic
churches have emerged and maintained their traditions. We
might mention some of these famous churches: in London, All
Saints', Margaret Street (the Anglo-Catholic equivalent of the
chapel of King's College, Cambridge), St Alban's, Holborn,
St Magnus-the-Martyr, in the city, and St Peter's in the docks;
and outside London, St Bartholomew's, Brighton, St Mary
Magdalene's, Oxford, Frome parish church, and both the
shrine and the parish church of Walsingham in Norfolk. There

have been hundreds – thousands – of such churches up and down the land, some of them well known, some of them scarcely heard of beyond the parish.

Anglo-Catholic clergy and laity have to gain inside information as to where these churches are – where, as people used to say amongst themselves, 'Catholic privileges' are to be found, or where the priest is a 'definite Catholic'. In times past many people obtained much of their knowledge of such churches through *Church Guides*, published by the English Church Union from about 1900 until 1931, and from notices in the *Church Times*, where the times and types of services were advertised. Today, the notices are less extensive than they used to be. If one wishes to see a flourishing Anglo-Catholic church in London which manifests much of what this book is about, no better example can be found than that of St Mary's, Bourne Street, in the West End. This was the church where Lord Halifax was a regular worshipper (see ch. 2.1). But what in fact do Catholic privileges and the priest being a 'definite Catholic' mean? What tests can be applied so that ordinary people know whether a church is Catholic or not? Obviously, the first thing to observe is whether the word mass appears on the notice-board or whether confessions can be heard at specific times. These public proclamations leave no doubt that the church is Catholic! Another sure mark of identity beyond which it is hardly necessary to go is whether or not there is a service of adoration or benediction. There are other criteria relating to furnishings and services, mentioned at the beginning of the chapter. But as to the priest himself, if he wears a Latin cassock, that is, a cassock buttoned down the front, often with a cape over the shoulders, which in France is called a *soutane*, then clearly the wearer is an Anglo-Catholic priest. The Sarum type of cassock was introduced in the late nineteenth century through the influence of Tractarians and, despised by Anglo-Catholics, is often referred to as a maternity dress. A negative indicator is that no Anglo-Catholic priest would wear a moustache – only Protestant ministers are as vain as that! Other identity marks of Anglo-Catholics are mentioned further on (see ch. 2.7).

Despite what has been said already, the problem of identifying Anglo-Catholics and of defining Anglo-Catholicism is by no means easy. The reason is simply that great variation is to be found within Anglo-Catholicism itself. There are degrees of Anglo-Catholicism, varying from the moderates to the extremists. The problem, as we have already said, arises from the fact that it is a movement without a well-defined organization. We have mentioned some obvious externalities which are to be found in parish churches. These are manifold and therefore are open to a large number of possible combinations. Much trivial talk amongst Anglo-Catholics has centred on rivalry about 'quantities' of ritual which different churches have adopted. In searching for some kind of litmus test, many Anglo-Catholics in the past held that the reservation of the Blessed Sacrament was a clear mark of Anglo-Catholicism (see ch. 2.7). Today, however, many churches have reservation but have no wish at all to be identified with Anglo-Catholicism and adopt no other practices to make them so.

The problem of identity is all the more difficult because of the changes made over the past twenty years or so as a response to the changes in the Roman Catholic Church after Vatican II. The effect on Anglo-Catholics has been to create uncertainty and division between those who wanted to follow the changes demanded by the Council and those who wished to retain the old tradition (see ch. 11.9). Many Anglo-Catholic parishes have adopted some of the practices emerging from the Council but not others and so have created yet more problems in trying to define and identify Anglo-Catholicism today. There is now more infighting and a lack of cohesion compared with former times (see ch. 11). A similar splintering can be seen in the existence today of many left-wing political parties based on socialism or Marxism. The difference, however, is that the political parties have established their own separate identities and rules of membership. Such social characteristics do not apply to Anglo-Catholicism. The nearest political analogy is the Labour Party being like the Church of England and Anglo-Catholics representing the so-called hard or loony left.

To understand Anglo-Catholicism one needs to see it in all its fullness and it seems generally agreed that the movement reached its peak during the 1920s and 1930s. Certainly the series of Anglo-Catholic congresses held between the wars bears witness to it. What is also remarkable is the large number of books written by Anglo-Catholics during those decades – theological, historical, and devotional. Some were meant to contribute to the academic world; others were polemical and little more than penny tracts. But they witness to a certain vitality and to the fact that Anglo-Catholicism had some appeal among English intellectuals.

In this chapter we have tried to wrestle with problems of definition and identity and in the face of these difficulties some solution comes in an examination of the congresses, along with a few of the spate of the books that came from Anglo-Catholic and other presses. Before these great effervescent gatherings are described, however, a word must be said about some of the problems which emerged in the Catholic revival and which have some bearing on the issues of definition and identity.

5 Tensions and dilemmas

It has been necessary to make a distinction between Tractarianism and Anglo-Catholicism. The difference has been symbolically expressed in terms of the relation of a mother to her daughter. But within great areas of agreement there also existed points of difference and even tension.

As we have already stated there was complete accord on the notion of the Catholic heritage of the Church of England and on an appeal to the creeds of the church. In more practical terms, not surprisingly, there was also an initial consensus on liturgical matters. From the early days onwards, the followers of the Oxford movement and of Anglo-Catholicism were united in a common policy of making the eucharist, the holy communion, the mass, whatever term is used, the central and most holy act of worship. The ideal to be set before the congregation was Sunday-by-Sunday attendance at such a service. There might be some disagreement, and certainly there was in the early days, about how quickly the ideal could be realized. Although more moderate churches would have matins and evensong as the main services on a Sunday, the directive of the clergy was that attendance at holy communion, perhaps once a month, was of far greater importance than participation in other acts of public worship. Tractarians were great advocates of attendance at early morning communion services (see ch. 11.5).

There was another point on which followers of the Oxford movement and Anglo-Catholics were agreed. In restoring the Catholic heritage of the Church of England the reintroduction of the religious life was necessary, that is, the fostering of vocations in men to be monks and women to be nuns. Ascetics and religious have existed in Christianity from the third century onwards. One of the great successes of the Oxford movement was the re-establishment of religious orders in the Church of England from the mid-nineteenth century onwards (see ch. 5.2). Tractarians and Anglo-Catholics were completely united in this and they became even more united in the face of considerable opposition from Protestant-minded people to such 'Romish ideas' (see Walsh 1897).

The same thing can be said about the introduction of auricular confession. This practice goes back, some might argue, to New Testament times. Or, with stronger evidence, it can be shown to have been widely practised in the early church. On this point there was little division between Tractarians and Anglo-Catholics, although there was considerable divergence on how it should be carried out. Certainly the establishment of absolution and penance gave rise to great controversy (see ch. 3.5). It is argued that confession and absolution are legitimate practices within the Church of England since there are indications in the Prayer Book that they are sanctioned.

One issue which caused division between the Oxford Fathers and Anglo-Catholics was devotions to the saints and, above all, cultic practices centred on the Blessed Virgin Mary. Such prayers have also had a long history in the church and their extensive use in the late middle ages was one of the causes of the Reformation. The Prayer Books of the Church of England, and especially that of 1662, made it quite clear that prayers and devotions to the saints were no part of Anglican practice. Here Tractarians were cautious about prayers made directly to the saints. Not so Anglo-Catholics. And they had history on their side because if an appeal is made to the early church, say up to the fifth century, there is plenty of evidence to show that prayers made directly to the saints were not unknown and were therefore obviously sanctioned. Similarly, it can be seen that in the early church relics of the saints were highly valued and pilgrimages were undertaken. From these facts, the problems of a principle arise. If appeal is made to the beliefs and practices of the early church for their inclusion in a refurbished Anglican Church, on what grounds is one component or practice accepted and another overlooked or rejected? The Tractarians were prepared to sift and to select in a way they believed was acceptable to the Church of England. Anglo-Catholics had no such hesitation and therefore did not have to face the problem of establishing a principle of selection.

A similar point was made by Hensley Henson about the reserved Sacrament. He was a liberal churchman and was as much opposed to Tractarians as he was to Evangelicals. He held that the reserved Sacrament was clearly in existence in the primitive church. Anglo-Catholics wanted it on various grounds but in Henson's mind it was clearly illegal according to Anglican tenets and practices. To appeal to the early church in trying to establish a norm could not in itself be an adequate principle (Henson 1898:9).

A crucial issue which emerged in the early days of the Catholic revival is enshrined in the life and thought of Pusey, who became the undisputed leader of the Oxford movement in the late 1840s after the conversion of Newman to Roman Catholicism. He held this unofficial position until his death in 1882. It is reported that he did not wear eucharistic vestments until about forty years after the 1833 assize sermon. He had a fear of Rome and stood firmly against indulgences, the doctrine of purgatory, benediction, and the cult of the Blessed Virgin Mary. Above all, he was anxious to see that the process of catholicization should proceed within the bounds of lawful ecclesiastical authority. That Anglo-Catholics refused to accept such constraints brought him sorrow as he found himself forced to oppose the growing romanizing party. Tractarians attempted to repudiate the idea that what they were doing was leading the Church of England toward Rome. They maintained they were involved in nothing more than the attempt to bring about, in the restoration of Catholic practice and doctrine, that which could be justified by the Prayer Book. Their arguments did not seem very convincing in the light of the activities of the extremists. Pusey wanted to introduce only those things which could be held to be both Catholic and Anglican. He was a firm advocate of auricular confession (see ch. 3); he practised asceticism in so severe a way as to cause many to label him a Roman Catholic; and he was instrumental in introducing the first religious orders into the Church of England (see ch. 5.5). Although Walter Walsh in his book, *The Secret History of the Oxford Movement* (1897), musters a great deal of evidence to show that Pusey was in fact a Romanizer, history shows that he never identified himself with extreme forms of Anglo-Catholicism.

The case of Pusey reflects the eternal controversy that has raged in high-church and Anglo-Catholic circles from the 1830s until the present time about the nature and authority of the Prayer Book. Since the Church of England has no constitution or confessional statement, such as the Westminster Confession, the Prayer Book has been for centuries the sole foundation of doctrine and practice in the Church of England. Whether the Church can be labelled Catholic and whether the services in the Prayer Book are Catholic in nature rests on what is to be found in that book alone. The followers of the Oxford movement were on the whole prepared to accept not only the implied doctrine of the Prayer Book but also the structure of its services. For Anglo-Catholics, especially Anglo-Papalists, the main argument against the book was that it did not contain a set of services, along with the necessary rubrics, which could really be seen to be Catholic. Hence, despite the legality of the Prayer Book, some Anglo-Catholics argued that it was necessary to introduce changes and additional services which were Catholic in form. Some argued that the new services merely supplemented what was already in the Prayer Book and therefore their loyalty to it was not at issue. What was at stake, however, was the question whether or not the new services could be said to be within the tradition of the Established Church. Throughout the history of Anglo-Catholicism there has been a constant examination of the Prayer Book and arguments have raged as to how far it has to be taken literally or interpreted according to its alleged spirit. Anglo-Catholics on the whole were critical of certain aspects of the book. Here they were quite unlike Tractarians. Also unlike Tractarians, they often joked about the Prayer Book, but they would not joke about the Roman missal. However, when it suited them they would uphold the Prayer Book and reject any alteration to it (see ch. 2.7).

One way in which the more sensitive Anglo-Catholic clergy overcame the dilemma of wanting to use Roman Catholic forms of service which they knew would be unacceptable to their congregations was as follows. Priests said private prayers, held weekday services and performed other acts of devotion which they knew would be attended by only a few people. Here they felt free to do more or less as they wished. On Sundays at the main services they would show an outward loyalty to the Prayer Book. Some Anglo-Catholics did not, however, adopt this dual standard and were consistent in having Roman-like services on both Sundays and weekdays. In certain churches and on some occasions Latin was used. These alternative paths gave rise to the existence of two fairly well defined groups within Anglo-Catholicism, although each contained a number of variations. The extremists, including the Anglo-Papalists, had no hesitation in paying scant respect to the Prayer Book, even going so far as to reject it, whereas 'Prayer Book Catholics' were those who were rather more cautious and who attempted, at least in public, to base their services on the Prayer Book, claiming to hold to it in letter and spirit. The term Prayer Book Catholic had some validity and value until the introduction of new services in the Church of England in the 1970s, which culminated in the Alternative Service Book of 1980. (The many alternatives that then became available have made a confused situation even more confusing.)

It might be said that the more moderate Prayer Book Catholics were quite near to the Tractarians, indeed at this point the lines of demarcation may become very blurred. As we have indicated, Pusey, as a key figure in the cleavage between Tractarians and Anglo-Catholics, claimed complete loyalty to the Prayer Book.

Shortly before he died he said: 'our only safeguard under God is to keep our Prayer Book as it is' (quoted in Chadwick 1970:309). These moderates realized that their only intellectual defence against attack from the outside was to take a firm stand on the Prayer Book itself. They also saw the absurdity of the argument, so often advanced by the extremists, that, since no priest in fact ever obeyed all the rubrics of the Prayer Book, the Prayer Book could be totally disregarded or altered according to fancy. The argument, of course, opened the door to the catholicization of the Church of England along post-Tridentine lines. Appeal to the Prayer Book always divided Anglo-Catholics and weakened their corporate position. The Anglo-Papalist, Hugh Ross Williamson, wanted to say a private mass at All Saints', Margaret Street, in the 1950s, but the vicar refused his request 'because, my dear, you'll use that horrid Roman book and the rule here is music by Mozart, choreography by Fortescue [a Roman liturgiologist], décor by Comper, but libretto by Cranmer' (Williamson 1956: 157). There was amongst Anglo-Catholics, and especially Anglo-Papalists, a restless, angular spirit as they embarked on many controversies, not least over the Prayer Book: this was in marked contrast to the quiet, serene disposition which was so evident in Tractarians, epitomized in someone like Keble.

To return to an earlier point – the search for a simple, concrete mark of distinction between Tractarians and perhaps Prayer Book Catholics on the one hand and extreme Anglo-Catholics and Anglo-Papalists on the other, no better criterion can be found than in that relating to devotion to the saints, and above all to the Blessed Virgin Mary. The Prayer Book makes no reference at all to such devotions. Pusey and Gore, the latter a notable theologian and bishop of a later period who was a representative figure of Prayer Book Catholicism, both held the saints in great reverence. Both, also, were prepared to accept statues of saints in churches and to see the saints as worthy examples of Christian life and witness, to be emulated wherever possible. These ideas are evident in the Alternative Service Book of 1980 but the book does not go beyond them (see Keast n.d.:38ff.). For Anglo-Catholics, invocations made directly to the saints, for example, 'Mary pray for us', were to be encouraged. Without a shadow of doubt, many Anglo-Catholics and Anglo-Papalists can be identified by their Marian devotions, by their recitation of the rosary, the angelus, and the litany and vespers of the Blessed Virgin Mary, and so forth, together with visits to the shrine of our Lady of Walsingham. Indeed, the very use of the term our Lady, as distinct from the Virgin Mary or the Blessed

Virgin Mary, can identify Anglo-Papalists from the less extreme followers of the movement (but see ch. 2.7). The cult of our Lady involves several feast-days, some of which are mentioned in the Prayer Book, but there were two points of contention. Anglo-Catholics made a great deal of the feast of the Assumption (the ascension into heaven of our Lady), which is not mentioned in the Prayer Book and which most Anglicans would hold to be unscriptural. The second is the feast of the Immaculate Conception of our Lady, which in the Prayer Book is known simply as the feast of the Conception of the Virgin Mary.

This criterion applies as much today as it did in the mid-nineteenth century. At the 1978 Catholic Renewal conference, Bishop Michael Marshall said that devotion to the Blessed Virgin Mary was 'crucial in any Catholic spirituality' and the response from the floor of the assembly was a sudden burst of applause (*CT*, 7 April 1978; see ch. 11.2).

In 1891, *Catholic Prayers for Church of England People*, commonly known as *Catholic Prayers*, was published by W. Knott & Son, who were associated with St Alban's, Holborn. Indeed, Fr Stanton and another priest, Fr Harris, who were curates there, compiled the book. It was the first prayer book published for Anglicans in which large sections were given to Marian devotions and devotions to the saints, contained in litanies and offices. Included in its list of holy days of obligation 'on which Catholics are bound to hear Mass' is the feast of the Assumption of the Blessed Virgin Mary celebrated on 15 August. (It was not until 1950 that the pope declared that the Assumption was a dogma of the Roman Catholic Church.) By 1936 the book had sold over 100,000 copies and its importance in spreading Marian devotions in the Church of England cannot be overemphasized. For sixty years or more this book has been *the* devotional manual for Anglo-Catholics. In 1933 a similar book appeared, *Centenary Prayer Book*, which went through many editions, and which was very similar to *Catholic Prayers*. The foreword was by Lord Halifax. An interesting point was made in the prayer book, namely, that 1933 was the nineteenth centenary of Christ's Crucifixion and also the centenary of the Catholic revival in the Church of England. To understand the Anglo-Catholic movement one must understand these great treasuries of devotion.

As we have said, as the Catholic revival proceeded mother and daughter inevitably quarrelled. Tractarians criticized Anglo-Catholics and Anglo-Papalists for their extremism, their idolization of Roman Catholicism, and their lack of loyalty to things Anglican. Their excesses in doctrine and practice prevented the wider acceptance of the Catholic movement within the Church of England. On the other hand, convinced Anglo-Catholics accused Tractarians and those who might loosely be called high church of not teaching the full Catholic doctrine and practice. They were frightened to be committed to the true faith: they were nothing more than 'Protestants in chasubles'. Far from being consciously Catholic they merely played with ritual. At heart they were just ordinary 'C. of E.'. These tensions between those who were Anglican before all else and those who were Catholic before all else are derived from subtleties inside the movement for Catholic revival. There has been a vast amount of infighting which is virtually incomprehensible to the outsider and which has much weakened the movement.

To help summarize the problems of differentiation which have been raised in this chapter we offer the following diagram:

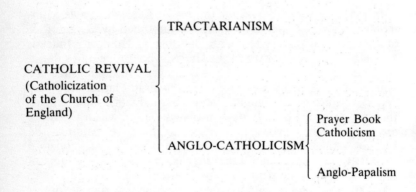

CATHOLIC REVIVAL
(Catholicization
of the Church of
England)

TRACTARIANISM

ANGLO-CATHOLICISM

Prayer Book
Catholicism

Anglo-Papalism

Chapter 2

From strength to strength: the glorious congresses

1 The early days of Anglo-Catholicism

As we have defined it, Anglo-Catholicism began to appear very shortly after the beginning of the Oxford movement. Quite quickly a number of individuals who readily accepted the Catholic status of the Church of England went beyond the practical aims of the Oxford Fathers and openly pronounced that the process of catholicization was best achieved by borrowing heavily from the Roman Catholic Church.

In the early days there were not many such individuals but they became prominent figures because of their unflinching and outstanding position. These first overt Romanizers were based in Oxford and consisted of such people as W. G. Ward, F. Oakeley, F. W. Faber, and J. B. Dalgairns. They were prominent in matters of piety and learning and, not surprisingly, many of them quickly or later jumped the narrow divide and made their submission to Rome (see ch. 9). While it is doubtful if Newman could be called an Anglo-Catholic, it was his secession which electrified the Tractarian movement and which made the Anglo-Catholic trends within the Catholic revival more prominent. That Newman did not take the step of joining the Church of Rome suddenly and without very careful theological reflection is apparent in his movingly written *Apologia pro vita sua*, which appeared in 1864. He was not an imitator of all things Roman, yet his influence amongst his contemporaries and those whom he taught in the university was enormous. Many of those influenced by him were more extreme and less cautious than he was. They soon adopted an unashamedly Anglo-Catholic stance and were far more concerned with liturgical and ecclesiastical matters than with theological issues. Some of them had in fact become Roman Catholic before he did: others, however, only followed him once he had set the example. We mention two cases in this very brief account of the development of Anglo-Catholicism up until the time of the First World War.

Perhaps the most colourful of all Anglo-Catholics in this early period was F. W. Faber (1814–63), who was greatly attached to Newman and who quickly embraced what might be called Catholic excesses. When he was rector of Elton in Huntingdonshire, he wrote in 1845 a life of St Wilfred for the *Library of the Fathers*, a precursor of the *Library of Anglo-Catholic Theology*. Faber's book contains sentences which openly showed adulation of all things papal. He introduced services in Elton which were entirely Roman and throughout his life had an 'exuberant fondness for Italian devotions' (Chapman 1961:139). It was obvious that what he had written was outside the boundaries set by the Oxford Fathers and as a result he and a group of men and women who led a semi-monastic life in Elton joined the Roman Catholic Church a few weeks after Newman took the same step. He later became an Oratorian, in London, again following the example of Newman; and his flamboyant personality, his love for continental Catholicism, and his enthusiasm for his newly found faith were often an embarrassment to the Catholic hierarchy.

A contemporary of Faber was W. G. Ward (1812–82), who seceded to Rome just before Newman. He was a philosopher, and also a fervent disciple of Newman. As a Fellow of Balliol College, Oxford, he wrote *The Ideal of a Christian Church* (1844). In it he openly demonstrated, like Faber, his admiration for the Roman Catholic Church and saw it as the only true church. He was charged with heresy by Oxford University and deprived of his degrees. Logically there was only one thing for him to do and that was to be received into the Roman Catholic Church. After his conversion he taught philosophy as a layman in Ware College, a Catholic eminary. He was one of the few lay converts of the period who was able to establish himself academically, although he was strongly anti-liberal and was opposed to allowing Roman Catholics to study in Oxford and Cambridge (see Adams 1977, chapter 6).

As it moved out of Oxford and into the parishes, Anglo-Catholicism began to grow rapidly, despite many conversions to Roman Catholicism and the opposition it brought upon itself from fervent Protestants both inside and outside the Church of England (see ch. 9). This was a period when heroic parish priests such as Fr Lowder, Fr Mackonochie, Fr Stanton, and others, began to emerge. Although convinced Anglo-Catholics and un-compromising in their use of Catholic ceremonial and devotions, these and others remained loyal to the Church of England. During this period and for some time after, the problem which faced authorities in the Church of England was how to curb, if not eliminate, the Catholic revival which was gathering such strength. The bishops, due to the limited power they could exercise within the Church, found it extremely difficult if not impossible to remove clergy, except for offences of a criminal or moral nature (see ch. 6.3). One answer was to bring ritualistic clergy to courts of law. Canon Newbolt of St Paul's cathedral is reputed to have suggested that the clergy who were prosecuted felt that the best way to get a bad law changed was to break it (see Walsh 1900:78). Many of the involved clergy would not accept law in the narrow sense as being applicable to them in ecclesiastical matters. As they saw it they had no right to be judged by the State but only by the Church, and in some instances clergy who were charged refused to attend the court. Active in prosecutions was the Church Association, which came into being in 1865 with the purpose of stemming the tide of extremism. It was instrumental in bringing to trial in the 1860s Fr Mackonochie of St Alban's, Holborn, for using what now seem such innocuous practices as a mixed chalice (water and wine) and altar candles. The Association was also bold enough to bring a bishop to court in 1888, the saintly Edward King of Lincoln. In 1874 the archbishop of Canterbury, Tait, worried by the continued spread of Anglo-Catholicism, persuaded Disraeli to take action and so came into force the Public Worship Regulation Act. As a result, from 1877 to 1882, four priests in various parts of the country were sent to prison, one for as long as 595 days. There was mounting opposition from moderate-minded people to the bill and the way it was put into practice and bishops vetoed cases of prosecution, as was their right in the Act. By the mid-1880s it was virtually obsolete.

It is an interesting fact that during this period and subsequently there was enough feeling in the country as a whole, encouraged by the powerlessness or lack of determination on the part of bishops, for the Church Association to gather sufficient financial resources to pay for the enormous expenses of court cases. But the opponents of ritualism found the overall results of legal action extremely disappointing and the Oxford and Anglo-Catholic movements were in no way deflected from their determined and persistent actions. Those who went to prison or suffered in any way were considered to be virtually martyrs. In this way the Anglo-Catholic cause was strengthened and became more widely known: it was certainly not weakened.

Mob violence did not do much good either. As is well known, a number of Anglo-Catholic parishes received a great deal of harassment from aggressive crowds, particularly parishes situated in working class areas. Much of the violence was generated by the Kensitites. John Kensit (1853–1902) was an ardent Protestant who, in 1890, became secretary of the Protestant Truth Society, which was rather more militant than the Church Association. He originally owned a Protestant bookshop in the city of London. The 'rent-a-mob' tactics which he originally organized were particularly in evidence in the period just before the First World War but continued afterwards. He founded and controlled the 'Wyclifites', who went all over the country stirring up trouble and taking part in acts of violence and profanation in Anglo-Catholic churches. They interrupted services by shouting, particularly at the moment of consecration in the eucharist. In a less threatening way, they held meetings and distributed pamphlets. (For a summary of the work of the Kensitites, see Munson 1975:385.)

In 1898 and 1899 the House of Commons had shown concern over extreme clergy not being disciplined. A motion condemning such clergy was passed at the time but no bill which called for action was put forward. Such was the concern about the unchecked growth of Anglo-Catholicism that the movement entered the heart of party politics. In 1904 the government was urged once again to act, and against its better judgement. This time it was by setting up a Royal Commission on Ecclesiastical Discipline. Randall Davidson, archbishop of Canterbury at the time, wrote to the Prime Minister, A. Balfour, that bishops did 'their best to discourage exaggerated Sacramentalism' but their task was made difficult if they had 'to look helplessly on while ignorant fanatics bring into court the very men who they are trying to guide into sounder paths' (quoted in Munson 1975:385). The findings of the Commission were interesting but their effect on curbing ritualism was virtually zero (see Lloyd 1946:144ff.). (The reports on parishes constitute a considerable source of material which still has to be carefully analysed (see ch. 4.2).)

Two important societies emerged which were particulary successful in fostering Anglo-Catholic ideals. One was the English Church Union, formed in 1860 to defend and at the same time spread high church ideals in the Church of England. It supported priests who were threatened by legal action or mob violence. As has just been noted, the Church Association formed by Evangelicals in the Church of England came into existence five years later. These two bodies stood in direct oppostion to each other (see Crowther 1970:186ff.). Charles Lindley Wood (1839–1934, later Viscount Halifax) became president of the English Church Union in 1868 and was the leading lay figure in the Anglo-Catholic world for many years, almost to the time he died in his nineties. The English Church Union was and still is the centre of the Anglo-Catholic party. Membership grew rapidly and in 1934 it changed its name to the Church Union (Crowther 1970:387; see ch. 4.2). The original aims of the English Church Union, which today seem extremely modest, were to encourage the priest to face east when celebrating holy communion (i.e. with his back to the people), to have candles on the altar, to use eucharistic vestments, unleavened bread, a mixed chalice, and incense, and to support reunion with Rome. The first five of these aims have today found their way into most parish churches; the last two may have been accepted by large numbers of Anglicans who would not necessarily wish to call themselves Anglo-Catholic.

The other society was for clergy only, the Society of the Holy Cross, and is described in the pages ahead (see ch. 3.3). It continues to this day, though with fewer members.

Several other important Anglo-Catholic societies also came into being in this early period. There was the Guild of All Souls, founded in 1873, which is still active, and the Confraternity of the Blessed Sacrament, which was started in 1857 and continues to this day, although it almost dissolved itself in its early days owing to the conversion of so many of its leaders to Roman Catholicism. Its main aim was to inculcate fasting before holy communion and the practice of confession.

What has been said so far constitutes a few indicators of the fact that by the end of the Victorian period and certainly up to the First World War radical changes were taking place in the Church of England through the Catholic revival. It moved steadily ahead without serious obstructions. The Oxford movement was making even greater progress. Clergy were accepting its ideals and many bishops were becoming sympathetic towards it, even if they did not identify with it (see Munson 1975:393). Anglo-Catholics were gaining strength, but under the cloak and protection of the more mature mother. They pushed ahead with their alien liturgical practices and religious ideals and met more opposition than did the Tractarians. Their following was never as great as that of the Tractarians but had a more vociferous presence and had a fair following in the cities, in the south of England, and amongst the middle classes (see ch. 4.3). Nevertheless they were very conscious of the opposition which they faced and this to some measure made them defensive. The truth of the matter is that both the Tractarian movement and – especially – the Anglo-Catholic movement caused strife and discord in the Church of England. In all probablity the Church would have enjoyed much more peace had the movements never existed and it was only after the First World War that the tension showed signs of decreasing. Today it is still present, though at a minimum. The Kensitites no longer exist, although they were still active in parishes where clergy defied bishops as late as the 1930s (see Walke 1935:292ff.).

Most observers would agree that Anglo-Catholicism expanded enormously in the last decades of the nineteenth century (see, for example, Yates 1975:30). Supporting such assertions, however, is by no means easy as statistical evidence is hard to come by and there are the ever-present problems of definition and statistical criteria (see ch. 4). But that is not the end of the story. From the initial uprise the movement was destined to grow even more and, above all, to become gradually accepted in the Church of England.

2 The effects of the 1914–18 war

For Anglo-Catholics the watershed of their history is without doubt the Great War, as it used to be called. The transition has been well analysed by Alan Wilkinson in *The Church of England and the First World War* (1978a). The appalling sufferings which the nation endured, with three-quarters of a million dead and double that number wounded, some of them seriously, found the Established Church ill-prepared to deal with the excessive suffering and bereavement. Never before in the history of Europe, indeed in the history of mankind so far as we are aware, had there been so much loss of life and maiming as took place in a matter of only four years. How could a religion – how could any church – comfort its members who experienced such carnage? The Christian doctrine of suffering within the context of belief in a creator God, who is all-powerful and at the same time absolute love, but who allows such terrible suffering, does not in itself provide very satisfying answers. Nevertheless, in the face of the tragedies they endured, millions of families had to be comforted in simple, practical terms. It was precisely here that Anglo-Catholicism offered something which the rest of the Church of England could not.

Although Anglo-Catholics had no alternative but to accept the traditional doctrines of God, creation, and man, they had for a long time adopted, in line with Roman Catholic practice, the tradition of praying for the dead and holding requiem masses. The aim of the Guild of All Souls, which was mentioned above, was precisely this. Of course it could be argued that such practices were, in the end, based on a doctrine of purgatory or some similar teaching. These beliefs and practices were the object of considerable attack by strong-minded Protestants, and middle-of-the road Anglicans were, to say the least, unhappy about them. With the advent of the war and as the death toll began to rise, criticism became less marked as praying for the dead began to be slowly accepted. Street shrines were erected in various places, notably in the East End of London, during and after the war. They recalled those who had died and there were also remembrance services where the names of the dead were specifically mentioned. After the war, memorials were erected in almost every local community, often by way of a stone cross, and sometimes a crucifix, together with the names of those who had fallen in battle. If one remembers the dead in prayer or in an act of silence, one is very near to actually praying for the dead. And, if this is accepted, then a requiem mass does not seem far out of place. In the face of so much suffering and death, denominational hostilities tended to melt away. Churches which had something comforting and hopeful to offer, some action that could be embarked upon, were at a great advantage over those which remained silent and only proclaimed doctrines that seemed cold and remote.

Throughout the war Anglo-Catholic priests displayed great spiritual qualities and their response to the crisis, not only at home but also at the front, made them generally admired, and even revered. Wilkinson has maintained that chaplains as a whole were ill-equipped to deal with the war situation. At the front they were often given protected status and did not know how to behave as chaplains in a positive and creative way. By contrast, perhaps because of their work in the slums, many Anglo-Catholic clergy showed great heroism and singleness of purpose, which was apparent when they were at the front. In particular, those who were members of the religious order of the Community of the Resurrection (Mirfield Fathers), appear to have given sterling service (see ch. 5.5).

Another reason for Anglo-Catholic priests becoming much more widely accepted also had its origins at the front. Chaplains generally became known as padres, basically the Portuguese, Spanish, and Italian word for father. Those soldiers and sailors who were lucky enough to come through the war very often continued to address their local clergy as padres. Despite the origin and meaning of the word, it became generally used and was appreciated by the chaplains themselves, irrespective of their denomination and churchmanship. It helped to overcome class distinction between officers and men and at the same time avoided the secular and 'common' Mister. Its use symbolized the degree of comradeship created amongst all those who had to face the terrible conditions of trench warfare and other forms of fighting during that ghastly war.

The years 1914–18 witnessed great social changes in Britain. In contrast to the nineteenth century, there emerged a more tolerant attitude towards religion and social mores. Notably there was a strong movement towards the liberation of women. Hostility against Anglo-Catholicism also mellowed and Protestantism lost its rigid dogmatism. Some bishops became more sympathetic towards Anglo-Catholic clergy than their predecessors and even welcomed them as hard working and pastorally effective priests. Others realized that the days of curbing Anglo-Catholicism through litigation were almost something of the past. Aggressive Protestantism had little or no following. With the end of the First World War and with many prejudices eroded, all seemed set for a steady, unhindered, even rapid growth of Anglo-Catholicism.

3 The congresses: introduction

As soon as peace had been established in 1918, Anglo-Catholics began to enter a triumphal period. There was no longer any need to be on the defensive or to be apologetic. For a long time the movement had seemed to be a movement in opposition. Now, with great self-confidence and openness, Anglo-Catholics could proclaim their ideals, knowing they had a strong following. They had much to be proud of – heroic priests working in the slums, clergy who had been sent to prison and highly regarded wartime chaplains. The opportunity for coming of age appeared in a rather unpremeditated way in a series of congresses. The first took place in 1920: subsequent gatherings were held in 1923, 1927, 1930, and 1933. The initial idea was the brainchild of a little known East End priest, the Rev C. R. Deakin, vicar of Christ Church, South Hackney. Quite rightly he has earned the title 'Father of the congresses'. A small group of priests, most of whom had been influenced by the Society of Saint Peter and Saint Paul (Keast 1984:52; and see below), became interested in the possibility of arranging a congress. The chief organizer and real leader, however, was the outstanding Marcus Atlay, vicar of St Matthew's, Westminster (see Wilson 1940:41ff.). It was really Atlay's great ability and enthusiasm which was able to realize the wildest dreams of the founding executive committee of fifteen members: twelve priests and three laymen (no women). The great success of the first congress in 1920 led to the subsequent ones. Atlay's strong personality, his constant devotion, and his deep conviction dominated the proceedings and gave the congresses, at least in part, a spirit of adventure that was not lost until the late 1930s (Keast 1984:52). He was president and chairman for the first congress. For the second, the chairman was the colourful Frank Weston, bishop of Zanzibar, who was a former curate of St Matthew's. The first congress was followed by a convention for priests held in 1921 in Oxford – about 1,200 attended (see ACPC 1921:viii–ix). The congress was at first intended to have a similar policy and plans were made to accommodate about 1,500 priests (Wilson 1940:79). The Catholic laity seemed to have got wind of the congress and showed a desire to come. An advertisement then followed which produced 2,000 positive replies by return of post. One possible venue was the Central Hall, Westminster, but this bastion of Methodism found its governors facing problems of conscience and the application was refused. It was pointed out by the applicants that the hall had been used for a prize fight and a meeting of the National Socialist party, but to no avail. The Queen's Hall was booked and immediately found to be too small. Finally, the largest hall in London, the Royal Albert Hall, was taken for what were by now 16,000 applicants. The programme consisted of eight sessions and lasted for the best part of a week.

There were probably two sources of inspiration for the congresses. One stemmed from the Church congresses. They began in 1861 in Cambridge and were held almost annually in different provincial centres or cathedral towns until 1913. After the war they began to dwindle away. On the whole they were supported by Anglicans of all shades of churchmanship, both lay and clerical, and they attracted a large number of bishops (see Crowther 1970: 198ff.). There were also contingents from the Tractarian and Anglo-Catholic camps and the main points of interest at the congresses were lectures by theologians and church leaders. The second source of inspiration was probably the Eucharistic congresses of the Roman Catholic Church, which began in France in 1881 through the intitiative of a local priest. They later became international and one congress was held in London in 1908. They were intended to be spiritually uplifting gatherings designed to heighten devotion to the Blessed Sacrament. They consisted of talks and addresses, but the main attraction was highly staged cultic devotions, which generally took place out of doors. Anglo-Catholics, as we shall see, combined the dominant characteristics of these two types of congresses in the organization of their impressive assemblies.

4 The congresses: a display of worship

From the very outset, the Anglo-Catholic congresses were gatherings for worship and devotion, as well as for theological education and enlightenment. (For accounts of the congresses given by the organizers, see ACC 1920 and subsequent reports.) Every congress opened with a great central act of worship. In 1923 it was held in St Paul's cathedral, when 900 robed clergy filled the nave for the high mass of the Holy Spirit, and where on the steps of the cathedral was the notice, 'Cathedral Full' (*The Times*, 11 July 1923; Wilson 1940:110). To pack the cathedral was a remarkable achievement when one thinks of the early days of Anglo-Catholicism. There was an even more spectacular opening in 1930 when the high mass was no longer at St Paul's, because it was not big enough, but in the White City Stadium, at which between 15,000 and 20,000 were said to be present (different estimates have been given in different sources). Three years later, to mark the centenary of the Oxford movement, there was evensong, not the most popular service with Anglo-Catholics, which 15,000 attended and which was also held in the White City Stadium. This time the high mass concluded the congress, at which between 45,000 and 50,000 were said to be present and which again took place in the Stadium (*CT*, 21 July 1933). The only diocesan bishop present, Bishop Furse of St Albans, was sheltered under a canopy in a manner reminiscent of the Roman Catholic eucharistic congresses. There was a fanfare of trumpets at the time of the consecration but no general communion of the people.

As well as these official acts of worship, Anglo-Catholic churches in London provided additional, more 'advanced' services. Here, after all, were to be found the great shrines which were so much part and parcel of Anglo-Catholic life. In 1920, nine such churches had services to commemorate the opening of the congress (Wilson 1940:43). At St Alban's, Holborn, about 1,200 attended mass, before which there was a great procession of bishops and clergy wearing birettas (*The Times*, 30 June 1920). And the secretary of the congress, Fr H. A. Wilson, at that time curate of St Matthew's, Westminster, wrote:

> No one who witnessed the procession through the streets to St Alban's, Holborn, will, I am confident, ever forget the

impression made upon them, as the column of priests moved slowly by, each priest reciting his Office, and all of them manifestly filled with the spirit of prayer for God's blessing upon the great venture.

(Wilson 1940:88)

There were also other churches where the opening was marked by the holding of services – St Paul's, Kinghtsbridge, St Augustine's, Kilburn, and even the less markedly Catholic St Margaret's, Westminster, where 500 intending worshippers were turned away because it was already full (*CT*, 2 July 1920). There were repeated accounts of the fact that the great centres of Anglo-Catholicism could not contain all those who wanted to take part in the worship which preceded the 1920 congress. At St Matthew's, Westminster, which, as has already been noted, was the organizing centre of the congress, the clergy 'certainly anticipated that there would be a great congregation for the High Mass, but we certainly did not expect that there would literally be hundreds who would fail to get into the Church at all!' (Wilson 1940:88). But Wilson was also impressed with other services connected with the 1920 congress.

I think on the whole that perhaps the Thanksgiving Services were in some ways the most striking feature of the congress. I am told that by 7.30 on Friday evening the queue of people waiting to get into Southwark Cathedral stretched from the Cathedral gates right across London Bridge to the Monument. It is the first time, surely, at any rate since the Reformation, that London Bridge heard a great crowd singing to the honour of the Mother of our Lord, as the waiting multitude sang again and again, 'Hail Mary, Hail Mary, full of grace.' These are some of the things which passed practically unnoticed in the newspapers; but which *we* shall never forget.

(Wilson 1940:88–9)

In addition to parish church and cathedral services, as well as to those in the White City Stadium, later congresses had special acts of worship in the Albert Hall itself. In 1933 there was a high mass or requiem for the souls of the founders of the Oxford movement, and then on another day in the same week, a high mass of the Blessed Sacrament (*CT*, 20 July 1933). In the same year there were other religious events, including pilgrimages to convents and monastic houses in and around London as well as to well-known Anglo-Catholic churches.

It would seem that a great deal of controversy went on behind the scenes about the propriety of being so openly Catholic and about the form of worship and devotions openly used at the congresses. Many Anglo-Catholics wanted to project an image of their party in the Church of England as one which, if it was not acceptable to the vast marjority of people, would at least not be offensive. Others, more aggressive, more extreme, less inhibited wanted to throw all caution to the wind. This policy became dominant after the first congress. It was in part due to the chairman of the 1923 congress, the forceful Frank Weston. The second morning opened with telegrams sent to the king and queen, the archbishops, the bishop of London, and the Patriarch of Constantinople. All this was agreed on (Hughes 1961:69). Then Weston proposed that a telegram of greetings also be sent to the Holy Father. This motion immediately caused disruption but was passed. Later it was seen to be a great mistake and W. H. Frere of the Community of the Resurrection said so two days later at the congress. It seems that no telegram was sent to leaders of Protestant churches. What some felt to be offensive, however, was that the pope was addressed as the Holy Father and that the intentions of the telegram would be misunderstood (see letters in the *Church Times* following the issue of 13 July 1923). There were even those who felt that the telegram fostered an underground rift which marred the sense of triumph by forcing people to side either with Weston or with Frere (see Hughes 1961:74). Incidentally, Frere was made bishop of Truro shortly afterwards in a diplomatic move to have one Anglo-Catholic bishiop on the bench, but his later restrained attitudes did not in the long run please Anglo-Catholics (Hughes 1961:70–1).

For many, this congress was the greatest of them all. Certainly never before had participants experienced such fervour, enthusiasm and effervescence in an Anglo-Catholic gathering as they did on that occasion (Wilson 1940:114). It was largely due to the influence of the chairman himself. Professor C. H. Turner of Oxford, an Anglo-Catholic layman, said of him: 'I think that the Bishop of Zanzibar was the greatest man I have ever met. I know he was the greatest orator I have ever heard' (Wilson 1940:121). Alec Vidler, a former dean of King's College, Cambridge, and in his early days a keen Anglo-Catholic, has expressed similar sentiments about Frank Weston – '[He] moved and inspired me when he visited Cambridge more than any other speaker' (Vidler 1977:31).

It was commonly said that the 1923 congress was very much Weston's. To over 10,000 people he delivered a deeply stirring address covering many aspects of religious life. Let two paragraphs speak for themselves.

> O brethren! if only you listen to-night your Movement is going to sweep England. I am not talking economics, I do not understand them. I am not talking politics, I do not understand them. I am talking the Gospel. And I say to you this. If you are Christians, then your Jesus is one and the same: Jesus on the throne of his glory, Jesus in the blessed sacrament, Jesus received into your hearts in communion, Jesus mystically with you as you pray, and Jesus enthroned in the hearts and bodies of his brothers and sisters up and down the country. And it is folly – it is madness – to suppose that you can worship Jesus in the sacrament and Jesus on the throne of glory, when you are sweating him in the souls and bodies of his children.
>
> (quoted in Wilson 1940:120)

> To put it quite clearly, our present duty as Anglo-Catholics is to make a far deeper surrender to our Lord Christ, and to make it over a far wider area than ever before. We are to make such a surrender of self to him over the whole area of our life that, were he to choose to come on earth to reign in his own person, neither you nor I would find it necessary to alter the principles upon which we conduct our work, our prayer, our worship. That is the point. Were he to come, our principles would not require to be altered.
>
> (quoted in Wilson 1940:114–15)

There were some who thought he was destined to be the leader of Anglo-Catholics in England. He was eminently qualified: he had been given a DD by Oxford university for a thesis on Christology, and, as a result of his activities in East Africa during the Great War, he was mentioned in despatches and awarded the OBE. Anglo-Catholics at this time were much in need of a dynamic leader and in Frank Weston many felt they had found one (Hughes 1961:69). Some questioned whether he would ever leave his beloved Africa. The issue was shortly settled when he died there in 1924 (see Maynard-Smith 1926).

Great adulation there might have been for Frank Weston at the 1923 congress, but there were many, especially those on the borders of Anglo-Catholicism, who saw a great deal of harm in the excesses displayed in the congresses, particularly in connection with Marian devotions shown by the hymns sung to the Blessed Virgin Mary (see ch. 1.5). Objections to these were raised by the popular, and high-church, bishop of London,

Winnington-Ingram, who had been persuaded to be the president of the congress. He was not often present at the congress because the National Assembly of the Church of England was then meeting in London to revise the 1662 Prayer Book – a revision for which Anglo-Catholics were the main cause and which they later so strongly opposed. When he knew these hymns were to be sung, Winnington-Ingram openly stated that they were contrary to the doctrine and practice of the Church of England. Such objections were dealt with publicly and disarmingly by the chairman. Frank Weston said: 'I appeal to you who reverence our Lady Mary to remember that she is the Queen of Courtesy and, out of courtesy to our President, let us deny ourselves the joy of singing these hymns [cheers]' (*CT*, 13 July 1923). In connection with the cult of the Blessed Virgin Mary, the bishop of Zanzibar appealed to the bishop of London, and addressed his words also to members of the National Assembly:

> Let his Lordship tell the members that if we invoked the saints and gave special honour to our Lady, it is because we see them in the heart of Jesus. It is to Mary within the heart of God that we sing our hymns, and all of us are of one mind in this, that you cannot invoke the saints outside the heart of Jesus.
>
> (*CT*, 13 July 1923)

The Hail Mary was said from time to time during the main sessions and there were, at least in the special reports, references to the Paternoster, not to the Lord's Prayer, the name usually used by Anglicans. It is not certain whether the actual words were recited in Latin or in English: one suspects it was the latter.

Dominating the Albert Hall was a large crucifix placed on the rostrum, alongside which was a panel displaying a verse associated with post-Tridentine Catholicism rather than Anglicanism:

> Blessed and praised for evermore
> Be Jesus Christ on His
> Throne of Glory
> And in the most Holy Sacrament of the Altar

Sensitivity about loyalty to the Prayer Book and the ethos of the Church of England as it had evolved echoed in the *Church Times*, which in general gave very strong support to Anglo-Catholicism (see ch. 1.5). In reporting the 1923 congress, and referring to the holy communion service at St Paul's cathedral, where it seems there was no general communion, although it was the 'most beautiful High Mass in Europe', it was noted that the service was entirely according to the Prayer Book, including the recitation of the Decalogue. Again, in 1933, a reporter stated that as the clergy entered the Albert Hall, many genuflected before the giant crucifix, but that the office of evensong was according to the Prayer Book, by 'men who loved the Book'; and, one of the services was 'absolutely Prayer Book from beginning to end' (*CT*, 14 July 1933). Again, at the high mass which concluded the congress (except that the Gloria followed the Kyrie) 'the Prayer Book was exactly followed' (*CT*, 21 July 1933). Here were attempts, perhaps rather pathetic ones, to show that Anglo-Catholics generally were committed to the language, structure, and ethos of the Prayer Book. The *Church Times* tried to make out a case for those who thought they were loyal to their Church but where their formal and informal language implied something else. To the general public it was obvious that the ideal which Anglo-Catholics aspired to was that of the Roman Church. How else could the outsider interpret the following words of the chairman? 'Take courage, then, the Eastern Patriarch smiles on you; the Bishop of the Diocese loves you; the Holy Father waits' (*CT*, 13 July 1923). For what does the pope wait? For Anglo-Catholicism to become yet more extreme? For Anglo-Catholics to convert to Roman Catholicism? For the union of the Anglican and Roman Catholic churches? It is in such assemblies that conventional barriers break down and hopes and ideals become unfettered. Certainly such language completely lacked that degree of carefulness and diplomacy that is so much associated with the Roman Catholic Church itself but which at the same time is alien to the general ethos of the Church of England.

5 The congresses: their popularity

The great sense of euphoria which permeated the 1923 congress was a reflection of the state of hope and triumph to be seen in the Anglo-Catholic movement in this period. In varying degrees such a state of jubilation was found in all the congresses, although towards the middle of the 1930s there were some who felt it was tailing off. The success of the early congresses readily caught the attention of the national press and they were widely reported in church newspapers. In times past, Anglo-Catholics had been in the news, usually on account of court cases or because of extreme practices carried out in individual churches and irritating to ecclesiastical authorities or to Protestant protagonists. Now, the story was one of going from strength to strength and the newspapers seemed to suggest that Anglo-Catholicism was, despite its romanizing tendencies, a respectable force which had to be accepted. It had become established within the Established Church.

As we have hinted, some indication of the popularity of the congresses can be gauged from the fact that the largest public buildings in London had to be used to accommodate all the participants. In addition, there were secondary congresses held in provincial cities in the months that followed some of the congresses. They were addressed by some of those who had given talks in the Albert Hall. There were day conferences as well, held in most dioceses, and at the time of the centenary of the Oxford movement special services with commemoration sermons were organized at some cathedrals, notably Canterbury and York, as well as Westminster Abbey, and a high mass was held at Keble College, Oxford. In addition, high masses were celebrated at various churches in the centre of the city and a noonday sermon was preached at St Mary's, the university church. Many of the events were held simultaneously: all were reported to be well attended.

Something of the growth in popularity of the congresses may be seen from the numbers who enrolled or who were called members. But here there are divergencies in the published statistics. The first set of figures refers to those given in the *Church Times* (21 July 1933) and the second to statistics from the official reports:

Year	Number enrolled (CT)	Number enrolled (Reports)
1920	18,000	13,000*
1923	not given	15,000
1927	24,000	21,000
1930	28,000	29,000
1933	70,000	70,000

*16,000 (Wilson 1940:79)

No matter which set of figures is accepted, both show great increases with the passing of years. The leap in numbers from 1930 to 1933 may be attributed to the fact that the latter year was the centenary of the Oxford movement and drew, one suspects, many sympathetic to that movement who may not have wished to be totally identified with Anglo-Catholicism. They were, however, prepared to support the congress. It was said that 100,000 commemorative cards were printed for the congress, displaying Leonardo da Vinci's *Last Supper* together with a verse written by John Keble.

Certainly the congresses could pack the Albert Hall for from three days to a week, with three sessions a day, morning, afternoon, and evening (the 1927, 1930, 1933 congresses lasted for seven days). The chairman of the 1920 congress, Fr Atlay, wrote:

> Again, we knew that if all the ticket-holders used their tickets the Albert Hall would be filled at each session; but we did not expect that a queue would begin to form outside the hall, at 7:30 each morning, of enthusiasts who were prepared to wait two hours and a half if only they might obtain a good seat. It is worth recording, I think, that one of the attendants at the Albert Hall told me that no boxing match had ever filled the place as it was filled, eight times over, during our congress.
>
> (quoted in Wilson 1940:88)

In 1923, overflow meetings were held concurrently in the Queen's Hall, where tickets were cheaper and where the organizers hoped to attract more working-class people than at the Albert Hall. Reports said that the hall was constantly full with 3,000 people in attendance and many of the speakers gave lectures in both halls. Other overflow meetings were held in Kensington Town Hall. With numbers of this size it was obvious that the congresses were not being attended just by clergy! The vast majority of those who did attend were lay people and at the 1923 congress only 13 per cent were clergy (Wilson 1940: 110 n.1).

6 The congresses: their unpopularity

It has been noted that the general support given to the congresses was far more extensive than the early organizers had, even in their wildest dreams, hoped for. The success of one congress after another made priests and laity jubilant. Yet behind such optimism and celebration there was a dark and foreboding shadow. That shadow was something which some Anglo-Catholics had seen for a long time and it was there at the congresses. The unpalatable truth was that the movement was still not popular amongst English bishops. The fact saddened the hearts of most Anglo-Catholics. As Anglo-Catholics saw it, central to church order is the bishop, who is the *sine qua non* of validly ordained priests who are the true dispensers of the sacraments. There can be no church without priests, no priests without bishops. Bishops are the very life-blood of the church and yet it was the English bishops who rejected Anglo-Catholicism despite its loud proclamation concerning their prime importance (ch. 6.3).

Even when a diocesan bishop was present at the congresses, it was not always a happy occasion. We have already referred to the ambiguous position in which Winnington-Ingram found himself when he was president of the 1923 congress. He gave the opening address and attended it once or twice but it is clear that his criticisms prevented him from being more enthusiastic about the congress. He was known as 'Uncle Arthur' amongst Anglo-Catholics, and although he had high church sympathies he was suspect in their eyes. He was in fact caught up in a number of unpleasant Anglo-Catholic controversies in his diocese (see p. 62).

Yet it was the virtual absence of bishops as a whole that was so galling to the organizers. At the 1920 congress, all the diocesan bishops were invited. Out of more than forty, only two, it seems, Bishop Ridgeway of Salisbury and Bishop Furse of St Alban's, responded positively. Ridgeway preached at St Alban's, Holborn, and not surprisingly was cheered at the congress and called 'the bravest bishop in England' (Wilson 1940:82). Furse preached at Southwark cathedral at the closing service.

Three years later, several bishops were present for part of the time, the bishops of London, Salisbury, Guildford, St Alban's, and Peterborough, along with Bishop Gore. The Evangelical bishop of Chelmsford would have attended but died the day after the congress opened (*CT*, 13 July 1923). In 1933 the only diocesan bishop at the final service was the bishop of St Alban's, although one or two other bishops had come to earlier sessions. Sometimes a suffragan bishop or two attended the congresses, but on the whole those bishops who were committed to the congresses were from overseas, from such places as Nassau, Milwaukee, Accra, and, of course, Zanzibar. These dioceses were known to be strongly Anglo-Catholic in ethos and it can be convincingly argued that Anglo-Catholicism functions much more coherently and satisfactorily in missionary dioceses far removed from England (see ch. 3.7). At the Overseas Association of the 1930 congress seventy-five bishops were present and nearly all of them must have been from abroad.

It was not only the lack of bishops that was felt so keenly, but also the absence of other ecclesiastical dignitaries in the hierarchical ladder. In 1920 the dean and chapter of St Paul's cathedral refused to allow a thanksgiving service which would have included a solemn Te Deum and sermon although a promise was given that no incense would be used (Wilson 1940:82). But in 1923 the cathedral authorities changed their minds and, as we have already noted, allowed a high mass to be celebrated. The dean, however, was absent on this occasion, perhaps conveniently, receiving an honorary doctorate from the university of Edinburgh.

The virtual absence of English bishops at the congresses made many Anglo-Catholics feel they had been let down. They believed themselves to be loyal to the Church of England – or at least the vast majority did – their priests worked extremely hard, and yet they were rejected – rejected not so much by people at large but by the highest authorities in the Church. The lack of episcopal support was noted in 1930 by the *Church Times*, which stated that bishops cold-shouldered the congresses and that 'Catholics are still inevitably made to feel strangers in their Mother's house' (11 July 1930). In 1927 the archbishop of Canterbury, Randall Davidson, sent a short and rather curt letter to the congress, which did nothing to reassure members. This was a time when changes to the 1662 Prayer Book were coming before Parliament, and the reason they were was in part due to what Anglo-Catholics were doing to parish services. The intended changes were not to their liking, for they were not Catholic enough. Their well organized opposition to the reforms, which were supported by those of Tractarian sympathies, was sufficient to defeat the planned changes and prevented the emergence of a new Prayer Book. In 1930 Anglo-Catholics received encouraging overtures from the new and slightly more sympathetic archbishop of Canterbury, Cosmo Gordon Lang (1864–1945), who sent a letter to the congress saying that Anglo-Catholics were 'a great body of eager and enthusiastic members of the Church' (*CT*, 4 July 1930). The message received tumultuous applause. Nevertheless, he took the opportunity of criticizing Anglo-Catholics:

> I dare say some controversial things have been, or may be, said or done in your Congress, possibly some things of which I might not personally be able to approve. But I do not dwell on these matters.
>
> (*CT*, 4 July 1930)

So here, even from this kindly primate, was a double-edged compliment. But Anglo-Catholics were being paid back in their own coin (see ch. 6.3).

7 The congresses: marks of identification

The congresses showed the Anglo-Catholic movement at its peak. They publicly stated what it was about, for they demonstrated the aims and ideology of the movement. In worship and in verbal proclamation there stood an unequivocal declaration of its ideals, hopes, and achievements. What happened at these congresses encapsulates what is implied by Anglo-Catholicism in this book.

What should any layperson who calls himself an Anglo-Catholic, or simply a Catholic, be required to do? What rules should he follow? What precepts should he try to live by? The answer came out quite clearly in the 1930 congress in an address by Fr Biggart, a member of the Community of the Resurrection. He enumerated the following duties for men, and one wonders how different they were for women (see *CT*, 11 July 1930)!

1 Hear mass on Sundays
2 Receive holy communion at least three times a year
3 Go to confession at least once a year
4 Observe Fridays as a fast-day
5 Give alms liberally
6 Observe the forbidden degrees in marriage

Some of these rules of life, of course, might be followed by Anglicans who would in no way wish to be identified with Anglo-Catholicism. It is interesting these days to note the distinction made between hearing mass and receiving holy communion (see ch. 11.5). Fr Biggart admitted in his talk that confession was not compulsory in the Church of England – and of course there is no service for it in the 1662 Prayer Book – but he claimed it was allowed and should be encouraged (see ch. 3.5). Such rules appear simple enough and perhaps it was their simplicity and directness that had a great appeal. They were certainly practical and no doubt fulfilling them provided the person with a great deal of satisfaction (see ch. 5.8).

During the congresses, leaders were shrewd enough to put forward a policy which would help to strengthen and advance the Anglo-Catholic cause. There was one issue which at that time seemed of vital importance, a veritable fortress to be scaled, the achievement of which would ensure Anglo-Catholic victory. This fortress concerned the reservation of the Blessed Sacrament. Priests and laity alike were encouraged to demand that it be reserved in every parish church. Were this ever to be achieved, Anglo-Catholics believed that they would then have fully catholicized the Church of England. In 1933 Fr Pinchard, secretary of the English Church Union, made an appeal to the effect that no one should rest 'until every parish church has the right to reserve the Blessed Sacrament for the benefit of the sick and dying' (*CT*, 14 July 1933). This was a call to increased determination in the battle which was raging in the 1920s and 1930s between Anglo-Catholics and certain bishops over the right to reserve the Sacrament. The formal and 'legitimate' reason for wanting reservation was for the purpose of giving communion to the sick and dying. If this were the sole function of the reserved Sacrament there would have been no problem, for on the whole bishops would accept such a laudable intention. But in one Anglo-Catholic church after another the reserved Sacrament, as in Roman Catholic churches, was given a place of great prominence, either on the high altar or in a side-chapel. There, with a lamp burning perpetually before the aumbry or tabernacle, it readily became a focus for private prayer or devotion. All this was probably quite acceptable to bishops and most Anglicans. The point at issue was that, in addition, the reserved Sacrament was used for extra-liturgical services such as adoration, benediction and exposition. The services usually, but not always, took place on a Sunday evening in addition to or instead of evensong, and called for the elevation or carrying of the Blessed Sacrament in such ways as to evoke veneration. In the 1930s the bishop of St Edmundsbury and Ipswich was reported in the congresses to have said that he had refused to grant permission for reservation of the Sacrament as he realized that if a church were allowed it the incumbent would soon begin to use it for cultic purposes. Pusey himself held that there was no authority for reservation except for giving communion to the sick (see ch. 1.5; Simpson 1932:253). But it was in the 1923 congress that Frank Weston stirred up great enthusiasm for the worship of Christ in the tabernacle. He said: 'He calls you from the tabernacle: we adore Him on the altar'; and, in concluding words which became famous, he made a passionate plea to Anglo-Catholics as they left the congress to 'fight for their tabernacles' (*CT*, 20 July 1923).

The call for reservation to be allowed generally was the battle-cry of Anglo-Catholics during this period (see Simpson 1932:253–66). But it might also be argued that reservation was a hallmark of Anglo-Catholicism itself. Anglo-Catholics reckoned that a church which had reservation would at least be potentially one of theirs. In their call for the right to have the Sacrament reserved they also implied that they had the right to extend this 'privilege' of using the Elements of the eucharist from a 'cold', non-action context, that is, simply reserved for the sick, to one in which the Sacrament was the centre of private and corporate adoration. As two moderate Anglo-Catholic priests, writing in criticism of the 1923 congress, said, it had become obvious that 'the extra-liturgical cultus of the Blessed Sacrament is of the *esse* of the Catholic position (*CT*, 20 July 1923). It was estimated that in the 1920s there were 700 churches in England which had reservation, together with 80 chapels not associated with parishes (Stewart 1929:362). Some have thought these figures low.

The bishops, quite rightly, felt that there was a degree of dishonesty in the application of Anglo-Catholics to have the Sacrament reserved. Anglo-Catholics said one thing to the bishop and did another, and they were well aware that what they were doing was contrary to the wish of the bishop (see ch. 6.3). Most Anglo-Catholic clergy knew that if they applied to the bishop to have the Sacrament reserved for the purposes of benediction or adoration (sometimes called devotions) they would have their application rejected. Charles Gore (1853–1932) was very much at the centre of the controversy over the reserved Sacrament. As bishop of Worcester, then Birmingham, and finally Oxford, he might have been seen as one of the few diocesan bishops who supported Anglo-Catholicism. After all he had founded the Community of the Resurrection. He was an unashamed Catholic, but his place amongst Anglo-Catholics was ambiguous. He seemed to be identified with them, but, when it came to reservation, he certainly was not. He stuck to the rigid position that the reserved Sacrament was not to be used for cultic purposes and in this he gained the respect of only a limited number of Anglo-Catholics (see Mary 1968:56).

It is doubtful, however, in the 1920s and 1930s and certainly today, whether the presence of the reserved Sacrament in a parish church is a sufficient reason to identify that church as being Anglo-Catholic (see ch. 1.4). The reason is quite simply that high church clergy and Prayer Book Catholics both in the past and in the present keep the reserved Sacrament in their churches for the sick and dying and for no other purpose. Using the reserved Sacrament for extra-liturgical purposes can be seen as a point of issue between 'true' Catholics and 'pseudo' Catholics: it is a way to sort out the men from the lads! After Anglo-Catholics had helped to defeat the reformed Prayer Books of 1927 and 1928 in Parliament, Winnington-Ingram tried to impose upon the clergy of London the regulations about reservation laid down in the 1928 book. Of the 149 incumbents of the diocese whose churches had reservation, 21 refused to accept the demand to stop holding cultic services (Williamson 1956:151 states that, in total, 71 clergy had devotions at the time of the imposition). The bishop's demand caused consternation amongst Anglo-Catholics. About this time the Federation of Catholic

Priests, with a membership of 1,400 in the country as a whole, stated that it would not change its position over reservation and would continue the policy of: '(i) Communion from the Reserved Sacrament of the whole, as well as the sick; (ii) Corporate Devotions before the Reserved Sacrament; (iii) Reservation of one kind; (iv) Perpetual Reservation in spite of the prohibition of the diocesan bishop' (quoted in Hughes 1961:93–4). Small wonder that Anglo-Catholics felt, as well as most bishops, that with the rejection of the reformed Prayer Books, and with the defiance of their clergy, such as those of the Federation of Catholic Priests, the last attempt to curb Anglo-Catholicism by coercion had been made (Hughes 1961:92). The more realistically minded would have put the date much earlier.

We have been dealing with the issue of identity. It is clear that, in itself, reservation is not a criterion, but that cultic services associated with it are. Another indicator which has already been put forward – and usually the two indicators go hand in hand – is Marian devotion coupled with invocation of the saints (see ch. 1.5).

8 The congresses: further observations

Each congress was addressed by about twenty theologians and church leaders, both clerical and lay. The speakers were generally, but not always, sympathetic to Anglo-Catholicism. One of the less sympathetic, who appeared at an early congress, was the Rev Professor H. Relton, whose paper was given a very unfriendly reception. Not all the subjects were related to the peculiar characteristics of Anglo-Catholicism. Some considered traditional doctrine, the Gospels, worship, Christian unity, modernism, and social and industrial problems, and some, perhaps more pointedly, considered the nature of Catholicism and 'the case against Rome'. Generally speaking the papers were given by leading Anglo-Catholic theologians such as L. S. Thornton, N. P. Williams, and K. E. Kirk, to mention but a few. There seems little merit here in describing or analysing the many papers that were presented.

Those who attended the congresses were not only prepared to worship and to be mentally stimulated, they were also ready to donate money. At the 1920 congress, in response to the call of the chairman, Fr M. Atlay, £43,000 was raised, nearly all of it given there and then. Some £7,000 came from the sale of gifts which those who attended gave on the spot – valuable jewels, brooches, and furs were amongst those things spontaneously given (Wilson 1940:43). The intention was for the money to be given to foreign missions, especially to the Anglo-Catholic oriented Universities' Mission to Central Africa (see ch. 3.7). Earlier on in the congress a hurriedly convened committee agreed to the idea of asking for what was thought to be a wellnigh impossible sum – £50,000. In the event the target was almost reached (Wilson 1940:81). In 1923 there was rather less money raised – £27,000 for the church at home, as well as £1,600 for foreign missions (Wilson 1940:114).

9 Conclusion

The intention of the first congress was 'to deepen catholic consciousness' (*CT*, 6 July 1923). There seems little doubt that such an aim was fulfilled more adequately than the organizers had prognosticated. The 1923 congress appears to have run amok with enthusiasm; that of 1933, because of its large numbers, spoke of strong, unshakeable success. There can be no doubt that the early congresses witnessed a heightening of religious devotion and that the effervescence of the common gathering gave rise to much religious fervour as new peaks and hopes were achieved for the devout, and the semi-committed were given greater assurance (see Pickering 1984, chapters 21 and 22). The effects extended well beyond the congresses themselves. Fr H. A. Wilson noted that on the last day of the 1920 congress, a priest in the church at which he was curate, St Matthew's, Westminster, 'heard confessions for very many hours, of which a number were made for the first time and not only by the laity' (Wilson 1940:89).

But the sense of triumph could not last for ever. Like any series of effervescent gatherings, an end has to be reached. Novelty wears off; the steam runs out. There were some who felt that even at the very height of the congresses the tide was beginning to turn and so indeed it was. The peak of Anglo-Catholicism had been reached and a downhill path awaited it (see Kent 1987:92). Some could see the future decline in the early 1920s. The point of triumph heralded a diminution. John Gunstone has observed that, with hindsight and taking into account the subsequent history of Anglo-Catholicism, one can see that the magnificent high mass of the 1933 congress was in fact a requiem mass (Gunstone 1968:202). Indeed, one could argue that the early congresses reflected the achievements of a preceding decade and that they were not a true indication of the situation in the period between the two world wars. What happened thereafter is taken up in a later chapter (see ch. 11.2).

Chapter 3

A missionary movement?

1 An evangelical streak in Anglo-Catholicism

What at first seems a strange fact about Anglo-Catholicism is
that, despite its strong anti-Protestant stance, notions of mission
and conversion were very much part of the movement. It is true
that the terms have not been as extensively used amongst
followers as they have been in Evangelical circles but their
circulation, especially in the early days of Anglo-Catholicism, was
much greater than is commonly realized (see Voll t.1963). To be
devoted to mission work – to deliberately go out to convert
people – is to give religion a serious dimension in which truth is
at stake to such a degree that people are asked to forsake one
position and embrace another. In the nineteenth century, and
even today, some Anglo-Catholics and Evangelicals, because of
the seriousness with which they regarded religion, often found
themselves on the same side. They had two common enemies.
The first was religious indifference, commonly found amongst
people who viewed religion in an easygoing and nonchalant way.
The second was religious liberalism where certain fundamental
beliefs were rejected in the name of reason – the enemies here
were often found to be theologians themselves, who gave the
impression of betraying the religion they professed. Both types of
enemies had little or no time for mission and conversion. For
Anglo-Catholics and Evangelicals, on the other hand, religion
was something to wax enthusiastic about. The very last thing it
should be considered to be is a cultural cloak for a comfortable
social life. And comfortable, ordinary Church of England religion
was seen to be precisely that at the time. For Evangelicals and
Anglo-Catholics, to be religious meant swimming against the
stream: it certainly was not sitting at ease in Zion. Their task was
to convert Anglicans themselves and make them take up
positions where religion was an either/or way of life. Either one
should be sincerely and devoutly religious or else abandon
religion altogether.

65

In order to make Anglicans see that they were indeed Catholic and to encourage them to be so in deed as well as in word, it is hardly surprising that Anglo-Catholics were quite happy to speak about conversion. Priests so persuaded wanted to 'convert parishioners' to Catholicism (see Mackenzie 1924:60). They started their task of conversion by introducing architectural changes and liturgical innovations, as we have already seen (see ch. 1). Conversion therefore often meant converting churches so that they looked like Catholic churches. Conversion in this sense was a turning away from old things and old services to the new, to the catholicization of the Church of England.

But the work of conversion was carried out with a further object in view. It was not only a question of converting members from position *A* to position *B* inside the Church of England, but that of the conversion of people to the Church itself – people who were totally outside any religious body at all. Even those who are only marginally acquainted with the history of the Church of England in the nineteenth century will know that one of the most serious problems confronting church leaders at the time was that a large number of citizens living in what was considered the leading Protestant country of the world were indifferent to the call of the Gospel and the church. With the growing industrialization of Britain and the expansion of towns and cities, there emerged a level of secularization which was the cause of considerable alarm amongst very many clergy and dedicated laity. The issue has been extremely well documented (see, for example, Currie *et al.* 1977). Anglo-Catholic clergy were as much alarmed about the situation as were clergy generally, but they were unique in so far as they held that the panacea for the problem was to be found in the distinct way of life that was theirs. More than any other approach it constituted, they thought, the most likely instrument for bringing the unchurched masses to Christianity. Rightly or wrongly, leaders of all denominations held that it was the impoverished working classes, not the middle classes, who were indifferent to the Christian message. As Fr Lowder said in the 1860s, the system that was adopted in the London church of St Barnabas's, Pimlico, where he was curate, was the only one that would remedy the conditions of the poor of London and offer them a way out of their prison of poverty (Embry 1931:xxxix). Throughout the industrial revolution the efforts of the Church of England had been singularly unsuccessful in coping with the changes in population, and enthusiastic Anglo-Catholics were convinced that what they had to offer unsophisticated working folk was a religion with colour, movement, action, and, above all, simple rules for being a Christian. This was in contrast to the dull dreariness of an average Anglican service, the centre of which was a long and often boring sermon – sometimes little more than an intellectualized interpretation of Christianity. Before the advent of Anglo-Catholicism one could point to Methodism with its inherently warm appeal to ordinary people and contrast it with the coldness, formality, and perhaps middle-class pomposity which characterized the Church of England. But Methodism had lost its initiative and had had only limited success in many working-class areas. Something different was needed and Anglo-Catholics held that in the second half of the nineteenth century theirs alone was the movement which could rescue the Church of England from its ineffectualness in working-class areas.

Anglo-Catholic priests enthusiastically entered the slums with a great sense of mission and a deep concern for the welfare of the poor, together with the conviction that they could succeed in the work of conversion where traditional Anglicanism had failed. Such a concern comes out very clearly in the words of an early Anglo-Catholic priest, James Skinner, writing in the 1850s about the ritual court cases which charged Anglo-Catholic priests with responsibility for illegal practices. He wrote: 'We cannot build up poor men's souls and fight against such foes as these anti-ritualists at the same time' (quoted in Embry 1931:xxxi). Many Anglo-Catholic priests involved in mission work boasted happily of their Evangelical outlook. Fr James Adderley (1861–1942), a well-known mission priest, was pleased to call himself, and others like him, 'Gospel Catholics' (Stevens 1943:27). He criticized the sermon of a famous Nonconformist theologian, R. J. Campbell,
• saying: 'There isn't enough Gospel in this to save a cat!' (quoted in Stevens 1943:23). In Fr Stanton, the great, popular Anglo-Catholic preacher, there was a strong Evangelical streak. It was probably this which prevented him from becoming a Roman Catholic. He wrote to an undergraduate hindered from making his confession: 'Nothing must ever take away our rest in the old Evangelical love and our trust in Jesus' (Russell 1917:75). He relied on a simple Gospel message: his biographer called him 'from first to last a "Bible-Christian"' (Russell 1917:50). Fr Dolling of Portsmouth, who was always looked upon as a Romanizer, and who invariably wore a biretta and cassock, was in many respects 'an Evangelical to the backbone'; he was very warmly disposed towards non-denominational Evangelicals (Voll t.1963:109). Fr Waggett of the Society of St John the Evangelist, who was always highly regarded as a preacher, spoke of the need

in the Church of England for old fashioned Evangelicals to preach about the atonement (see Knox 1918:58). His position with regard to the Church was described as that of 'Catholic Evangelism' (Nias 1961:211). The Rt Hon G. W. E. Russell, friend and biographer of Stanton, gave a lecture to the English Church Union in 1898 with the intention of demonstrating that Catholic theology is at heart Evangelical and that Evangelical doctrine in 'so far as it is constructive and affirmative' is 'truly Catholic' (Russell 1902:314). Certainly on the grounds of basic doctrine Catholics and Evangelicals have much in common, far more than either group has with liberals. Those of the Catholic mould wanted to combine the experience of a personal Saviour with the sacraments and ritual of their brand of churchmanship. How far these high church and Anglo-Catholic Evangelicals assumed the cloak of early Wesleyanism, as some have maintained, is doubtful (Voll t.1963:88). The Evangelical Catholic component was at its height in the second half of the nineteenth century and was particularly influential on Anglicanism as a whole (Voll t.1963:136). (For an understanding of the complicated relations between Tractarians and Evangelicals, see Brilioth 1934, especially chapter 3.)

2 Two models of mission work

Although Anglo-Catholics and Evangelicals frequently respected one another from a distance, modes of mission and conversion were quite different in the two camps.

Probably no one has shown more clearly the differences between contrasting models of mission and conversion than Raoul Allier. In his monumental work, *La Psychologie de la conversion chez peuples non-civilisés*, he posited what we might call ideal types projected by Catholic and Protestant in connection with the conversion of preliterate peoples (Allier 1925,1:15–18). For much of his work he relied on the accounts of missionaries and his analysis is very much that of the *anthropologue de salon*. For our present purpose one can adapt what he says about the models or ideal types in this way. The object of mission and conversion is the same for both Catholics and Protestants – to make Christians of people who were formerly not Christian. To this end, two different methods are employed. For the Catholic, the initial point is to 'plant the church' through the agency of a missionary, who is nearly always a priest, and who erects a building, a chapel or church. He invites non-Christians in the neighbourhood to enter the church, obviously an innovation for them, and to listen to what he has to say. By their continuing presence and by, it is hoped, a growing interest in what they see and hear, the Catholic missionary trusts that those interested will gradually become Christian. After instruction they will seek baptism and so they will have entered the Christian fold. By contrast, the Protestant missionary, usually sent by a society of his own country, will not create a church or attempt to erect a building until he has a sufficient number of converts to constitute a community. These converts are made as a result of the missionary's direct preaching to people wherever he may find them – on the street corner, in the market place, in friends' houses. As a result of conversions a group is established, consisting of men and women who have shown that they possess a firm, common faith. A church building is then erected but only after sufficient people have been converted. This means that church life is a subsequent result of their acceptance of Christianity. It is added to their confession of faith. Thus, it can be argued that the first generation of converts hardly know what they are letting themselves in for, since they cannot experience church life beforehand.

The two models reflect different policies with regard to baptism. Both Catholics and Protestants agree on the importance of baptism. But Protestant missionaries will not as a rule administer it until they have seen a radical change in the life of the individual who claims he or she is converted, or who seeks to be a Christian. Catholic missionaries, believing in the grace present in the church viewed as an organic body, and therefore an instrument through which a person can be helped, administer baptism relatively early on, even to children. Protestant missionaries, on the contrary, rarely, if ever, baptize babies unless they are the children of parents who have themselves been baptized. Further, they rely almost entirely on the Bible and its exposition as an instrument of conversion and therefore have to translate the New Testament into the native languages at the very outset of their work. In this respect they depend on a literate population. If the people are not literate, one of the tasks of the missionaries is to teach them to read. Not so the Catholic worker, who relies more on the instruction he gives by word of mouth and on the liturgical and devotional actions which take place in the church.

One can extend these contrasting models put forward by Allier by stating that Protestant conversion turns upon a change of belief and action. The process is both more precipitous and more cautious than the way it is seen by Catholics. It is precipitous because it often takes the form of sudden conversions, exemplified by that of St Paul and encouraged by certain types of preachers. On the other hand, particularly through the experience of missionaries overseas, there exists a cautionary note about those who claim to be suddenly converted. It gives rise to a strong belief that converts should grow slowly and surely in their full acceptance of the Christian faith. This is to make sure that the individual who claims to be converted really grasps the nature of Christianity and its practical consequences, which must be lived out in the community where he resides. Within Protestantism, therefore, there is some divergence, largely based on expediency, which may be manifested in different denominations where various attitudes towards conversion exist. It also means that in the long run Catholic and Protestant policies tend to converge. No attempt is made here to try to establish in detail which of these two models the Church of England has adopted in its work of mission at home and overseas. Suffice it to say that, as a *via media* church, it has tended to adopt elements of both models but with a strong bias towards the Catholic ideal. Some evidence for this comes from a nineteenth-century sermon preached by Bishop G. W. Doane, bishop of New Jersey in the United States. He said:

> This is what is meant by a missionary bishop: a bishop *sent forth* by the Church, not *sought for* of the church; going *before* to organise the church, not waiting till the church has been partially organised: a leader not a follower.
>
> (quoted in Rowell 1983:162)

Not surprisingly Anglo-Catholics have invariably followed that model. For them mission work always proceeded from a given base, the local church, and to that base, with its rituals and avenues of grace, priests tried to draw potential converts. One cannot start mission work unless one starts with the church. The 1947 report by leading Anglo-Catholic scholars of the day and commissioned by the archbishop of Canterbury stated: 'The right order is not: Christ – faithful individuals – the Church; but Christ – the Church – faithful individuals. . . . The visible Church is a part of the Gospel' (Abbott *et al.* 1947:13).

When Anglo-Catholic priests began to consider missionary work, they meant 'the establishment of a continual Mission' (Embry 1931:11). Their problem was where and how to get started. They had some limited access in parishes which were sympathetic to their ideology. Rather than use the parish church as the base of mission, they frequently built small mission churches, especially in large slum areas, as offshoots of parish churches, where the Christian or Anglican witness seemed to be slight and ineffectual. There were several advantages in this strategy. Mission churches were relatively inexpensive to erect and maintain: often the parish church had sufficient funds to build one without much difficulty. The buildings did not require much land, they could be erected often where land was cheap, where it was thought the 'battle' would be the toughest, and where priests could make bridgeheads in a hostile region. It also meant that, tucked away in remote poor areas, the Anglo-Catholic clergy had more freedom to do what they wanted to do liturgically than in larger parish churches which had a long tradition of a particular form of worship and where there might be more hostility to changes in the services. Again, it was sometimes thought that the size and grandeur and also the wealth associated with a parish church, even when that church had an Anglo-Catholic ethos, would be offensive to the poor and dispossessed. These 'mini-parish' churches were generally run by a curate, more often than not unmarried, who was given a relatively poor stipend. Where mission churches were successful in terms of the growth of their congregations, they later became parish churches in their own right and the 'tin tabernacle' gave way to a larger and more permanent building. Others were totally unsuccessful and faded away. They were always seen as second-class churches, both by those who were their members and by those who worshipped in the main parish churches (see Pickering 1981:175). It must be remembered that mission churches were created by Anglican clergy working in cities irrespective of their churchmanship and also that they are to be found associated with other denominations.

3 Mobilization

Anglo-Catholics not only adopted the Catholic model of mission but also tended to follow the Roman Catholic Church in various aspects of its implementation.

Amongst the first notable attempts to respond to the missionary situation in England, as some Anglo-Catholic priests envisaged it, was the creation of a religious society, the Society of the Holy Cross (or the SSC, derived from the Latin, *Societas Sanctae Crucis*). It came into existence as early as 1855 through the inspiration of Charles Lowder, a convinced Catholic-minded priest. He had originally wanted to do missionary work in New Zealand. Instead, he turned his energies to being curate in the newly built church of St Barnabas in a poor district in Pimlico. In

1854 he was forbidden by the bishop to take an active part in parish life for six weeks on account of his ritual activities. During that time he visited France. He read the life of St Vincent de Paul (1580–1660) and was much moved by the incredible pastoral achievements of the man who initially worked so bravely amongst galley slaves. He was convinced that mission work could not be achieved by a rector, vicar, or curate working in an isolated situation. Something more was required, something collective, and this Lowder envisaged in the creation of a religious order along the lines of the Vincentians or, as they are known in France, the Lazarists. This was an order of secular priests which St Vincent de Paul had encouraged and which came into being in 1625. Their work was really an extension of what Vincent de Paul himself was doing, for the order was concerned with the spiritual and social well-being of the poor. Its members had as their aim to teach and to bring comfort to those who were little cared for by the official Church. They also became chaplains to the armed forces, to hospitals, and to prisons, as well as amongst galley-slaves. Another part of their work was the running of seminaries, not least for members of their order. They were secular priests who lived under a common religious rule. Vows were taken for life and were dispensed only by the pope.

What Fr Lowder created was not a religious order in the sense that the Lazarists were, or that the Cowley Fathers were in the Anglican Church (see p. 74). Members did not pool their economic resources and the notion of community life was minimal. More important, there was no vow of obedience to the corporate will of the Society. Members constituted a confraternity of priests who bound themselves together by rules of life (Embry 1931:58; and see Pickering 1977:75). The rule related to daily attendance at holy communion, private prayer, self-examination, meditation, ascetic practices, and fasting (Ellsworth 1982:65). There were three sets of rules: the White Rule for celibates, the Red Rule for single and married priests, and the Green Rule for deacons and candidates for holy orders. (How much should one read into the symbolism of the colours?) To accept the last rule was, as it were, to be a novice. Lowder wrote in 1856 that the objects of the SSC were to defend and strengthen the spiritual life of the clergy, to defend the faith of the Church, and to carry on and aid mission work both at home and abroad (Embry 1931:2). In line with the work of St Vincent de Paul, retreats were encouraged by the Society and the first ever held in England took place in 1856. The Ignatian form of meditation was adopted. In the early days several parishes in the poor parts of London were run by clergy who were members of the SSC, notably St George's mission in the East End and St Barnabas's, Pimlico. Fr A. H. Mackonochie (1825–87) developed and master-minded the SSC. He, like Lowder, was fully convinced of the importance of evangelistic work, which was one of the ideals initiated by the brotherhood. He summed it up in an expression which was to become well known – '"to dig a pit for the Cross" in London' (Embry 1931:52).

Despite the vigorous and determined opposition to Anglo-Catholicism in the latter half of the nineteenth century, the Society grew steadily from 105 members in 1866 to 376 in 1882. There was a yearly synod and the elected Master was assisted in the organization of the Society by four elected vicars or rectors, who were responsible for specific geographical areas in England and Scotland. Hardly surprisingly, the SSC was one of the main targets of attack by anti-ritualistic Protestants. It openly advocated auricular confession, published manuals on hearing confessions, and was labelled a secret society by its opponents. It was impossible to contradict the first two charges. The third also seemed in many respects to be correct. Members of the SSC did not openly proclaim their membership, as did members of the Lazarist order. A church would be known to be run by members of the latter order but those who belonged to the SSC tended not to parade the fact of their membership, although when challenged they would say they were members of the Society. It was and still is today a somewhat private association which does not go out of its way to publicize its existence. Such a characteristic caused Walsh, in his attack on Anglo-Catholicism, to criticize the movement for its secrecy (see Walsh, 1897).

The ideal gleaned from France was not altogether successful when transplanted on to Anglican soil. Quite apart from the fact that the SSC was not really comparable to the Lazarists, the original aims of the Anglican society were too diverse to be realizable. As well as being concerned for mission work, Lowder and those who followed him as Master of the confraternity were intent on bringing about a change in the outlook of the clergy of the Church of England as a whole towards their work. Lowder wanted them to realize 'the supernatural power of the priesthood' (Embry 1931:xxxix). In practice this turned out to be the main concern of the SSC. To bring about the catholicization of their church was clearly no part of the aim of the Lazarists! As time went on, mission work received less and less attention. The Society became overwhelmingly concerned with the general well-being of the Anglo-Catholic movement and in this respect it made a great contribution to it. It still holds a very prominent place within the Anglo-Catholic party.

The Society of St John the Evangelist, the members of which are commonly called the Cowley Fathers, was established as a mission order in 1865 by the Rev R. M. Benson. It was the first successful order to come into existence in the Church of England. Because of the asceticism and deep attachment to the Church of England of the order, some, such as Voll, would argue that it was not really Anglo-Catholic but stood within the high church wing of the Church of England (see Voll t.1963:46ff.). It could be argued that their work was much more in line with that of the Lazarists. They had a strong sense of community and were always based in a religious house. Their hope was to bring into existence an order of priests who would always be ready to undertake mission work in England, especially parish missions and retreats. In addition, they worked overseas and established centres in India, Canada, the United States, and Japan. But the plain fact of the matter was that the Cowley Fathers never recruited sufficient members to make them a force in any way comparable to the Lazarists and other Roman Catholic mission orders. In recent times they have suffered a considerable decline (see ch. 5.5; and Anson 1964:72ff.).

A more recently founded Anglican order is the Society of St Francis, which began in the 1930s. While it is not strictly a mission order, its interests are much associated with mission work, such as the conducting of parish missions and work in public schools and amongst down-and-outs and those convicted by the courts. By tradition Franciscans have always been associated with preaching and therefore conversion. If numbers alone constitute the criterion, it can be stated that the order has turned out to be the most successful of orders founded in the Anglican Church. It reflects a moderate form of Anglo-Catholicism (see ch. 5.5; and Anson 1964:200ff.).

Because religious orders and communities have only recently emerged in the Church of England, and because they have never had the following they have enjoyed in the Roman Catholic Church, they have never reached the dominant position in mission work anywhere in the Anglican Communion that they have had in the Catholic Church. The mission activity in England has largely rested on the shoulders of individual priests who have had the responsibility of parishes. Over the years there have been those who have been particularly successful in this work and have often been in demand to conduct parish missions. On account of the preaching abilities of their own clergy, some parishes have become famous for their mission work *in situ*. Probably the most famous of all such churches was St Alban's, Holborn, where for many years the curate, Fr Arthur Stanton, in fact a member of the SSC, drew thousands through his extraordinarily powerful Evangelical sermons (see Russell 1913). People would come many miles to hear him, including those (like my father) who had no wish to be associated in any way with Anglo-Catholicism. But there have been many mission-minded priests, among them, Fr Adderley (see Stevens 1943).

4 Techniques

Many techniques were used by Anglo-Catholics in their mission work. Although priests such as Fr Lowder in the parish of St Peter's, London docks, maintained that mission work was a continuous activity, most priests felt it was desirable to emphasize such work at particular times of the year. The most notable of these was Lent. Indeed, it might be said that, within the Church of England as a whole, the rediscovery of Lent and the devotions associated with it became prominent in the nineteenth century through the efforts of the followers of the Oxford movement, and not least through Anglo-Catholics. The penitential season that preceded Easter was a legitimate occasion to inculcate personal piety and to promote self-discipline, fasting, and additional attendance at public worship. As well as being present at preaching services during the week, especially Holy Week, Anglo-Catholics were also urged to make the Stations of the Cross, a practice which had been introduced by many Catholic-minded clergy. Lent was generally seen to be the time for Christians to bestir themselves, and by stressing this fact, Anglo-Catholics realized that they would not be subject to the sort of criticism they faced in upholding certain doctrines and practices which have already been noted. To have a parish mission during Lent seemed particularly appropriate. Mission services were made as simple as possible so as to cause no offence to the outsider. Hymns of a rousing, emotional kind, even choruses, were used, often borrowed from Protestant sources. The priest wore a cassock. There was nearly always a lesson, prayers, and the talk or sermon. Incidentally, Fr Stanton inaugurated watch-night services on New Year's Eve which were modelled on similar services in Methodism and were very well attended. These have subsequently been ridiculed by Anglo-Catholics as being 'Protestant' (see Voll t.1963:97). In churches in the centre of cities, Lenten services were often held during the lunch hour to attract office workers. At the popular Anglo-Catholic church of St Matthew's, Westminster, it was said that during the First World War, when Fr Atlay was vicar, there were never less than two hundred people at such midday services (Wilson 1940:70).

The climax of the Lenten services was the Three Hours service held on Good Friday. This act of worship was to become very popular in the Church of England as a whole. It was introduced by Fr Mackonochie in the 1860s when he was vicar of St Alban's, Holborn (see under Mackonochie in *ODCC*). The service was actually invented by Jesuits in South America in the seventeenth century. Perhaps one of the reasons why it spread so quickly in the Church of England – it was used at St Paul's cathedral in 1876 when there was little sympathy with Anglo-Catholicism – was that, as meditations on the last seven words of Christ from the Cross, the service was essentially a biblical one, which could not be doctrinally faulted. In England it was to become far more popular in Anglican parishes than in English Roman Catholic churches.

In general terms Anglo-Catholics and Tractarians pressed for a more 'religious' keeping of Lent and Holy Week than had been the custom. They pleaded for more services to be held during the season and for churches to be kept open. From society generally they requested that less entertainment be available for the public. Thus, the English Church Union supported a motion addressed to Parliament in the latter part of the nineteenth century asking for London theatres to be closed during Holy Week (see Roberts 1895:41; and ch. 4.2). Although supported by the archbishop of Canterbury the motion had no impact on the government of the day. At about the same time the Union on one occasion distributed 100,000 handbills asking for a better observance of Good Friday and Ascension Day (Roberts 1895:77)

When missions as such were started, it is difficult to say. Voll has mentioned the claim that the first parish mission was in Wednesbury under the high-church vicar, Richard Twigg (Voll t.1963:45). In 1869, on the initiative of the founder and head of the Cowley Fathers, R. M. Benson, a great Twelve Day London Mission was held which included a large number of high church and Anglo-Catholic clergy. In all, 120 parishes were involved (Voll t.1963:49). A second similar mission was held in 1874. In these and other cases a mission would last a week or ten days, during which time there would be increased pastoral visiting. This might also occur immediately before the mission began. Through personal contact, those on the periphery of the church were urged to come to the services held during the mission. In later years theological students were often sent to parishes holding missions and they would help with the visiting.

Early Anglo-Catholic priests saw that one of their chief tasks was to be a pastor to the people whose spiritual responsibility was theirs. This was in part achieved by constant visiting. The vicar and his curates 'must visit, visit, visit' (Wilson 1940:62). There were many reasons for this kind of work, which had no end. It demonstrated to ordinary people of the parish that the clergy were indeed concerned with their well-being. Reciprocally, it brought home to the clergy the way their parishioners lived, and the condition – sometimes very terrible – of their houses and home life. It provided an opportunity for preaching the Gospel in an informal way, for bringing people into contact with the church and of encouraging them to attend worship. In assessing the Church of England as a whole, it could be argued that it is not a profoundly theological church, or one of moving ritual, or one which possesses great administrative genius. Rather, it is a pastoral church in which the clergy in a particularly gentle way have shown concern and care for their parishioners. Whereas this might be seen to be a general characteristic of long standing, full credit has to be given to Anglo-Catholic priests, especially those of the early generations, who reinforced such pastoral work at a time when some thought it was languishing.

5 The proof of conversion: confession

We have already observed that in their mission work Anglo-Catholics adopted, not surprisingly, a Catholic model of conversion rather than a Protestant one and therefore, on the whole, rejected the notion of a sudden, emotional spiritual change. Certainly they looked for a change in the individuals whom they hoped to influence by preaching and by religious instruction. But the change that was anticipated was a gradual one, of the will as well as of the heart, and to be grounded in some intellectual assent, no matter how simple it might be. But, given all this, was there not some ritualized point where the change was declared and confirmed? At the end of their preaching or instruction, Anglo-Catholic clergy did not ask their hearers to raise their hands to indicate that they had experienced conversion, nor did they request them to come forward to kneel at the altar rail. They did, however, in many cases, press for another sign of conversion. As John Kent has noted, this sign was in making a first confession to a priest, or in making a confession after a long period of abstention (Kent 1978:243ff.). Fr Adderley was uncompromising in his call for sacramental confession during a mission (Stevens 1943:22). Interestingly enough, an aim at the centre of Lazarist missions was to encourage individuals to make their confession. Anglo-Catholics realized that for members of the Church of England to take such a step was to perform an act attended by emotional pain or embarrassment, just as much as standing up in a church and signifying openly that one had been saved by Christ.

First confessions, and indeed confession itself, contained unique problems for Anglicans. Until the time of the Oxford movement, auricular confessions were not practised at all in the Church of England (see ch. 1.5; also Simpson 1932, chapter 6). It was the Oxford Fathers, certainly Pusey and Newman, who were the first to make use of it in recent times. Within Anglo-Catholicism itself, the making of a confession was often seen as the seal upon one's embracing the ideals of the movement. If anyone made a confession she or he was indeed Anglo-Catholic! The problem which faced high churchmen and Anglo-Catholics alike was, of course, the fact that followers had not grown up in a church where it was the custom to go to confession. It was no part of their religio-cultural world. Anglican penitents had to be led into a new country – to something that was lonely, private, and strange. They had to be encouraged to perform an unusual act and to be convinced of its merit in a milieu where it was not practised at all. People knew that the sacrament of penance was very much part of Roman Catholicism and therefore anyone calling himself or herself a Catholic would practice confession. They also realized, perhaps after the initial event, that a ritual of this kind – like a *rite de passage*, although confession is not really a *rite de passage* in the technical sense – is strengthening and reassuring, and this Anglo-Catholic clergy knew.

Priests who wished to encourage parishioners to make their confessions were placed in an entirely different situation from that of their Roman Catholic counterparts. They could not openly enforce confession as a required preparation for receiving the sacraments, especially holy communion, as Roman Catholics have traditionally done and which was part of a generally accepted procedure. The whole ethos and tradition of the Church of England had been against such a system. Anglicans had to be persuaded of the merits and desirability of confession rather than being told that they had to practise it as a sacrament and gateway to the other sacraments. The gentle advocacy of confession by most clergy associated with the Oxford and Anglo-Catholic movements has been summed up in the expression 'some should, all may, none must'. There have been many Anglo-Papalists who were much more demanding. For them it was not optional. In a small village in the Lichfield diocese at the turn of the century, there appeared in the church magazine: 'You will come to the church sometime before Easter and make your confession and if you want Absolution, you will make your confession in the hearing of God's priest' (quoted in Heitland 1903:40). Such policies led to tensions within the Anglo-Catholic movement itself. E. S. Talbot, the first warden of Keble College, Oxford, wrote the following words in a letter concerning the reappointment as tutor of someone called Mylne.

> Mylne gives me much cause for hesitation in his views on Confession. His practice is to urge Confession as a general rule on all his pupils [undergraduates] with whom he gets intimacy and influence upon such subjects; and where he thought a person would confess to himself and none other he stipulates to be free to hear a Confession.
>
> (quoted in Stephenson 1936:23)

From evidence in a subsequent conversation between Talbot and Pusey, it is clear that they both disagreed with Mylne and upheld what they considered to be the Church of England's position in 'treating it as exceptional for those who could not quiet their own consciences' (Stephenson 1936:23). Mylne differed from the other two in that he saw that there were many in this state in which their consciences were deeply troubled. The usual example of a case where Anglo-Catholic priests make demands concerning their first confessions comes when young people are about to be confirmed and where priests demand that each confirmand make a confession. The penalty for not conforming to the demand is to refuse to allow the person to proceed with confirmation (see Yates 1975:12ff.). There have been some clergy who wanted to make it generally obligatory on theological grounds, holding it to be the only way in which sins could be forgiven – a position almost identical to that supposedly advocated by Roman Catholic priests (see Yates 1975:12ff.). Such a rigid outlook was condemned by Pusey, as is clearly evident in his response to certain Anglo-Catholic clergy, who in 1873 submitted to Convocation a request that clergy be trained in the matter of hearing confessions (Kent 1978:27). Probably no priest was sought out as a confessor more than Fr Stanton, yet he appears never to have tried to force people to make their confession. Confession was not necessary for salvation, he argued (Russell 1917:74). His approach was pragmatic, not dogmatic.

And this raises the second problem which beset the clergy from the beginning. They were totally unskilled in the hearing of confessions. They had to learn about the subject *de novo* in a church which as a collectivity had had no experience of it (see Yates 1975:12ff.). One might almost say that priests and penitents had to learn from each other. Several books began to appear on the subject, the most notable was *The Priest in Absolution*, which appeared in 1877 and aroused a great deal of controversy. It was a translation by Pusey of Gaume's *Le Manuel des confesseurs* (1837). The project of translation and publication was strongly supported by the SSC. In such a venture Anglo-Catholics were particularly vulnerable, not only on account of the practice of confession and absolution, but also because of the moral theology involved in the instructions to clergy in dealing with penitents. Despite certain alterations by Pusey of contemporary Roman Catholic ideas, he made no criticism of the ideas themselves and did not seek out other traditions in the matter of moral theology. Anglo-Catholics could only defend themselves pragmatically with the simple assertion that, if anyone was convinced of the need to use the sacrament of penance in a church which knew very little about it, there was nowhere to turn for advice and help but across the Channel.

The outcry against auricular confession was extremely strong in the second half of the nineteenth century, partly on the grounds of the alleged evils in its use perpetrated by Roman Catholic clergy. The hostility was so strong at the time of the translation of Gaume's book that members of the SSC considered disbanding the Society (Embry 1931:57). Pusey himself felt that tactical errors had been made in publishing the book at that time. Anglo-Catholic clergy continued to press for the use of confession and received a ready response. A horrified Church Association accepted the evidence of a 'Father Black' that in 1896 between 1,200 and 1,500 clergy regularly heard confessions and that in St Bartholomew's, Brighton, in 1898 10,000 confessions were heard (Church Association 1900:v; see also ch. 4.2). On an average throughout the year, this would mean twenty-seven confessions a day – a rather remarkable claim! There were some clergy who nevertheless felt that the degree to which parishioners made their confessions was a mark of catholicity or spirituality. So one priest wrote, in his magazine in a poor parish:

> Then as to the number of confessions made. To my mind this is by far the truest test of progress of spiritual work. And this is certainly increasingly becoming better proportioned to the

Communions made – even more amongst men and lads, as I
have before more that once noted.

(in Booth 1902,7:63)

Today, the cries of condemnation are no longer heard, even
from ardent Evangelicals who often see the need for some form
of counselling or semi-confession, some occasion to unburden the
self in the presence of another person within a Christian context.
But one point needs to be mentioned briefly. It is connected with
the Protestant criticism that through confession the priest
exercises control over people's lives. The matter that is raised
here is not so much the effect on individual penitents but the
effect on confessors. To clergy of the Anglican tradition,
especially to those who have come unexpectedly to the hearing of
confessions, there is borne in upon them the realization of the
power the priest holds in such an act. It gives him an entrée into
the innermost regions of a person's soul, and, if required, the
confessor may penetrate as deeply as he wishes without being
challenged by the penitent. In this way the confessor has wellnigh
absolute power, for if certain conditions are not met he may
withhold absolution. Of course, there is the question of natural
curiosity, but, for some, 'working in the box', that is, hearing
confessions, can have its own secret fascination as well as a deep
wish to control and therefore to have power over other people's
lives. This possibility is openly admitted in the biography of
F. W. Faber (see ch. 2.1).

Then there was unpleasant gossip that Dalgairns had a 'regular
passion' for hearing people's confessions – which Faber
described as the very worst that could be said of a convert
priest. '. . . . I have told him that I think he fishes for penitents
and looks greedily about him when sitting outside his
confessional,' he reported . . . . It was said that the Fathers
'were too new in their catholicism to hear confessions'

(Chapman 1961:227)

Some advocates of confession have made out a remarkable
case for administering the sacrament. Certain of the Oxford
Fathers, and in this case one has in mind John Keble, believed
that the hearing of confessions was of pastoral value to the priest
because by such means he would know how people were
behaving and what their innermost thoughts and motivations
were (Kent 1978:249). Thus, the sacrament would bridge the gulf
between clergy and laity. This may be true but it is hardly a

legitmate theological reason for pressing for the use of the sacrament.

Anglo-Catholic clergy faced a situation which was essentially voluntary. It was one without the pressure derived from a tradition. Some clergy, despite their wishes and endeavours, found themselves without penitents. Others seemed to have an innate ability in encouraging people to make their confessions. One notable example was an eccentric member of the SSC and a well-known mission preacher, the Rev Joseph Leycester Lyne (1837–1908). He was later known as Fr Ignatius, who revived the Benedictine order by creating a small monastery at Llanthony in south Wales (see Anson 1955/1964:51ff.). He once conducted a mission in Claydon, near Ipswich, in Holy Week 1863. On Maundy Thursday, after his address, fifty people, mainly dissenters, made their first confessions. As he was only a deacon he was not allowed to hear confessions but people made their acts of penitence to an accompanying priest until two o'clock in the morning. Twenty more made their confessions before Easter Sunday (Embry 1931:27). He was a great orator and frequently used secular buildings rather than churches for his missions. The extremely colourful Fr Ignatius was very much in the tradition of the Evangelical Anglo-Catholic. He drew enormous crowds when he conducted missions in the city of London. It was reported that at one lunch-time at St Edmund's, Lombard Street, he drew a crowd of 60,000 and preached in the street. The police had to control the people. Fr Ignatius was probably one of the first Anglo-Papalists, and certainly the most flamboyant of his day: he remained an Anglican all his life (see Calder-Marshall 1962).

6 Popular missions and Anglo-Catholicism

John Kent, in his book, *Holding the Fort* (1978), has drawn attention to the enthusiasm for missions that occurred in England in the late nineteenth century. As is well known, there had been for a long time a deep concern in most of the traditional churches for reaching the many hundreds of thousands who were reckoned to be outside the Christian fold. What happened during that period was the advent of a new technique to redress the situation in the form of large, non-denominational Evangelical missions, such as those carried out by the American, Dwight Moody (1837–99), in London in 1875 and 1884. They gave impetus to the churches to press on with their work of mission. In addition, one might point to a particular organization initially dedicated to the conversion of the working classes, the Salvation Army, which was inaugurated some ten years before Moody's first campaign, and which, under its leader, William Booth (1829–1912), appeared to be so initially successful.

It is interesting to note that the early endeavours of Anglo-Catholic clergy antedate the arrival of Moody in this country. Lowder had conducted a mission in Bedminster near Bristol in 1862 and Bishop Wilberforce (1805–73), sympathetic to Tractarianism, had held missions about the same time in every part of his Oxford diocese (Russell 1917:80) In 1866 Fr Stanton took a mission in rural Lincolnshire and thereafter became an extremely popular mission priest in his own parish of St Alban's, Holborn, as well as throughout the country (Russell 1917:80). When the American evangelist took London by storm, Fr Lowder and members of the SSC were placed in a quandary. Their Catholic ideals prevented them from whole-heartedly supporting Moody's mission. All churches had been asked to assist and many Anglican parishes did so. Of course there was no question of Moody promulgating what Anglo-Catholics saw as their faith. Yet Lowder and his followers could appreciate the fact that here there were elements of a common position and that many of Moody's techniques were to be admired. They decided in the end to remain entirely neutral, publicly neither condemning nor praising the great missions – missions attracting numbers they knew they could never command. And, if numbers were the criterion, the influence of Anglo-Catholic priests was pitifully small.

7 Success and decline

Anglo-Catholics, from, say, the 1860s onwards, gave considerable impetus to mission work within the Church of England. Some of the policies and techniques which they either initiated or developed, such as holding special Lenten services, conducting intensive pastoral visiting, and building mission churches, were all soon to be found within the Church at large. The most notable of these was the keeping of Lent. The concern for first confessions during a mission had little influence outside Anglo-Catholicism itself. Nevertheless the practice of confession and absolution grew gradually amongst middle-of-the-road Anglicans, high churchmen and Prayer Book Catholics. Once again, however, it is impossible to determine with any precision the extent of their use. Certainly church people became much more tolerant towards confession as time went on and, as we have noted, today even Evangelicals do not stand strongly opposed to it. Kent, nevertheless, has maintained that the confessional was too esoteric and sophisticated to be used by English people at large (Kent 1978:273). But there are two issues at stake which he fails to differentiate. As a technique of missions – as an occasion for making a first confession – it is probably true that Anglo-Catholic policy had limited success and the technique was not widely used in missions conducted by more moderate clergy. On the other hand, confession began to spread throughout the Anglican church and particularly in churches which saw themselves as generally high church. Today, confession to a priest is much on the decline, not only amongst Anglo-Catholics, but amongst Roman Catholics as well, where there has been a tendency towards a more open position and where the use of corporate confession and absolution shows signs of being a substitute for auricular confession. This is very much the position of Anglicans in general. In the Roman Catholic Church the change has largely been brought about by decisions made at Vatican II.

At the present time, missions, especially parish missions, have virtually ceased in the Church of England except, perhaps, amongst Evangelicals. They have ceased because they have become ineffectual. All they have done in recent years is to rally a smaller and smaller number of the 'converted' who feel they must support the missions – outsiders and those on the fringe are seldom drawn into a local church on such occasions. At the same time, the evangelistic type of mission, with its emphasis on a distinct turning-point, has remained unchanged and, if anything, is now strengthened, not least through the campaigns which have transcended denomination and which are associated with Billy Graham and the Anglican evangelist, David Watson, who died a few years ago. Further, the Evangelical streak which was so strong in Anglo-Catholicism right up to the 1920s and 1930s – it runs through the First Anglo-Catholic Priests' Convention, which followed the first Anglo-Catholic congress – has now largely disappeared despite recent calls that it should be restored to the centre of the movement (see ACPC 1921; also *CT*, 18 July 1986). There are those who argue that one of the reasons why the movement was so successful up until the inter-war period was that its missionary policy was of paramount importance. When that was abandoned, Anglo-Catholicism seemed to decline.

There still remains the problem of assessing the success of Anglo-Catholic missions. Statistics are difficult to come by. There are only a very few case histories available for examination. In the last resort one can only make some general observations and intelligent guesses.

There can be no doubt that many Anglo-Catholic parishes grew and flourished through the mission work of clergy. Certain names such as Lowder, Stanton, Mackonochie, Lyne, Adderley, and Atlay have been mentioned. They appear to have been singularly successful, not only in building up churches to which they were appointed but also in the conducting of parish missions. Fr Lowder's dream of creating an Anglican equivalent of the Lazarist Fathers by forming the SSC was never very successful for reasons we have observed. Nor was the attempt of the Cowley Fathers any more successful. The Franciscans also, in recent times, have tended to follow the trend in the Anglican Church as a whole in doubting the value of parish missions. It is true also that Anglo-Catholicism in its depleted state at the present time, and indeed this applies to most of the Anglican Church, has lost the sense of mission and the expectation of making converts within a mission setting. The simple reason is that a change of heart in individuals, arising directly out of a mission, does not appear to occur, except amongst Evangelicals with their particular techniques and type of preaching. The notion of mission is still widely adhered to in Anglican circles but its sense has been so widened as to make it almost a meaningless expression. The Evangelical dynamism of former Anglo-Catholic priests has virtually disappeared.

Perhaps the Catholic model for conversion is no longer applicable in a society which seems to have lived through its Christian phase. This does not mean that work done according to the model does not produce any conversions but that the cultural state of society is such at the moment that response to the policy and techniques of the model are exceedingly thin and sporadic.

8 Missionary work overseas

One of the charges levelled against the Oxford movement was that it showed little or no concern for missions overseas at a time when missionaries were being sent out by churches of many denominations and countries to various European empires (Clarke 1932:289). The charge contained a certain element of truth. Tractarians found themselves very much absorbed in propagating Catholic doctrines in England. But, as we have seen in the previous chapter, Anglo-Catholic congresses were supported by bishops from overseas and were very conscious of the misionary situation abroad. At the 1920 congress £40,000 was raised for missionary work and the Anglo-Catholic Congress Overseas Association was able to raise £12,000 per annum. Thus, the charge levelled against the Oxford movement was hardly applicable to Anglo-Catholics in their heyday. In a brief consideration of these statements it ought to be mentioned that Tractarians became influential in the Society for the Propagation of the Gospel (SPG) founded in 1701. They also helped the Society for Promoting Christian Knowledge (SPCK), established a few years earlier, which worked mainly in Britain but with some overseas concern. Anglo-Catholics from an early period were much involved in 'the conversion of the heathen'. Their contribution may not have been very great compared with what other churches and societies achieved, but it was quite sizeable in relation to their following and indeed their contribution was in many ways unique (see Rowell 1983, chapter 8). As always it is not easy to draw a precise line between Tractarians and Anglo-Catholics. We have already referred to the contribution of the Cowley Fathers to overseas work; Anglo-Catholics were also behind the creation of the Society of the Sacred Mission, which was established in the 1890s and finally moved to Kelham, near Newark, in 1903. One of its aims was to send men overseas and a number went to Korea and Africa. It drew postulants from the lower middle classes, for whom a degree at Oxford or Cambridge was out of the question. Later, the Society concentrated much of its energies on training such young men for the priesthood in England. A number of the community who taught, such as Kelly, Hebert, and Every, were academically of a high order. The Community of St Denys in Warminster, Wiltshire, was a women's nursing and missionary order founded in 1879. The sisters, who have not been many, worked in South Africa. The Oxford Mission Brotherhood, originally based on the Oratorians, began in Calcutta in 1880 to work amongst high-caste Hindus. A daughter order for women was started in 1902. In Delhi there was a parallel brotherhood, that of the Ascension, which was founded in 1877. Apart from such orders, which were never numerically large, one can point to the creation of missionary colleges, notably St Augustine's college, Canterbury, and St Boniface college, Warminster, Wiltshire, in 1869. The latter was founded by the vicar of Warminster, the Rev Sir James Erasmus Philipps. It trained missionaries, usually non-graduates, until the end of the Second World War. Both colleges were Tractarian or Anglo-Catholic in ethos. Another college was Dorchester Training College, which had as vice-principal the learned Anglo-Catholic theologian, Darwell Stone.

Beyond any shadow of doubt the greatest contribution to missionary work came with that unequivocally Anglo-Catholic society, namely, the Universities' Mission to Central Africa. It began with the enthusiastic response to David Livingstone, actually a Scottish Presbyterian, when he addressed the universities of Oxford and Cambridge in 1857 on the subject of his journeys of discovery in Africa. By a series of coincidences the committees formed in the two universities both encouraged the Rev Charles Frederick Mackenzie, who was on furlough from Natal, to lead the newly founded society. He was consecrated bishop in England and the mission began to establish itself in Zanzibar. It worked for the abolition of slavery, built a cathedral on the slave market and also extended its influence into Nyasaland and Northern Rhodesia and amongst the Masai. The history of the mission has been written up in great detail (see Anderson-Morshead and Blood 1897, 1957, 1962). It undertook medical and educational work, and Frank Weston, one of its most famous leaders, encouraged the formation of a women's community, the Community of the Sacred Passion, in 1910. The mission was also assisted by the sisters of the Community of the Resurrection of our Lord from Grahamstown in South Africa. In 1957 there was a centenary celebration in the Albert Hall in the style of the Anglo-Catholic congresses. Like so many missionary societies it found itself forced to reduce its work after the Second World War. In 1965 it combined with the Society for the Propagation of the Gospel. Anglo-Catholics have nothing to be ashamed of in their missionary endeavours. In a more academic vein they contributed to a series of theological studies on missionary work, *Essays Catholic and Missionary*, which appeared at a not insignificant time in the 1920s (Morgan 1928).

Finally, it might be said that, in contrast to the opposition and difficulties which Anglo-Catholicism encountered in Britain, overseas it seems to have enjoyed more successful and less difficult times. The proposition cannot be developed here but one might point to the fact that the ritualistic services might be very acceptable to Africans and Indians and that distance in rural areas would prevent Christian converts coming easily into contact with Anglicans of other churchmanship. Further, priests could exert a paternal influence more easily and effectively on the native peoples of countries overseas than on English parishioners, and bishops could rule as bishops, often in conjunction with a synod (see Pickering 1988b).

Chapter 4

The extent of success

1 An impossible assessment?

How successful has Anglo-Catholicism been? As we have stated, the movement reached a peak in the period between the wars. But that in itself is no clear guide to the influence of Anglo-Catholicism within the Church of England or in society at large. Although ultimately one can never measure accurately the success of social movements, at least some attempt has to be made in establishing possible ways of measurement. But, that said, one immediately faces the hazardous task of discovering statistics which apply to Anglo-Catholicism. Such statistics are even more patchy and unreliable than are those for larger and more official church bodies. The fact that Anglo-Catholics have no unifying organization to which they belong makes the task wellnigh impossible. Nevertheless, this is no reason for abandoning some sort of assessment in objective terms. An attempt must be made to gather such statistics as have been used in connection with Anglo-Catholicism and to search out as many other types of indicators as possible.

2 Some early estimates

Kaye-Smith in her book on Anglo-Catholicism produced some statistics, the sources of which are not stated. They demonstrated the very considerable growth of the Catholic revival over a period of about sixty years.

> In 1854 a daily service was held in only 650 churches in England, whereas in 1919 Matins and Evensong were read daily in 5,427 churches. In 1854 there was a weekly Mass only in 128 churches, the others contenting themselves with one a month or even one a quarter; in 1919 the Mass was offered

weekly in 11,842 churches, while the offering of a daily Mass has risen from three churches in 1854 to 1,215 in 1919.

(Kaye-Smith 1925:118)

More statistics are available about Anglo-Catholicism at the turn of the century than for any part of its history. This is largely due to the fact that it was at the time when the ritualistic controversies were at their height and stood very much before the nation and in which party politics were involved (see Munson 1975:386).

Within the controversy a book appeared in 1900 with the title, *The Disruption of the Church of England*. In it the Church Association printed the results of a detailed survey which had been taken during the year 1899. The Association, as has already been noted, was a strongly Protestant body made up of members of the Church of England, dedicated to the task of opposing the growth of the Oxford movement, especially in its ritualistic forms (see ch. 2.1). The rest of the title of the book was therefore hardly surprising: *by more than 9,000 clergymen who are helping the Romeward Movement in the National Church*. This was the number of Anglican clergy who by name were implicated in the survey and were held to be traitors to the Protestant cause. The details were precise and contained emendations, and on the whole the veracity of the facts cannot be doubted. The book went through four editions and the last was published in 1908.

The late nineteenth century was very much a period of statistics and surveys, especially those dealing with the subject of poverty and the conditions of life in English cities. On the whole, the Church of England, as the Established Church, paid little regard to statistics which related to their Church (see Pickering 1972). This was not the case in Nonconformist churches, which gathered statistics about themselves, not least in the hope of demonstrating their growing strength as serious rivals to the Church of England. The anti-Catholic extremists of the Church Association were thus to be congratulated on being one of the few Anglican bodies to apply statistical methods to ecclesiastical institutions.

It has been estimated from other sources that around 1900 there were about 23,500 clergy in the Church of England in the provinces of Canterbury and York (Paul 1964:304). It is extremely difficult to obtain precise numbers of clergy with regard to geographical boundaries and the percentages given below must be seen to be only approximate, but they are at least an acceptable guide to the situation. The survey of the Church Association included all clergy, whether or not they were working overseas. In the second edition of 1902, out of the 9,600 named clergy, 748 were listed as working outside England and Wales, the majority of this number being in the colonies, and 419 who were not in parish work.

On the basis of 8,850 'offending' clergy in England and Wales, it would seem that just under 40 per cent were 'highish' but not necessarily Anglo-Catholic according to our definition. Such a large proportion of clergy, however, indicated the great success of the Catholic revival in the Church of England and for the Church Association it was evidence to confirm its contention that the Church of England was on the point of taking the slippery path to Rome!

The surveyors used nine indicators, applicable to any priest, of what they saw as Romeward tendencies. They were:

1   membership of the English Church Union;
2   a priest-associate of the Confraternity of the Blessed Sacrament;
3   membership of the Cowley Fathers;
4   membership of the Holy Cross Society;
5   adopting the eastward position to celebrate holy communion;
6   mixing ceremonially water and wine for the holy communion service;
7   the use of incense in public worship;
8   the use of 'sacrificial' vestments at holy communion;
9   burning candles at services in daylight hours.

Indicators 5 to 9 were shown to be illegal as a result of court cases. A further item was held to be illegal, although it was not used, for some unknown reason, as an indicator. It was the employment of wafers instead of bread in holy communion.

There was also an appendix giving a list of churches which supported the Guild of All Souls (see ch. 2.2). Not only was the name of the church given but also the days and times when public services were held for the dead. It was noted that about 500 clergy (2 per cent) were members of the Guild and that according to the annual report of the Guild in 1892 'Requiem Celebrations' were held in 328 churches every month. The survey printed the names of 209 of the churches.

Just over 4,000 clergy (17 per cent) were members of the English Church Union which openly lobbied for the practices used as indicators (see p. 93).

The question of bishops is interesting. For England in the 1903 edition, six diocesan bishops were named, together with three suffragan bishops (in the first edition there were only two bishops named, Edward King of Lincoln and Johnson, the suffragan bishop of Colchester); but there were nineteen other bishops, most of them working overseas, though some had been ordained abroad and held appointments in England (Church Association 1903). The indicators against bishops were minimal – in the main, the eastward position, membership of the English Church Union, and even that of the Alcuin Club, which was an academic society devoted to the study of liturgy, membership of which was not an official indicator.

In the second edition some attempt was made to relate the findings to geographical areas, namely, dioceses, but little was done to draw any conclusions from such a demographic exercise, even in relating absolute numbers to percentages. It was a pity that more analysis was not employed (but see pp. 98–106). The issue was somewhat complicated by using nine indicators. Thus, some clergy had only one indicator placed against their names; only a tiny minority could have the full number on account of membership of the Society of St John the Evangelist being one of the indicators. Looking at the diocesan analysis in a wide sweep, and based on absolute figures, most 'offending' clergy were to be found in the diocese of London, followed by the diocese of Oxford, and then St Albans. Joyfully the surveyors noted that the one diocese where there were no 'offenders' was the diocese of Sodor and Man: other diocese which had low scores were those in Wales and those of Liverpool and Carlisle (see Church Association 1903:104).

Of the items categorized by the Church Association, the first four can still be said to be applicable to Anglo-Catholicism as we have defined it, perhaps along with item 7. The membership of the Guild of All Souls is another indicator. All the other practices could reasonably be adopted by Tractarians or high churchmen. Today, these practices are very widely accepted without comment throughout the whole of the Church of England. There could be no greater hallmark of success of the Catholic revival, judged in terms of ceremonial, than in such changes. Tractarians created a sense of dignity in public worship, which was coupled with rich church furnishings and fine architecture. These ideas quickly spread to clergy of every kind of churchmanship.

The controversy over candles on the altar, heightened by the efforts of the Church Association, rested on the criterion of whether or not candles in a church were necessary for people to read by. If they had no such obvious function, they were seen to have ritualistic, symbolic, and therefore Romish purposes. It has been argued that originally candles were used on the altar solely for the purpose of enabling the priest to read in a dark church. The practice might even be traced to the early church when members had to hold their services in secret in the catacombs. In the nineteenth century candles were still being used to give light for reading. Hence the emphasis by Protestant extremists that candles used in daylight hours could only have one sinister purpose. Now only a minority of Anglican churches in England do not have candles on the altar or in the sanctuary.

In the second edition great alarm was sounded that there was 'no abatement of the plague' (Church Association 1902:iii). Bringing their statistics up to date, the Association showed that there had been increases over a year or so in nearly all the indicators, especially in the use of the mixed chalice (700), altar lights (431), and the eastward position by the celebrant for holy communion (353).

Perhaps prompted by the Church Association, Anglo-Catholics also provided some similar statistics, though for a diametrically opposite purpose! One of the reasons was to help Catholic-minded Anglicans find places of worship to their liking. At the turn of the century the English Church Union had a book printed with a title which has a modern ring about it: *The Tourist's Church Guide 1898–9*. This survey, which covered the years 1882–98, may not have been very accurately compiled. But the figures have many advantages, not least because they are based on churches and not clergy, and because they cover a large number of years. Table 4.1, which is from this publication, was reproduced in several of the editions of Church Association reports as if to confirm the Association's own findings. There is no clearer picture than this of the rapid growth of ritualistic practices during the last decades of the nineteenth century. It bears out the worst fears of the Church Association. From

Table 4.1 Findings of English Church Union Surveys 1882–98

Particulars	1882	1886	1888	1890	1892	1894	1896	1898
Churches	2,581	3,476	3,776	4,455	5,042	5,957	7,062	8,183
Daily holy eucharist	123	156	200	253	306	406	474	613
Vestments	336	509	599	797	1,029	1,370	1,632	2,026
Incense	9	66	89	135	177	250	307	381
Altar lights	581	968	1,136	1,402	2,048	2,707	3,568	4,334
Mixed chalice							2,111	4,030
Eastward position	1,662	2,433	2,620	3,138	3,918	5,037	5,964	7,044

all sources the three most popular changes related to the east-ward position, altar lights, and the mixed chalice. These practices are not, as we have noted, in themselves indicators of Anglo-Catholicism but do show the influence of the movement beyond its own boundaries. If one assumes that at the turn of the century there were about 14,200 churches which could have been included in the survey, then about half used the eastward position, 30 per cent had altar candles, and – a more 'Catholic' criterion – in 14 per cent eucharistic vestments were used (Brown 1980:2). The proportion of churches involved with one indicator or more was as much as two-thirds, which confirms our contention that the *Guide* and the List of the Church Association indicate high-churchmanship rather than Anglo-Catholicism *per se*.

Membership of the English Church Union is one of the best indicators of the strength of Anglo-Catholicism. In many respects, both in the past and in the present, the Union stands very much at the centre of Anglo-Catholicism and is some indication of the strength of the movement. When it began in 1860 it had only about 200 members. By 1894 there were 35,000 followers (see Roberts 1895:40–5). From 1860 to 1880 it grew to 17,700, and from 1880 to 1894 it doubled its membership (Roberts 1895:40–5). By 1901 membership was put at 39,000 (Munson 1975:387). In one year alone, 1889, it recruited 5,870 new members. Women were allowed to join but were called 'women associates'. The Union was well organized into a number of district unions, in which there were local branches. In 1893 there were 64 of the first and 377 of the second. By any reckoning the growth of the English Church Union must be seen as a great achievement for an organization closely identified with Anglo-Catholicism. Of course, not all its members would necessarily call themselves Anglo-Catholic: some were Tractarians. But, then, as we have often noted, not all Anglo-Catholics would be members. The figures given are a very clear indication of the growth of the movement at the end of the nineteenth century.

Alas, this is about the sum total of general statistics for the country as a whole which relate to Anglo-Catholicism. Beyond the turn of the century, and apart from what went on at the congresses, no one seems to have made any attempt to produce statistics which would apply to the movement. The enthusiasm of Protestant-minded Anglicans for statistical reports at the turn of the century evaporated as it became evident that the mere production of statistics had no effect on curbing the Catholic revival. Perhaps it should be mentioned that around the turn of the century, when there was a great national furore about disciplining ritualistic priests, a considerable amount of published material appeared describing what went on in specific parish churches. The difficulty is to deduce meaningful conclusions from a welter of detailed and mostly repetitious material. A Royal Commission on Ecclesiastical Discipline was set up in 1904 and published its notes on 559 churches in four volumes in 1906. Before Parliament met in 1904, it would seem that the pattern for gaining information had been established by the Hon and Rev W. E. Bowen, a leading figure of the Church Association, who as a result of research published his *Ritualism in the English Church* (1904). He had organized descriptions of ninety-one churches and their furnishings and services, and concentrated on twelve indicators. His report also listed Romish manuals, published mainly by Knott and associated with St Alban's, Holborn. He also prepared a bill with the help of counsel to discipline offending clergy. Clearly Bowen's work and the report paved the way for the Royal Commission. He was doubtless helped by a similar report compiled in 1903 by Linden Heitland, who described the 'havoc' created by ritualistic priests in country parishes (see section 4 below). Once more we have in these reports a vast amount of detailed material but no way of easily deriving statistics. Those who actually recorded the information for Parliament and for private organizations used paid agents to visit the churches and this of course made such surveys extremely expensive. It also came to be realized that the time and money involved in such reports produced virtually no results in plugging the dike against Anglo-Catholicism

In examining Anglo-Catholicism in the past there is one area in England which might be claimed to be an exception to what has just been said. It concerns London at the turn of the century. A very interesting source which has generally been overlooked by those concerned with Anglo-Catholicism are church attendances for London used by R. Mudie Smith in *The Religious Life of London* (1904). Before any meaningful results can be produced for Anglo-Catholic churches as a whole a considerable amount of research and analysis is required. At least this book offers somewhat limited attendance statistics for every church in London for one Sunday in the years 1902 and 1903.

Another source, but one which is virtually without statistics for church-going, is Charles Booth's *Life and Labour of the People of London*, in which as many as six volumes were devoted to 'Religious Influences' (Booth 1902). The survey was particularly interested in issues of class and the churches, and some of the reports on individudal churches were of varying quality. The way people are said to think and act is not always convincing (see section 3 below). Once again, in order to extract material on Anglo-Catholicism in London as a whole, a great amount of research is required.

The only guide one has to the strength of Anglo-Catholicism in more recent times can be found in *ad hoc* statistics relating to particular gatherings or membership of societies. We have already referred to the Anglo-Catholic congresses (ch. 2.5). The Federation of Catholic Priests needs to be mentioned. It was founded in 1917 in Pusey House under the leadership of Darwell Stone. Its aims were 'thoroughly Catholic' in so far as it pressed for maintaining the doctrines of the virginity of the Blessed Virgin Mary and the physical resurrection of Jesus Christ, the reservation of the Blessed Sacrament, the invocation of the saints, penance and fasting communion, and finally Catholic order and discipline (Cross 1943:128ff.). In 1929 its membership was 1,230 and in 1943 1,350. Today there are about 1,000 members. These figures represent something in the order of 10 per cent of all full-time Anglican clergy at the various years stated, or perhaps a little less. Membership over this period has kept to roughly the same proportion of clergy. All its members would certainly be Anglo-Catholic, if not Anglo-Papalist, but of course there would be a good number of Anglo-Catholic clergy who would not be members. Again, it is not known how many members have been from churches overseas.

A recent survey based on a sample of clergy found that just under a quarter described themselves as high church but not all these would be Anglo-Catholic (Gallup 1986:25). One might hazard a guess and say that today about a fifth of all clergy are Anglo-Catholic, or, in absolute figures, about 2,000.The survey further showed that high church clergy were as a group younger than clergy of other degrees of churchmanship.

We now turn to a limited number of demographic character-istics and similar observations about Anglo-Catholicism as a whole.

3 Criteria of age and class

In the past Anglo-Catholicism was often known as a young man's religion. One of the conclusions which emerged from the Church Association's ritualist clergy list for 1902 was, Munson has argued, that 'just over half the men surveyed were in their twenties and thirties and three quarters were between twenty and fifty', although he does not show how he made the calculations (Munson 1975:388). The figures were for those who were generally defined as ritualists but for Anglo-Catholics, that is those who used incense, much the same observation could be made: 'six out of every ten priests were under forty years of age and just under three out of each ten were in their twenties. Indeed, only 16% were in their fifties and above' (Munson 1975:390). In the 1920s and 1930s it was often said that Anglo-Catholicism was for the young. In her book on Anglo-Catholicism, Sheila Kaye-Smith wrote:

> It is a remarkable and encouraging fact that it is a religion which appeals to youth. The numbers of young men and women in an Anglo-Catholic congregation is often in excess of the middle-aged and elderly, and if one compares a gathering of Anglo-Catholics in Congress or otherwise, with a gathering of some other type of churchmanship, the average age is seen to drop at once from fifty or older to thirty or under.
>
> (Kaye-Smith 1925:153)

Again, at the 1933 Anglo-Catholic congress, it was claimed that, at the back of the Albert Hall, the majority were young people in an audience which filled the hall almost to capacity (*CT*, 14 July 1933).

Today it is the Evangelicals who capture the attention of those who are young and interested in religion: an unexpected reversal indeed from fifty or more years ago. Nevertheless, in some respects Anglo-Catholicism is still attractive to men. A quip often applied to Anglo-Catholic congregations today is that they consist of old ladies and young men. That is only partially true. It is probably the case that congregations consist mainly of middle-aged women and men. And just as significant is the fact that congregations are made up almost exclusively of 'singles', that is, of the unmarried, male and female; the widowed; and, of those who are married, only the wife or husband. The 'family pew' and families are very much lacking in Anglo-Catholicism.

Some Anglo-Catholic churches rejoiced in the fact that they had a good following of men in their congregations. Fr Ommanney in Sheffield could claim; 'Not infrequently, at High Mass on Sunday, the proportion of males would exceed that of the females' (Belton 1936:21). National gatherings are often dominantly male. At the centenary mass for the death of Fr Mackonochie held in 1987 at St Alban's, Holborn, it was estimated that, out of a congregation of over 700, about 80 per cent were male, many of them clergy. It would seem that within the Church of England religious gatherings of Anglo-Catholics are relatively more male than similar groupings associated with other types of churchmanship (see ch. 8). Booth did not fail to note that in the popular church of St Augustine's, Haggerston, in the East End, the ornate services drew one to two hundred people, mostly women and girls of lower middle- and working-class background (Booth 1902,2:90–1). Booth admitted that the 'High Church' (the term he constantly used when referring to Anglo-Catholics) was able in many cases to draw men to its services. But then, after a reference to the ritualistic dressing up of clergy, he wrote:

> The men who find satisfaction for their religious nature in the High Church are of a quite peculiar type. I cannot think it a strong type, and the idea that on these lines the world of men could ever be won is utterly untenable. . . . The influence exercised on the male sex is indeed strong, but is very limited. With women it is more diffused, and with children it reaches its greatest numerical success.
>
> (Booth 1902,7:51)

The subjective bias of Booth against Anglo-Catholics is apparent in these remarks about what he thought was the effeminate nature of men who went to ritualistic churches. From such a reading of the situation he was clearly pointing to the presence – an extraordinarily large presence in the light of their numbers – of homosexuality defined in some vague way (see ch. 8). Incidentally his Protestant leanings emerge in the following quotation:

> Meanwhile, the High Church as a distinct branch of the Church of England is able to find men to teach her doctrines who unreservedly accept and, I suppose, unfeignedly believe them, and knows how to stimulate her servants to the highest point of devotion in her cause.
>
> (Booth 1902,7:52)

Booth's generalizations are impressionistic and are not based on carefully documented material. There are no overall statistics for church attendance, let alone those which relate to gender and age of worshippers, and which may be compared with wider populations.

The Anglo-Catholic movement, like the Oxford movement, was initiated and led by clergy and as such it has always been a clerical movement (see ch. 9.3). Clergy had to encourage rather than restrain the enthusiasm of parishioners. Of course, as we have seen, there was always a fairly good following of lay people.

So what of the clergy themselves? What was their background? What was their training? As in the case of the Church of England as a whole, at least up until the time of the Second World War, the majority of the clergy associated with Anglo-Catholicism were graduates of Oxford or Cambridge – around 70 per cent at the turn of the century according to Munson (1975:390). As time went on, more and more graduates went to a theological college as well and more than likely to one sympathetic towards things Anglo-Catholic. By social background they tended to belong to what we would call today the upper middle class or minor nobility. Very few indeed came from lower middle-class homes or further down the social scale. It is true that many worked in slum parishes – the point will be treated in more detail later on in this chapter – but their background had the obvious consequence that they brought with them middle-class ideals and consciously or otherwise imposed them on the people to whom they devoted their lives (see ch. 5.6). Although working-class parishes proved to be so attractive to Anglo-Catholic priests, virtually none of the priests, or at least very few of them, were of working-class background. In the face of the difficulties and opposition which Anglo-Catholic clergy encountered, one speaker addressing the full assembly of the 1933 Anglo-Catholic congress declared that the leaders of the Oxford movement 'met everything that came their way like Christians and gentlemen. . . . They were gentlemen in the finest sense of that much abused term, as well as scholars and saints' (*CT*, 14 July 1933). The Anglo-Catholic concern for and interest in the middle classes is evident in their effort to influence public school life, especially through the Woodard schools (see ch. 5.7).

Yet Anglo-Catholic clergy, although so often from a middle-class background, realized the weakness of the Church in having priests only of this class and they, perhaps more than those of other church parties, tried to encourage working-class lads to enter the ministry. To this end they deliberately cut the traditional boundaries and established theological colleges, such as Kelham, for working-class people (see ch. 5.7). A change took place after the First World War as more non-graduates were ordained (see, for example, Williamson 1963).

4 Geographical distribution

Anglo-Catholicism has been nicknamed the 'London, Brighton, and South Coast religion' – a name derived from the now extinct railway company. The designation, attributed to Dean Inge, is not inappropiate. If England's 'biretta belt' is to be found anywhere at all, it is located in the south-east corner of the country. However, the spread of Anglo-Catholicism is slightly more complicated than that indicated in the nickname.

As soon as it had burst out of its Oxford chrysalis, Anglo-Catholicism immediately developed a firm base in London. Two poles emerged: one in the West End, the other in the East End of the metropolis.

In the West End one might mention some of the famous churches not yet mentioned: St Augustine's, Kilburn; St Cuthbert's, Philbeach Gardens; St Thomas's, Regent Street; St Mary Magdalene's, Munster Square; St Mary's, Graham Street; St Cyprian's, Clarence Gate; the Annunciation, Bryanston Street; St Stephen's, Gloucester Road; and so on.

In the East End some of the most famous churches were: Holy Trinity, Hoxton; St Augustine's, Haggerston; St George's-in-the-East, Stepney; St Saviour's, Poplar; and several churches on the Isle of Dogs.

There were also many Anglo-Catholic churches in other parts of London. In the city itself there was St Magnus-the-Martyr and St Nicholas, Cole Abbey; to the south, St John the Divine, Kennington, and the Ascension, Lavender Hill; to the north, Holy Redeemer, Clerkenwell, and St Mary's, Somers Town. And, of course, in the suburbs there were many great centres of Anglo-Catholicism. Perhaps the finest of all the churches was St Alban the Martyr, Teddington, often referred to as the cathedral of the Anglo-Catholics or 'the cathedral of the Thames Valley'.

It is quite remarkable how quickly Anglo-Catholic churches appeared in almost every part of London and its sprawling suburbs. At the turn of the century, according to figures culled by observers for the Church Association, one out of every four Anglo-Catholic churches, that is, churches using incense, was in London (see Munson 1975:391). It would seem, without over-stating the case, that by the 1930s Anglican churches in the centre of London were dominated by Anglo-Catholic incumbents. And today, aided by the present bishop of London, it is beyond all shadow of doubt the most 'Catholic' diocese in England.

Remarkable, too, was the growth and spread of Anglo-Catholic churches in the East End and other slum areas. This trend began with the pioneer work of Fr Lowder at St Peter's, London docks, and has been encouraged, in some measure, by the influence of mission centres established and financed by Oxford and Cambridge colleges. The churchmanship of these centres was usually, though not always, Anglo-Catholic. During their vacations, students helped the official missioners by doing what they could to assist in social and religious matters. When the students had finished their time at the university, some of them joined the staff in a lay capacity and others went back to the missions as clergy. The point is that such missions were powerful agencies in attracting men to work in the slums (see section 5 below).

Outside Greater London, Brighton was the most important centre. The church of St Bartholomew, one of the most impressive parish churches to be built in England in the nineteenth century, was the centre of an ornate Catholic cult offering a feast of beauty in liturgy and music (see Hennock 1981; and section 5 below). In 1904 it was said that 'St Bartholomew's is probably the best known Ritualistic church in England. The St Bartholomew's Tracts, written in defence of Ritualistic doctrine and practice, are circulated by hundreds and thousands' (Bowen 1904:66). There were other churches as well, for example, St Paul's and St Martin's. And evidence of Brighton's importance as an Anglo-Catholic stronghold is the fact that anti-Catholic, Protestant associations made the town one of their main fronts of attack. For them it was a 'plague spot of Mariolatry' (Bowen 1904:386). And, interestingly enough, in Brighton at the turn of the century, John Kensit, the Cromwell of the Protestants of the day, stood as the 'Protestant' candidate for Westminster and polled just under a quarter of the votes cast.

Anglo-Catholicism grew rapidly all along the south coast, extending to towns large and small from Folkestone at one end to as far west as Devonport, and indeed beyond, into Cornwall, at the other, although, strangely enough, Evangelicals often found strongholds in Victorian seaside resorts.

To give the impression that Anglo-Catholicism in its development in the nineteenth century moved away from its mother in Oxford is to create a totally false notion. To this day the tradition lingers on that Oxford not only remains the spiritual home of the movement of that name but is also the home of Anglo-Catholicism. From an early date many parishes in the city became high and some very high indeed. One has but to recall St Barnabas (Jericho), St Paul's (one of the most Anglo-Papalist churches known, but now closed), St Mary Magdalene's (which today is the most popular of all Anglo-Catholic churches in Oxford), St Thomas's, St Frideswide's (patron saint of the city and university), St Margaret's, and St Philip and St James's (now closed). One must also mention Pusey House, the gathering point of male (and now female also) undergraduates who wish to experience Anglo-Catholicism in a somewhat restrained and academic setting, where good preaching and strong congregational singing could be found. Also in Oxford are several convents as well as the foundation house of the Cowley Fathers (see ch. 3.3). Apart from Rome itself, Oxford is a veritable Rome for Anglo-Catholics. By the 1930s most, but certainly not all, of the parish churches of the city were either high or decidedly Anglo-Catholic. The choice for church-goers lay between one form of Catholicism and another. (For the subtle differences between the various Anglo-Catholic churches in Oxford, see Hughes 1961:42–3.)

'Smells and bells' were never as popular in Cambridge as they were in Oxford. There have been a handful of churches which in the past embraced the Catholic revival with varying degrees of enthusiasm but such churches have not been as numerous as they have been in 'the other place'. In the *English Church Union Church Guide for Tourists and Others* for 1931, twelve churches were named as acceptable to Catholic practice in Oxford, and Pusey House was not mentioned, but for Cambridge there were only five such churches. In Cambridge, however, there was the Oratory of the Good Shepherd, an order of Anglican priests having some parallels with the Oratorians. The Oratory of the Good Shepherd, which still functions today, reached its height in the 1930s. About a hundred years earlier, in 1839, the Camden Society, which had as its centre of interest the study of ecclesiastical art and architecture, was founded by J. M. Neale. Seven years later it moved from Cambridge to London and became known as the Ecclesiological Society. Gorman's list of converts to the Roman Catholic Church from the begining of the Tractarian movement to just before 1900 showed that, for every Cambridge-trained person who converted, there were two (2.08) who had been undergraduates at Oxford (Gorman 1899). In the figures extending to about 1910, when there had been 274 more 'Oxbridge' converts, the ratio had changed a little in favour of Cambridge – 1 to 1.7 (Gorman 1910). Yet the number of those being ordained in this period in the Church of England was more or less equally divided between graduates of the two universities. This seems to show, if nothing else, the difference in influence in the matter of the Catholic revival between the two centres of learning.

Unlike the Oxford movement, which gained a considerable following in rural areas, Anglo-Catholics as a whole were far more successful in towns and cities than in the countryside. It has been said that eight out of every ten Anglo-Catholics were found to be residing in urban areas in the 1920s and 1930s. Munson has argued from statistics for an earlier period around 1900 and compiled by the Church Association that 'the larger the urban area, the greater was Anglo-Catholic strength' (Munson 1975:390; see section 5 below). Thus, its greatest following in comparative terms was in populations of 100,000 and over (Munson 1975:390). Three out of every four Anglo-Catholic churches were in towns or cities. From details of the 1851 religious census it has been shown that church-going was weakest in large urban areas: the bigger the city, the lower the level of church-going (see Pickering 1967). It is an interesting reflection that, where church-going was generally weakest, Anglo-Catholics appeared to be proportionally stronger.

Although the movement had its bastions in London and the south, it was fairly well represented in other parts of England. We mention the following places, together with the names (in brackets) of the well known priests associated with them: Sheffield (Ommanney, see Belton 1936), Birmingham (F. Underhill), Middlesborough (Burn), Newcastle (Vibert Jackson), Hull (W. H. Baker), Liverpool, Leeds, and so on. Places and names could be extended but, although there were no Anglo-Catholic wildernesses in the towns of the north and midlands, the fact remains that the numbers of 'advanced' parishes in such areas were much fewer on a per capita basis. From the 1930s onwards new housing estates mushroomed all over England, especially at the edges of older towns and cities. Anglo-Catholicism and Anglo-Papalism never seemed to gain a foothold in the estates (see Gunstone 1968:193). Therefore today it remains associated with older churches, not those more recently built. Middle-of-the-road Anglicanism – a mild form of semi-Catholicism centred around parish communion – is the prevailing churchmanship on estates built after the Second World War (see ch. 11.4).

Country parishes which had and still have a strong Anglo-Catholic flavour are often difficult to locate. They appear here and there with no obvious pattern of distribution. There have been, however, one or two exceptions. In Cornwall many rural churches adopted Catholic practices – indeed, Cornwall has gained a reputation for fostering extremes – Evangelicals and Anglo-Papalists, plus a powerful Methodist contingent (see Brown 1980; Walke 1935; Voll t.1963:83; the novels of Mackenzie 1922, 1923, 1924). Miles Brown has shown that around 1900 in Cornwall, according to statistics of the *Church Guide for Tourists* (English Church Union 1901) and judged by the indicator of the use of vestments, 25 per cent of the churches used them, whereas for Devon it was 14 per cent, for Lincoln 13 per cent, for Yorkshire 19 per cent, and for London 26 per cent (Brown 1980:2). For the country as a whole, as we have stated, the corresponding figure was 14 per cent. In earlier times Cornwall was the centre of a great Methodist revival. Did Anglo-Catholics think they had the Anglican answer for a take-over? Another exception is in north Norfolk, where a cluster of churches display Anglo-Catholic leanings. The chief of these is, of course, Walsingham, both the shrine and the parish church, which together make a great pilgrimage centre for Anglo-Catholics. Nor should one overlook South Creake, much beloved by Sir John Betjeman. Apart from these two rural areas, 'spiky' churches have tended to emerge singly in various places around the countryside. One such is the parish church of the small town of Frome in Somerset. W. J. E. Bennett (1804–86) had been the priest in charge of St Barnabas's, Pimlico, London; the church opened in 1850 and was subjected to so much mob violence that he was encouraged by Blomfield, the bishop of London, to resign. Subsequently he became vicar of Frome. Under his direction the church took on a very strong Anglo-Catholic ethos. To this day one may see giant Stations of the Cross outside the church. Not surprisingly, Bennett was taken before the courts for his Romish doctrines, particularly his writings on the eucharist. But nothing in fact changed in the parish church as a result of the court case. Due to the influence of Lord Halifax, no doubt, there are a number of parishes in Yorkshire which are Anglo-Catholic.

Such is the pattern which has emerged. Nevertheless, opponents of Anglo-Catholicism became alarmed at the turn of the century about the alleged spread of the movement into the countryside. Linden Heitland made a detailed examination of about 110 parishes, nearly all of them country parishes, which appear to have been selected on an *ad hoc* basis (Heitland 1903). He observed the services, the prayer books recommended, the association of the priest with Anglo-Catholic societies, and, in many cases, the numbers of those who attended church. The observations were made in great detail and in this respect they are interesting, for the author challenged anyone to fault him on the matter of accuracy. Counter-Reformation devotional literature was found available at the back of tiny country churches and many a time did the surveyors find the service of holy communion celebrated with only the priest communicating. In the introduction, written by the Lady Wimborne, several generalizations were made. Apart from the unexpected penetration into the countryside, the most telling criticism of the ritualist churches was the fact that congregations had dropped very seriously. Adults stayed away in the face of the alien changes but the priests were able to draw children, who, it was alleged, later dropped off. The statistics given bear out the first point. 'The village church has been the house of the poor', but now the poor have forsaken it (Heitland 1903:10). 'They turn in disgust from the new services. Nor do the priests seem to worry about their emptying the churches of the adults' (Heitland 1903:12). The laity who leave do not go to the chapel: they simply go nowhere. Incidentally, Heitland (1903) and Bowen (1904) made much of chidren's masses. For one thing they indicated an unhealthy influence which priests exerted over the defenceless young and for another, since there were no communicants except the priest, they implied a doctrine of the sacrifice of the mass, all of which was contrary to the Prayer Book.

Sabine Baring-Gould (1834–1924), an ardent ritualist and a prolific writer, spent most of his working life in rural parishes. He made the observation that, owing to the mentality of country people, changes in a Catholic direction had to be made very slowly if anything positive were to be accomplished (Purcell 1957:134). Although an extremist himself, he does not seem to have stridently imposed his wishes on any of the country parishes where he was the incumbent. Perhaps the fact was that Anglo-Catholic clergy generally had an urban mentality and little understanding of rural affairs.

That cannot be said of Bernard Walke, who spent virtually all his life in the west country and for twenty years was vicar of St Hilary, near Penzance. In his church he had a chapel to the Sacred Heart, apparently said mass in Latin (parts of it, or from time to time?), and had his congregation say the rosary. Yet he appears to have been a very lovable and understanding person who was generally called 'Parson' by his parishioners. He was apparently 'successful' in his Anglo-Papalist views, accepted on account of his understanding of country people and his warm personality. One or two people were strongly opposed to ritualism and successfully brought an action against him in the diocesan consistory court in the early 1930s. The locals on the whole did not really seem to understand what he was doing but they were willing to trust him (see Walke 1935; also ch. 7.4). By and large, however, such priests were rare. With a brutal foisting of ritual practices and their accompanying beliefs on to conservative country folk the charge could be laid at the feet of Anglo-Catholicism that it accelerated a creeping secularization in country areas. A priori such a contention is well worth examining in detail but it cannot be undertaken here.

From what has been said one can see that Anglo-Catholicism as the 'London, Brighton, and South Coast religion' exhibits a pattern something like this:

$$\left\{ \begin{array}{lcl} \text{strong} & : & \text{weak} \\ \text{south} & : & \text{north} \\ \text{urban} & : & \text{rural} \end{array} \right\}$$

Although Anglo-Catholic churches can be found in all large towns and cities, nevertheless it is evident, as we have said before, that both in the past and the present their presence has been stronger in urban areas in the south than in the north. From this a number of questions arise. If Anglo-Catholicism was relatively successful in the East End of London, why was it less successful in the back streets of Manchester, Birmingham, or perhaps Newcastle (where admittedly there have been one or two such churches)? Again, if Anglo-Catholic churches captured the centre and West End of London, why did it so lamentably fail in the centre of cities in the north?

But before we take up these issues, which will be considered for the rest of the chapter, something more must be said about the poor showing of Anglo-Catholicism in the countryside. A number of reasons for this state of affairs might be put forward. One would be that rural life was less attractive to the adventurous, dedicated priest who wanted to be stretched in situations which called for heroism. The slums of London obviously offered such an opportunity and, by contrast, rural life would be seen as a quiet, bucolic, pastoral, family existence. It should not be forgotten that many Anglo-Catholic priests supported the ideal of celibacy and as a consequence might find rural parish life lonely (see ch. 8.2). Further, the ideal of a group of unmarried priests working together in a clergy house was quite alien to rural parish life in the nineteenth century. From a purely liturgical point of view, a country parish would probably be more difficult to transform into a church radiating a Catholic ethos, not least on account of potential opposition. This might come, on the one hand, from the local squire vociferously objecting and complaining to the bishop and, on the other, from the less prestigious members of the congregation. These would most likely be farm labourers and tradesmen. It has often been said, and with some justification, that the mentality of rural people is stubborn and averse to change. Ritualistic changes would therefore, more than likely, be opposed by such a congregation, who might well leave to attend the local chapel, if there were one, or just go nowhere at all, as we have seen suggested. Lowther Clarke, a priest of strong Catholic sympathies, wrote of the English countryside:

> We have seen that the Christianity of the English countryside is far from strong. It is in possession, but in an attenuated form. It is rather a passive acquiescence of traditional religion than a triumphant living faith. No obvious cure can be suggested for such a state of things.
>
> (Clarke 1912:168–9)

5 Success in the slums?

Anglo-Catholic priests penetrated the dark places of London, the slums of Stepney, Shoreditch, Pimlico, Paddington, Holborn, and Lambeth, to name but a few. Through biographies and autobiographies a great deal has been written about their allegedly courageous exploits. The names of Lowder, Wainwright, Mackonochie, Stanton, Wilson, Williamson and many others are associated with pioneering work done by Anglo-Catholic clergy amongst people who were generally held to be pastorally uncared for by the Church of England. Other cities have also had their Anglo-Catholic slum priests. For example, so popular was Fr Dolling in Portsmouth that when he died it was estimated that 20,000 parishioners followed the cortège (see Dolling 1896). (For a moving account of the work of a priest working in the slums of Newcastle upon Tyne in the period 1927–44, see Pickering 1981, chapter 13.) At one time it was generally expected that all Anglo-Catholic curates would, for a time at least, do a spell in a slum parish. Nevertheless, despite the fame of slum priests in and outside London, and the great esteem in which they were held, how 'successful' were they? How full were their churches? No careful study has been undertaken of what, admittedly, is a complex subject and, until such an analysis has been made, all one can do is to put forward a number of observations and hypotheses which need to be carefully tested.

There can be no doubt that there were large numbers of Anglo-Catholic priests who wanted the movement to be deeply concerned with the welfare of working-class people. In this respect they wished to transform at least part of the Church of England into a church of the 'ordinary man'. They had no wish to be identified with squirearchy, with the privileged, with the cosy middle-of-the-road 'C. of E.'. This goal, which had long existed, was symbolically declared in the 1933 congress, when on the last day at the high mass, although there was no general communion of the people, 'six simple workaday men [no women!], varying in age and condition, proceeded to the altar and made their Communions'. This, commented the reporter, was 'the most impressive moment of the whole ceremony'. On the day before, evensong had been sung in plainsong 'by a choir from a working district from London' (*CT*, 21 July 1933). And the comment was that this sort of music could be achieved by working-class people. In 1923 one correspondent writing to the *Church Times* claimed that: 'Anglo-Catholicism is becoming more and more a movement of the people . . . which will bring perhaps England back to Christ' (*CT*, 21 July 1933).

Two forces appeared to be present amongst Anglo-Catholics relating to this issue. The first was a general and genuine pastoral concern for people who had to live in appalling social conditions. The second was a deep conviction that Anglo-Catholicism could make an impact on the unchurched in areas where those forms of Christianity which had been tried, especially 'ordinary Church of England', had failed.

So Anglo-Catholic priests plunged into parishes which were notorious for their appalling social conditions. When Fr Lowder went to work in St George's mission in the East End in 1856, it was reported that:

> There were large numbers of pubs, providing an escape from the misery of life, and numerous prostitutes unable to earn a living in any other way. Of four streets surrounding S. George's, 154 houses were brothels, and 40 were pubs, out of a total of 733 houses. Much of the opposition to the Mission came from the proprietors of these, rightly recognising a threat to their trade.
>
> (Trott 1983:6)

Anglo-Catholic clergy were constantly fighting against the degradation which prevailed in the slums of England's great cities. They were particularly prominent in times of crisis, as in the outbreak of cholera in the East End in 1860, and at times when other scourges reigned. Slum-dwellers quickly realized that Anglo-Catholic clergy were on their side and many clergy were not slow in calling for changes in the social conditions in which thousands were forced to live. They demanded, for example, the closing of brothels, the ending of sweated labour, and the improvement of rented housing. One of the first things which Fr Ommanney did when he went to St Matthew's, Sheffield, was to demand from the authorities that drains be installed in part of the parish where there was nothing but open sewage (Belton 1936:56–7). That was in 1882! Inevitably, the demands made by the clergy drew opposition and hostility from interested parties, from owners of factories and houses, and from other entrepreneurs.

Today, those clergy who show concern for the poor are, it is often said, to be found amongst those who profess liberation theology. If that means the churches being skewed towards the poor, Anglo-Catholic clergy had reached that conclusion in the nineteenth century. They preached and practised it. W. G. Ward, in the early days of the Oxford movement, was of the firm opinion that the Church of England had to be a poor man's church. And Fr Ommanney wrote:

> The Church of England was the religion of the rich and respectable, and the poor did not have the Gospel preached to them. . . . It is the fulness of God's love to all, rich and poor, learned and ignorant, that is manifested in the Catholic religion that will draw them back, and they will be true saints.
>
> (Belton 1936:56–7)

In preaching the Gospel and in being true pastors to the poor, many but not all Anglo-Catholic clergy felt that they could bring about social amelioration by personal intervention and individual action, not by joining a political party. The approach of the priest working by himself or with colleagues has been seen to be paternalistic: indeed the whole approach of Anglo-Catholicism in ecclesiastical and social matters is both individualistic and paternalistic, not least because it was a clerical movement (see Mayor 1967:45; also ch. 5.6).

The amount of social welfare carried out by the clergy in their parishes was enormous and cannot be adequately described here. Let one or two early examples suffice. When Fr Mackonochie established himself as vicar of St Alban's, Holborn, he organized the following societies and facilities:

> A Sisterhood; a Burial Society; Guilds and Associations for Men, Boys, Women and Girls; a Working-men's Club; an Infant Nursery; a Choir-School; Parochial Schools, built at a cost of £6,000, and educating 500 children; Night Schools for Boys and Girls; a Soup-Kitchen; a Blanket Loan Fund; a Lying-in Charity; a Clothing Fund; a Coal-Charity; a Savings-Bank and Clothing Club; a Shoe-Club; provision and food for

the destitute, and relief for the sick, to the amount of some
£500 a year.

(Russell 1902:85)

The number and types of services which were held in parishes
is mentioned in the pages ahead (see ch. 5.3). In and through the
great amount of service and help which Anglo-Catholic priests
bestowed on the poor, they showed a deep concern, not only for
the pious but, above all, for those working-class folk whose
attachment to the church was extremely tenuous. Fr Stanton's
heart was really with these people and it was his open love for
them which attracted so many people to his ministry. Non-
church-goers would probably only enter his church at his popular
New Year's Eve watch-night service (see ch. 3.4). Shortly before
his death he saw such people through the window of the clergy
house as they were coming to the service and he is reported to
have said to the nurse:

> These are my friends. They have come, I fear, many of them
> come straight from the Public House. It is the only time they
> think of coming to church. But these dear people are our real
> parishioners, the people for whom the church was built.

(Russell 1917:302).

But why should London and its slums be the main point of
attraction? It is a commonplace that London was the capital of
the world's greatest nation at the time, a nation, moreover, which
claimed to be Christian. But London also had some of the worst
slums of any European country. These facts prompted a number
of surveys on poverty and in such research England began to lead
the world. The most notable example was Charles Booth's *Life
and Labour of the People in London* (1902–3, 17 vols). London,
far more than Manchester, seemed to attract such surveys,
although in the latter city there was also great misery and
poverty, which was the subject of a book by F. Engels. English
life, with its contrast between enormous wealth and grinding
poverty, was epitomized by London with its sprawling population
of several million.

It was hardly surprising, therefore, that a priest with initiative
and a strong sense of mission should turn to London as a place of
challenge and of hope. But there was also another reason.
London was relatively near to Oxford and Cambridge and this
meant that undergraduates could visit it easily and venture into
the slums to see for themselves what they were like. Those of
Manchester were far away: there were no college missions there.

Birmingham grew much later and scarcely experienced slum life. Another factor was that Manchester was a city whose religion was dominated by Nonconformists and Evangelical Anglicans. It had a formidable 'Prot' as bishop from 1903 to 1921. He was the redoubtable E. A. Knox, who had little love for Anglo-Catholics, and whose son, Ronald, became one and eventually a Roman Catholic (see ch. 9.2). Such a diocese did not attract Catholic-minded students and junior clergy. Kaye-Smith, in admitting that far more progress was made in the south than in the north, places emphasis on such ecclesiastical factors. She pointed to the influence of Northern Irish Protestantism in such cities as Liverpool, and also to the fact that bishops in the northern dioceses were on the whole more opposed to Anglo-Catholicism than were bishops in the south. Some northern dioceses forbade the reservation of the Blessed Sacrament under pain of deprivation of church grants and the refusal of bishops to license curates to parishes where there was reservation (Kaye-Smith 1925:84).

Of course it must not be forgotten, in evaluating the work of Anglo-Catholics in the slums, that they were not alone in establishing missions in parishes in the East End of London: undergraduates of all shades of churchmanship were encouraged to help run missions (see ch. 3.2; Booth 1902,7:89ff.). And London was not the only city to be given such missions. The public school at Winchester created a mission at Landport, the slum in Portsmouth, where Fr Dolling was the priest in charge of the associated church of St Agatha (see Dolling 1896).

There was a strong conviction amongst many Anglo-Catholics, however, that the ritualized and elaborate services which they introduced would be particularly attractive to working-class folk living in abysmal surroundings. Many people bear testimony to the fact that to enter a large, colourful Anglo-Catholic church having come from a drab, dreary street – one of many exactly like it, all of them lined by mean terraced houses – is to enter a new and exciting world, a world which takes one away from the gloomy surroundings of ordinary daily life. In short it is to enter another world, a world of colour, beauty, and mystery. Whether or not the ritualist services in themselves drew people to church has always been open to doubt. Around the turn of the century Booth found churches which had ritualistic services which were 'entirely neglected' as at St Stephen's, Haggerston (Booth 1902,2:92). He seemed convinced that successful Anglo-Catholic congregations were dependent on the personality and devotion of the priest (Booth 1902,2:146). And Anglo-Catholics seemed to be able to produce such people. It would appear that some wealthy people were prepared to build churches in slum areas which would have an Anglo-Catholic ethos, because as such they would be effective as centres of evangelization and social care. That idea was obviously in the mind of Mr Hubbard, later Lord Addington, who built the church of St Alban the Martyr, Holborn, and appointed Fr Mackonochie as the first incumbent (Russell 1902:80).

But it was not only private patrons who secured the services of Anglo-Catholic priests. The influence of various types of patrons in the appointment of incumbents has never been analysed. The Church Association around the turn of the century was quite convinced that government bodies and bishops themselves were, by the power they had in making appointments, reponsible for the growth of churches which were distinctly Anglo-Catholic. In the third edition of the ritualistic clergy list in 1903 the compilers reckoned bishops had appointed 380 clergy with Anglo-Catholic tendencies and the government 180. Interestingly enough just under a fifth of the latter number related to chaplaincy appointments in India (Church Association 1903:iv–v). On the other hand, Bowen, also concerned with Anglo-Catholicism and patronage, puts a lot of blame on to Keble College, Oxford, for their appointments to livings (Bowen 1904:x).

To return to the main issue. How far in fact were the slum churches effective, the hopes realized? Today, one cannot escape the fact that these famous churches, often made so by biographies of their clergy, are patronized by dwindling congregations: some churches have completely disappeared, either through bombing in the blitz or through closure made inevitable by very poor attendances.

All observations made about church-going in the inner cities at the present time point to the extreme weakness of nearly all traditional churches judged by their very thin congregations, and that irrespective of denomination. Anglo-Catholic churches have shown themselves to be no exception. But what were they really like in their heyday? In the face of little or no research it is impossible to offer a general picture. Around the turn of the century they do not seem to have commanded the numbers people might have been led to expect. The survey of London churches with which Mudie Smith was associated reported figures for the East End which were below what was anticipated for high church Anglicans (Smith 1904:24–5). The comments were:

The High Church – or at least the Ritualist section of the High

Church – does not seem to have made the progress that everybody anticipated. Here and there an able, devoted man has built up a strong and flourishing church, but there are many instances of ineffectiveness and incapacity. So far as the working man is concerned, he seldom feels at home in a church with a highly ornate ritual, in which he takes little part. If he does attend, it is because he approves of the socialist leanings of the parson and finds in him a real friend and brother. Even the women are not attracted to the extent that we were led to expect.

(Smith 1904:37)

Although the opinions of the compilers of the report might have been skewed towards Protestantism, the total attendances at St George's in the East were 454 – there were plenty of other Anglican churches in the area with higher attendances – and St Peter's, London docks, had 1,092, but of these 670 were of children (Smith 1904:49). St Barnabas's, Pimlico, had 879, of which about 100 were children (Smith 1904:109). But St Augustine's, Haggerston, had only 314, of which about 120 were children (Smith 1904:59).

What one knows about Anglo-Catholic churches nearly always turns on the character of the priest, not on the size of the congregations. Evidence about the priests often comes from unlikely sources, even from a bishop! In this the witness of bishops should be reliable, as in the controversy between Fr Dolling and his bishop. The bishop of Winchester, in the 1890s, wrote to the secretary of the Protestant Alliance:

Mr Dolling . . . [whose work] though disfigured by errors and eccentricities, which, in common with not a few of his truest friends, I sincerely deprecate, is of a kind which very few other men are capable of accomplishing, and reaches a class of society too frequently left to itself out of sheer helplessness and despair.

(Dolling 1896:160)

To read Dolling's own account of his work in the slums of Portsmouth is to be made aware of his enormously effective ministry. Whether this was in fact the case has not been accurately assessed. Nor is it generally known whether other Anglo-Catholic churches, lesser known ones, were able to exert influence over those whom they served in their parishes.

In his *Class and Religion in the Late Victorian City*, McLeod has compared unfavourably the effectiveness of Anglo-Catholic priests with that of Roman priests. In referring to men like Stanton, Wainright, and Dolling, he noted that they

> won many individual converts; but their impact on the community as a whole was very limited. They were respected as individuals rather than as priests, and there was no special pressure to support their churches. The London pattern of life had grown up in independence of the Church, and when the church tried to recreate a traditionalist church-centred organisation of life, this sort of community was irrevocably a thing of the past.
>
> (McLeod 1974:80)

This may have been a telling factor in the long run but in the short term the churches were perhaps more successful than McLeod maintains. Let us take an optimistic position and assume that most Anglo-Catholic churches in the slums were successful and some of them were very successful. Why was this so? Was it to do with the personality of the priest? At the social level it clearly was. That priests would spend the best years of their lives in London's worst slums was greatly appreciated by those who lived in them, those who suffered and were trampled on. When priests like Dolling, Wainwright, and Lowder died, there were reports that thousands lined the streets for their funerals. Of course, in the long run, the question arises: what happens in the parish after the beloved priest dies? It is here that McLeod may have a point. While the popular priest ran the parish, all went well. But when there was a change of priest the continuity of his predecessor's work and influence was broken. It is the old story which is so common in non-Roman Catholic churches situated in a milieu characterized by religious pluralism. Anglo-Catholicism was and still is no exception.

At a more theological level, Catholic minded people have tended to criticize Protestants because their success in influencing people has depended upon the personality of the clergyman. They have failed to stress the objectivity of spiritual grace which comes through the sacraments and which is in no way dependent on the personality of the priest. But they are placed in a somewhat ambiguous position. Although Anglo-Catholics and indeed Roman Catholics believe that theologically the working of the Holy Spirit comes through objective channels and is without reference to the personality of the priest, they speak enthusiastically of heroes and saints whose influence on others has been enormous. They want to have it both ways. In trying to account for the development of Anglo-Catholicism there seems little doubt that it was largely due to the labours of devoted and high-minded priests. The force of the individual personality of the priest was more apparent in slum parishes, not least because of the social background and abilities in leadership which these clergy possessed. Some Anglo-Catholic clergy may have been eccentric but they show that on the whole they were good organizers, incessantly took the initiative, and gave to working-class parishioners the impression of being people in authority who could produce results. Rather cynically, but perhaps with a certain amount of truth, the Congregationalist writer, Stephen Mayor, has observed:

> The Anglo-Catholics always believed they had special advantages in dealing with the working classes, but in practice the only striking advantage they had from this point of view was that they were not acceptable themselves in many parishes other than the poorest, so that they necessarily made the close acquaintance of the poor.
>
> (Mayor 1967:336)

The clergy found that in working-class areas there was very little natural leadership. The problem of organizing the masses on some voluntary basis around a given ideal was one which Karl Marx faced. It has always remained a problem in Marxism and, in fact, in arousing any form of political consciousness. Everything seems to devolve around middle-class infiltration and leadership. Anglo-Catholic priests working in the slums could not fail to gain respect on account of their sense of duty, their incredibly hard work as pastors, their great sympathy with the poor, and their obvious powers of leadership. Of course this applied as well to clergy of other denominations, where such moral qualilties were also to be found.

An important factor in accounting for the success of Anglo-Catholic clergy was that they were nearly always unmarried, and often lived in Spartan conditions in a clergy house (see ch. 8.2). To this must be added yet another factor, namely that many clergy had their own private incomes, which meant that they did not often have to rely on their salaries and could use part of the salary to pay a curate. Fr Stanton was curate of St Alban's, Holborn, for fifty years and because of a private income it is thought that he never received a salary above five shillings a year (see Russell 1917:37). Arthur Tooth, vicar of St James's, Hatcham, in south London, who was imprisoned on charges of ritualism was another priest with an adequate private income (Russell 1917:53). Changes could be made to church buildings:

they could be beautified with money out of the pockets of such clergy. Clearly the poor could not produce the money themselves. Sometimes wealthy incumbents actually built new churches. For example, St Bartholomew's, Brighton, was erected through the magnanimity of the Rev A. D. Wagner, incumbent of the mother church, St Paul's. St Bartholomew's, completed in 1874 at a cost of £18,000, has magnificent furnishings and works of art (see Hennock 1981; also ch. 1.3). It has been described by John Betjeman as one of the great English churches of the nineteenth century. (That the parish of St Bartholomew was in fact situated in a slum could be contested.) Fr Wagner also paid for the building of three other churches in Brighton. One of these had money given by his two half-brothers as well. There can be no doubt that this unmarried priest, who, incidentally, was said to be much devoted to the Blessed Virgin Mary and who came from a local, very wealthy family was extremely generous to the Church. It was reported that he gave away £70,000 for churches and schools (Hennock 1981:180). That Anglo-Catholicism became known as the London, *Brighton*, and South Coast religion is largely due to him. Very high (in many senses) and large (it can hold 2,000), St Bartholomew's, reminiscent of Westminster cathedral in its interior, stands as an enormous building close to the railway station and symbolizes to the ecclesiastically inclined traveller that he or she has reached one of the great shrines of triumphant Anglo-Catholicism.

The wealth and generosity of many Anglo-Catholic priests of the period affected churches everywhere, but in slum areas it was particularly important. Pusey gave a large sum of money for the building of St Saviour's, Leeds, as a memorial to his wife (Yates 1975:3). Further, because of their contact with wealthy middle-class people, priests were able to find money from outside to help ameliorate the sufferings of the poor in their parishes and also for the upkeep and expansion of their churches. Some Anglo-Catholic clergy, James Adderley and Maryon Wilson to name two, were sons of the nobility.

The wealth of the clergy was employed in a different way to the benefit of Anglo-Catholicism. The costs of the court cases and legal battles over ritualistic practices were often borne by the English Church Union but there were cases where priests were able to pay themselves. It is said that Fr Fynes-Clinton, of St Magnus the Martyr in the city of London, loved litigation and used 'his not inconsiderable private means to finance appeals to the very highest courts' (Lunn and Haselock 1983:11; also ch. 1.3).

Despite their upper middle class or aristocratic background, most Anglo-Catholic clergy could be seen to be marginal compared with clergy as a whole (see ch. 7.4). Many of them, in the early days of the movement, never received preferment, to a canonry or a bishopric. Sometimes they were never offered it: on other occasions they refused for a host of reasons. It had the result, however, of experienced and able people remaining in front-line parishes and thus strengthening the movement where, some would say, it mattered most. As they were so often unmarried, they were not anxious to be in more valuable benefices for the sake of wives and families. As we have mentioned, Fr Stanton remained a curate all his life. It is said that when he went to the parish as curate, the bishop said that he could have no hope of preferment, but, just before he died, he was offered a prebendary stall in St Paul's cathedral and, with a certain kind of logic, turned it down. Another example was G. C. Rawlinson, curate of the famous St Barnabas's, Pimlico, who was there as curate for twenty-one years. Prior to that he was in another curacy for nine years. He was a scholarly priest, interested in French Catholicism. He died from pneumonia in 1922, aged 53, having been afflicted with asthma for much of his life (see Rawlinson 1924). A certain Fr E. C. Morgan was an assistant priest from 1918 to 1936 to the well-known and much loved George Campbell Ommanney, the leading Anglo-Catholic priest in Sheffield. After a curacy of these eighteen years, Morgan became vicar of the church (Belton 1936:34–5).

Another reason must be mentioned for the apparent success of some Anglo-Catholic parishes. Many of their congregations have tended to be eclectic, that is, made up of people who do not necessarily live in the parish. For reasons which were stated at the very beginning of the book, Anglo-Catholics are given to attending particular churches attractive to them on account of the subtleties of ritual and ceremonial found there. Sometimes it is the personality of the priest that draws them. Members cross parish boundaries in order to go to a church of their choice and they are therefore not representative of the parish in which the church is situated. To be sure, they might come from an adjoining parish, but in many cases this is not so and therefore, where public and private transport is readily available, many Anglo-Catholic churches find that the class structure of their congregations does not reflect that of the parish and that the large numbers are not really a good indication of the success of the church in influencing people at large. Today in some of the great Anglo-Catholic churches in the West End some members may live thirty, forty, or more miles away.

On the other side of the balance is the fact that Anglo-Catholics failed to make any lasting impresssion on the non-Christianized working-class masses and therefore failed to stem the forces of secularization. Those Anglo-Catholic laity who were of such a background, for better or for worse, were in no way drawn into the Labour Party or into socialism, either secular or Christian. Hence the fact that these movements were uninfluenced by Anglo-Catholic laity in the worst of the slums. They showed minimal interest or ability in entering into party politics (Mayor 1967:337) and were far from the 'aristocracy of labour' which gave rise to leadership at various levels in socialist movements in England. Thus, Anglo-Catholic thinking never penetrated the Labour Party: this is in marked contrast to that of Methodism. Nor must it be forgotten that the Anglo-Catholic thinkers in matters of social and political theory were unable to gain any large following for such ideas in working-class parishes – a fact which is commented on in the next chapter (see section 6).

Chapter 5

Further achievements

1 Success

Within a century of its inception, Anglo-Catholicism had established a firm hold on the Church of England. Pessimists within the movement no doubt wondered why it had not been more successful and had not in fact taken the Anglican Church by storm and completely catholicized it. The more realistically minded rejoiced in the fact that, in the face of Protestant opposition and the way the Church saw itself in the early nineteenth century, achievements had been as great as they had been. To them it seemed remarkable that in such a comparatively short time Anglo-Catholics had been instrumental in bringing about a great number of changes within the Church of England at large – changes quite unimaginable to anyone living in the 1830s. Given the general Protestant ethos of the Church of England which had been established over three centuries, what Anglo-Catholics and Tractarians had been able to achieve was indeed astonishing. We have referred to the triumphalism of Anglo-Catholicism in the 1920s and 1930s (see ch. 2). This triumphalism was not that of a victor over an enemy but rather the realization by Anglo-Catholics that their movement was now recognized as making an acceptable and irreplaceable contribution to the life of the Church of England. Anglo-Catholicism was not a movement of a few eccentric clerics but a widely established one in the Church, with a strong following of clergy and lay people. In the early days of the inter-war period it was openly declared that the triumphalism was certainly not 'an arrogant demonstration of conscious strength – a shout of triumph, ending, perhaps in a shriek of defiance' (ACPC 1921:x). The congresses showed that Anglo-Catholicism had arrived and had brought with it eager devotion, humility, thankfulness and spiritual enthusiasm (ACPC 1921:x). As we saw in the previous chapter, it is to be doubted whether Anglo-Catholicism had any lasting effect on the ever-growing threat of secularization in England. Some might argue that it hastened it. What is beyond all shadow of doubt is its effect on the Church of England.

But precisely at this point a note of caution must be sounded. To speak of the achievements of Anglo-Catholics within their own church is to speak of the achievements of the Catholic revival itself. Tractarians and Anglo-Catholics, including of course Anglo-Papalists, were all in it together and together they created beliefs and practices which became accepted and which spread throughout the institution (see ch. 1 and the diagram at the end). It is very difficult to see which component of the Catholic revival was responsible for which achievement. The majority of the developments were supported by everyone in the movement, for example, auricular confession, religious orders, and the centrality of the eucharist. To a man they laboured for these: where they differed was in matters of detail and pastoral execution.

The statement that could be made by many theologically inclined Anglicans that 'We are all Catholics now' speaks clearly of the success of the Catholic revival in altering the Church of England over the past 150 years. It resembles another statement, that 'We are all Marxists now,' which implies the acknowledgement by many intellectuals, not necessarily dogmatic Marxists, of the overriding influence of economic factors on social structures. So, in the Church of England, 'We all acknowledge an underlying Catholic structure in Anglican belief and practice.' Disregarding a precise definition of the word Catholic, the statement implies that the Church of England has within it a Catholic component which most Anglican intellectuals would now accept. No less a person than Cyril Garbett, archbishop of York in the 1950s, said: 'The Church of England is the ancient Catholic Church of this land' (in Slesser 1952:10n.1). And before, in 1890, Archbishop Benson of Canterbury declared that 'the English Church is a true faithful branch of the Church Catholic' (in Munson 1975:383). Tractarians and Anglo-Catholics together have exerted such an influence on the Church that very few people today would maintain that the nature of the Church of England is wholly Protestant. When the Lambeth Quadrilateral, stating the four basic doctrines of Anglicanism, was approved by the Lambeth conference of 1888, it was clear that the teaching of the Oxford Fathers had become widely accepted by those who would not necessarily call themselves Tractarian or Anglo-Catholic. In short, it embodied a moderate Anglo-Catholicism (Gunstone 1968:188). Whether they liked it or not, Anglo-Catholics have been able to create a true comprehensiveness in Anglicanism by introducing into it something of a Catholic ethos which was heretofore missing. If the destiny of the Church of England is to be comprehensive, then that comprehensiveness has indeed been brought about by the Catholic revival (but see ch. 6.2).

Some might argue differently. Anglo-Catholics were able to establish themselves in the Church of England over against opposition from bishops and Protestant organizations. They became a firm component of the Church of England because no one could impede them. Having therefore accepted their inevitable presence, the Church of England had no alternative but to rethink the very structure of the Church. Thus, the concept of comprehensiveness was introduced in a process of rationalization so as to include ideas and practices which were initially absent from it. In this way the Anglo-Catholic intrusion has been accommodated. At the time of the Reformation there was no idea that the Church of England was in any way 'comprehensive'.

In what has just been said no fine distinction has been made between Tractarianism and Anglo-Catholicism, despite attempts to differentiate them at the beginning of the book. It is quite clear that, in the general acceptance of the Catholic nature of the Church of England, both Tractarianism and Anglo-Catholicism have played a part and it is impossible in general terms to try to distinguish between the contributions that each component has made. The Church of England as a whole has been pervaded by ideas and practices which have stemmed from a synthesis of elements of Tractarianism and a mild form of Prayer Book Catholicism. While the existence of extreme Anglo-Catholicism or Anglo-Papalism has evoked a great deal of opposition and dislike from many in the Church of England, especially the bishops, it too has played a positive role. Just because Anglo-Catholics were able to carry on their work unhampered their presence brought with it a continual challenge to the question: in what way can the Church of England be called Catholic? The fact that the question is accepted as legitimate indicates in itself the success of the Catholic revival. There is probably no one today in the Church of England at large and in the Anglican Communion who has not encountered beliefs and practices which have been emphasized by Anglo-Catholics. But ardent followers might argue differently. Even at the time of the First World War, some Anglo-Papalists, for example, H. Hamilton Maughan, would maintain that what was happening was that the Church of England was becoming high church, not Catholic. The ideals of Anglo-Papalism and its Roman doctrines and ritual were still only being practised by a relatively small number of clergy (Maughan 1916:5). Maughan vigorously attacked all other possibilities of Catholic expression, especially the English use, except that of Anglican Papalism (see ch. 1.2 and 1.3). The fact remains that no matter what term is employed to explain the changes that were taking place in the Anglican Church, they were as a whole due to Anglo-Catholic influences.

We have already described many of the changes brought about by Anglo-Catholicism and, in trying to present a more general picture, we must glance at them again, but above all point to other achievements brought about by the movement.

2 Doctrinal emphases

In the matter of basic Christian doctrine, Anglo-Catholics have asserted traditional, orthodox beliefs which some might hold have been at the heart of the Catholic church throughout its history. Not least because the word Catholic appeared in them, Anglo-Catholics have rigidly stood by the traditional creeds and their orthodox interpretation. They have emphasized the transcendence of God, that He is essentially above and beyond the world, 'totally other', and this doctrine was strengthened by the symbolism of their churches and in their rich liturgy and furnishings. They have stressed the doctrine of the Incarnation as being central to Christianity, a doctrine in which God dwelt with man in the person of Christ. Christ was both God and man. From this emphasis a number of extensions had their *raison d'être*. For one thing, in stressing the Incarnation, rather than the Atonement which was a key doctrine amongst many Protestants, Anglo-Catholics have had a base on which to build beliefs and practices associated with the Blessed Virgin Mary. Also, the doctrine of the Incarnation gave rise to notions of the dignity of man and the need for creating some kind of Kingdom of God on earth (see ch. 5.7). The high doctrine of the Incarnation also tended to counteract the belief, held by some Protestants, in man's total depravity, which can in turn lead to a denigration of human life.

Perhaps the most important extension of the doctrine of the Incarnation, as Anglo-Catholics saw it, was that it gave a basis for the notion of the organic nature of the church. In an expression which one does not here wish to justify theologically, it was commonly seen by Tractarians and Anglo-Catholics that the church was an extension of the Incarnation. It might well be said that, as the Catholic versus Protestant controversies emerged over the past century in the Church of England, the most notable point of controversy was over the nature of the church. The conflict also affected thinkers of other churchmanship. To put it in an over-simplified form one could say that the issue rested on whether or not the institution of the church was man-made or whether it was of a divine nature. For Protestant and liberal thinkers, the church was like any other social institution. They thought of it as an organization which, during the course of history, men had devised to suit the needs of the times. It meant, therefore, that church order was not necessarily something that was fixed for all time but that its structure could be changed. Always, however, Protestants refer to the evidence of the New Testament as a guide for any overall organization of the church. The church was a gathered community of all those who held certain beliefs about Jesus Christ (see ch. 3.2). Whatever structure the church takes will be determined by pragmatic reasons with a modifiable pattern as seen in the primitive church.

Anglo-Catholics, believing along with the Tractarians that their position was truly Anglican, rejected the man-fabricated and individualistic concept of the church. Christ was held to be the founder and head of the church and his commands to the church are eternal and beyond the possibility of change (see ch. 6.4). Its existence in society stems from the apostles and its continued presence depends on the apostles' successors, the bishops. The church could only be itself if it had validly consecrated bishops and ordained priests. The linchpin was the bishop, who himself had been consecrated by other bishops and who alone had the right to ordain priests. This divine structure implied that the collectivity existed over and above the individual, who becomes part of the collectivity through a process of religious socialization and participation in the sacraments.

A high doctrine of the church was at the centre of the message of the Oxford movement and therefore of the Anglo-Catholic movement. Crucial to such a theological position was the assertion that the church was of divine origin and divine status. E. A. Knox has correctly asserted that: 'The essence of the Oxford movement was an attempt to assert the existence of a corporate body, wholly clerical, possessing a Divine Right to prescribe for the Nation its faith and worship' (Knox 1933:382). Above all stands the church, controlled and dominated by the clergy.

Not only did Anglo-Catholics and Tractarians continually proclaim the difference between the doctrine of the church as held by Catholics and Protestants, but they also stressed the difference in the function of sacraments between the two groups. Adopting what might be called a traditional Catholic tradition, Anglo-Catholics held that grace, that is religious nourishment, comes to the individual by partaking of the sacraments, of which there are seven. The foremost two are baptism and holy communion; the lesser sacraments are confirmation, penance, and extreme unction, which apply to all people; and marriage and ordination are also rites of passage which are for those embracing a particular form of life. For these to 'work' it is necessary to have them administered by validly ordained clergy. Of course, in extreme cases baptism may be administered by a layperson. The whole system is quite logical: no church without bishops; no sacraments without clergy. All is stamped with divine authority so that it cannot be altered. Such a position has a simplicity and coherence which to many is very attractive, and Anglo-Catholics were not slow to realize it (see section 8 below) There can be no doubt that such an entrenched doctrinal position proved to be a great stumbling-block when, from the 1920s onwards, serious attempts were made to create schemes of reunion with Protestant churches. These churches obviously would not accept such a rigid position as that which had gained so strong a foothold in the Church of England through Anglo-Catholicism and the Catholic revival generally. In fact the presence of Anglo-Catholics and their ideas has prevented the Church of England entering into any scheme of reunion, despite the concrete attempts to do so with particular churches during the decades following the Second World War (see ch. 11.6).

Evangelicals and Anglo-Catholics found themselves at loggerheads over the doctrine of the church, but there was a virulent and persistent enemy which undermined the positions of them both. It was religious liberalism. This movement, if it can be called that, had entered the field of biblical research, started in Germany in the early nineteenth century. It challenged the notion of the divine inspiration of the Bible and it also adopted current philosophical thinking about the nature of God which reached conclusions not in keeping with traditional doctrines, Catholic or Protestant. Here was a real threat, going to the very foundations of the Christian religion as it had been handed down over the centuries. In the early days of the Catholic revival, Tractarians and Anglo-Catholics were one with Evangelicals in asserting basic doctrines (see Crowther 1970:202). Trouble arose in the ranks of Tractarianism and Anglo-Catholicism when, towards the end of the nineteenth century, certain of their theologians felt it was necessary to come to terms with the changes occurring in the academic world, centred on the acceptance of scientific thought and its application to the Bible and early church history. A crisis occurred over the publication in 1889 of *Lux Mundi*, edited by Charles Gore, whose essay on the Holy Spirit caused considerable stir. A similar volume appeared in 1926, *Essays Catholic and Critical*, edited by E. G. Selwyn. This book gave some place to the findings of social anthropology and was also concerned with psychological theories relating to the nature of man and the person of Christ. This second set of essays did not on the whole arouse the controversy which the first did. The reason was probably the fact that 'liberal' ideas were now much more acceptable and their threat to revelation either unchallengeable or seen to be irrelevant.

Anglo-Catholics produced no outstanding theologians of international stature: perhaps that would apply to the Church of England as a whole in this period. But there were those who, as Prayer Book Catholics or staunch Anglo-Catholics, did make a great contribution to the theological world, certainly in England. Anglo-Catholics could muster a large number of very learned men, whose minds were steeped in the history of the church and in its theology. They could claim far more scholars of this genre than the Evangelicals or perhaps even the middle-of-the-road Anglicans. By way of example one might mention the names of Charles Gore, W. H. Frere, N. P. Williams, Darwell Stone, Gregory Dix, L. S. Thornton, B. Kidd, K. E. Kirk, C. C. J. Webb, A. E. Taylor, E. L. Mascall, and Austin Farrer. And amongst writers of a less strictly academic and theological kind were those who were extremely sympathetic to Anglo-Catholicism: T. S. Eliot, C. S. Lewis, and Dorothy Sayers, not to mention others not as well known. Where academic issues were involved, Anglo-Catholic contributions, though very important, were in the main concerned with the past. Such theologians did not tackle basic issues of the day by placing them in a theological setting, as some German thinkers were doing. None was what one call a systematic theologian. They followed very much in the path of Pusey. As in the emerging social sciences in the country, the basic attitude was one which did not call for evaluation but rather for letting the facts speak for themselves. The patristic fathers had in their own right an almost infallible status. Their 'infallibility' was not the subject of argument or debate. All this was far from creative theology. In the early days the Tractarians fielded a better side than did later Anglo-Catholics. Newman was their outstanding thinker, followed by Pusey who some might doubt to be an original theologian. Anglo-Catholics never had comparable theologians. The intellectual side of the movement tended to be weak (see Kent 1987:104). But that might be said of Anglicanism generally. By and large, as we stated at the beginning of the book, the achievements of Anglo-Catholicism have not been in the publication of learned theological treatises or in profound apologetics but in the realm of practice, in trying to bring home to people at large what it means to be Catholic and offering a powerful apologetic for it. None the less, one fact must never be overlooked: Tractarians and Anglo-Catholics produced a vast number of publications and showed themselves to be both skilled intellectually and determined to defend their position in a way far superior to that of Evangelicals (see Crowther 1970:23).

3 New ways of worshipping

We have repeatedly shown that Anglo-Catholics introduced new forms of worship in their churches, which were modfied and extended into the Church at large. The revival raised the level of solemnity and decency in all forms of worship and introduced furnishings which made churches more aesthetically attractive. Before the movement started, parish churches and their Sunday services seemed dull, cold, harsh, and unattractive. All this changed as the revival spread (see Chadwick 1970,2:308ff.). Clergy began to wear surplices and cassocks: and eucharistic vestments were used by the more Catholic-minded priests. Today, within the Anglican Communion, cassocks and surplices are universally used, while in many churches eucharistic vestments are the order of the day. Robed choirs were introduced, at first only for men and boys, but later women and girls joined them. As more singing was encouraged in the services, so hymns quickly became popular. Anglo-Catholics and Tractarians contributed greatly to the emergence of hymn books and they were directly responsible for the *English Hymnal*, which was first published in 1906 and which continues to be used extensively in the Church of England. At parish services no differences have been more marked between Anglo-Catholics and Roman Catholics than in congregational singing. Anglo-Catholics gladly inserted hymns into the mass. By contrast Roman Catholics had no such tradition, although with the conversion of F. W. Faber it was carried into that church. Faber as Anglican and Roman Catholic wrote many popular hymns. Tractarians and Anglo-Catholics translated and had set to music Latin and Greek hymns written by the early fathers. Anglo-Catholics also had no hesitation in using Evangelical hymns in mission services as well as in normal

parish worship (see ch. 3.4). To this day Anglo-Catholic
gatherings, parish as well as national, are often accompanied by
strong and powerful singing, usually due to the presence of a
large number of men who respond to the liturgy and its hymns.
Pusey House, Oxford, has become famous for this. The singing is
often reminiscent of that in Welsh chapels (see ch. 5.2).

Perhaps the most dramatic change in public worship was that
towards a frequent and ritualized celebration of the holy
communion. Before the Catholic revival it was celebrated at most
once a month, often less frequently. Today nearly every church
has a celebration at least once a Sunday. One of the direct
influences of the revival was to replace matins as the main
Sunday morning service with a sung holy communion service,
eucharist, or mass, whatever the name used. Fr Mackay, vicar of
All Saints, Margaret Street, could say in 1921 that matins was still
the main morning service of the Church of England (see ACPC
1921:73). That is hardly the case today. The general acceptance
of the eucharist as the main service on a Sunday emerged after
the Second World War, prompted by what later became known as
the Parish and People movement, which has had such a great
influence throughout the whole of the Church of England (see
ch. 11.5).

Something of the great amount of 'religion' introduced into
churches by Anglo-Catholic priests comes in this account of what
Fr Lowder was doing in St Peter's, London docks, around the
1860s. He wrote:

Let me speak more particularly of the services of the
church. . . . There had been always one, and for many years
there have been two celebrations of the Holy Eucharist daily in
St Peter's. The first is at 6.45, the second at 8 a.m., with
matins at 7.30. Choral evensong is at 8 p.m., with, on Fridays
and eves of festivals, a sermon. A communicant class is held on
Thursday evenings, and during a portion of the year a
confirmation class on Tuesdays. On Sundays we have
celebrations at 7, 8, and 9 a.m.; matins at 10.30; High
Celebration and sermon at 11.15, . . . Litany is said at 2.30,
the children's service at 3.30, and evensong at 7 p.m. During
Advent the *Dies Irae*, and during Lent the *Miserere* is sung,
and an instruction is given after evensong; at other times there
is a Bible Class. On weekdays during Advent and Lent there is
a meditation in church on Mondays; a mission service,
consisting of metrical litany, hymns and sermon, on

Wednesdays; and the Stations of the Cross on Fridays. Confessions are heard on Fridays and Saturdays, and on special days before great festivals. There are on an average fifty communicants on ordinary Sundays; at Easter, including those made during the octave, about 280, and at other festivals in proportion; while the total number of communications made during the year are nearly 5,000. These are all made at the early celebrations. The church is well filled on Sundays, on festivals often thronged, and has a good attendance during the week.

(in Ellsworth 1982:149)

It was the firm conviction of Anglo-Catholics that religion was communicated by visual means, by pictures, symbols, and ceremonies and not just by words. The poor and ignorant, and not only those either, embraced religion and were nurtured in it by the eye as well as the ear. This attitude is very much a Roman Catholic one and stands over against that of many Protestant churches, where the word is the sole means of communication (see ch. 4.6).

John Kent has observed that the impetus given to the study of liturgy by the Catholic revival, together with the great efforts that were made to create more dignified services, not only penetrated the entire Anglican Communion, but also spilled over into the Free churches themselves – the very bastions of Protestantism (Kent 1978:117). Probably nothing would have given Anglo-Catholics of the early days a greater sense of victory than to know that their point of view about the eucharist had to a large measure become acceptable to their opponents.

4 A new spirituality

It might well be maintained that the greatest contribution of the Catholic revival was to inculcate a sense of spirituality and piety amongst clergy and laity alike. This might certainly be said of the Tractarians, and Anglo-Catholic clergy might also well be proud of their achievement in introducing into the Church of England a new type of spirituality. Nothing like it had happened in the Church since the Reformation and it was a form of spirituality which infected lay people as well as clergy. It cannot be claimed that it was unique since it was modelled on various forms of Roman Catholic devotion which Anglo-Catholic clergy thought suitable for their parishioners (Lloyd 1966:131). In previous times various types of piety and devotion had spread extensively

127

throughout the Church with such movements as those of the Caroline divines and the Evangelicals. But the Anglo-Catholics introduced new ideals, for example, that of attendance at daily mass. Viscount Halifax, the most prominent Anglo-Catholic layman of his time, himself set the example. Priests were encouraged to say mass daily and, as a result, holy communion on weekdays became much more frequent throughout the Church of England. Saints' days, and not only those commemorated in the Prayer Book, were kept. People were encouraged to visit the church in order to say their prayers, if possible before the reserved Sacrament. It was said of Darwell Stone, the theologian and member of Pusey House, Oxford, that he spent long hours in the chapel where the Sacrament was reserved (Lloyd 1966:132).

To help people in their devotions, prayer books edited by Anglo-Catholic priests were published and sold in great numbers. They contain some of the Prayer Book services as well as a large number of devotions, litanies, and prayers, including those to the saints and the Blessed Virgin Mary. We have already referred to *The Catholic Prayer Book*, but mention should also be made of *The Centenary Prayer Book* and *St Hugh's Prayer Book* (see ch. 1.5).

Two main sources were used in the revival of the spiritual life. The first came from writings of the early fathers of the church who, as well as being theologians, were also men of piety. This source was much favoured by Tractarians, who helped by having some of their works translated into English, as well as by translating some of their hymns. One should particularly mention J. M. Neale in this connection. The other was, as we have often noted, of a more recent origin and was favoured by the Anglo-Papalists. They turned to aspects of spirituality which emerged with the Counter-Reformation, the works of Jesuits, to a cult such as that of the Sacred Heart, and to litanies of the saints. These devotions were often seen to be sentimental and were criticized by both Anglo- and Roman Catholics as being too Italian to be welcomed by the English. The books of prayers, based on Counter-Reformation ideology, had little influence outside extreme Anglo-Catholic circles. Other forms of devotion, especially those advocated by the Tractarians, became widely used in the Church. But, whichever way one looks at it, it is certain that Anglo-Catholics found enormous caches of spiritual devotion which had been hidden for a long time from Anglican eyes and they made full use of them (Lloyd 1966:132).

We have already had occasion to mention the great importance which Anglo-Catholics placed on auricular confession and how it became quite widely accepted (see ch. 3.5). One practice often associated with it is that of going on a retreat, where the participant often makes a confession. This form of spritual withdrawal spread extensively in the Church of England through Anglo-Catholics and Tractarians. Fr Lowder was said to be one of the first to organize a retreat (see ch. 3.3).

5 Religious orders and communities

Any attempt to catholicize the Church of England would have to include the more particular aim of introducing or, as followers might argue, reintroducing the religious life. This implies the creation of institutions in which men and women strive after spiritual perfection based on the acceptance of lifelong vows of poverty, chastity, and obedience. Monks, nuns, and similar seekers after perfection have been known in the church since the third and fourth centuries, and perhaps earlier. Very shortly after the beginning of the Oxford movement it became apparent that there were a number of people who wanted to create religious communities. Newman was one of the early advocates, and a disciple of his, J. D. Dalgairns, writing from the proto-community at Littlemore in the mid-1840s, said in his book, *Life of St Stephen Harding*:

A church without monasteries is a body with its right arm paralysed. . . . There is yet another excellent way of advancing the Catholic cause, some field for their zeal and of turning it into the poetry of religion. What poetry more sweet, and yet, withal, more awfully real – indeed hourly realized by the cuttings of the very cross – than the pursuit of holy virginity.
(quoted in Anson 1955/1964:36–7)

The development of the monastic life in Anglicanism has been extensively documented by Peter Anson in his book, *The Call of the Cloister* (1955/1964). Anson was a Roman Catholic convert, having once been a member of an Anglican religious order. There is little merit in trying to summarize this detailed and authoritative work. It might be worth noting, however, that after the early attempts by Newman to create a community for men, and later by F. W. Faber to do the same thing in his rectory at Elton near Huntingdon, the first group to become established and persist was the Society of St John the Evangelist – the Cowley Fathers – in Oxford in 1865. Its leader was the Rev R. M. Benson. Two years earlier the eccentric and highly emotional figure, Joseph Leycester Lyne (Bro. Ignatius), had founded a Benedictine monastery situated in Llanthony, in the Black Mountains of South Wales. The community lasted until he died in 1908. Notorious for its Roman practices was another Benedictine experiment, that of Benjamin Carlyle (Abbot Aelred), which eventually settled on Caldey Island off South Wales. The community, virtually in its entirety, made its submission to Rome in 1913. The largest orders for men have been (the founding date is given in brackets): the Community of the Resurrection (1892); the Society of the Sacred Mission (1894); the Benedictines of Nashdom (1914); the Society of St Francis (1921).

Women's orders appeared on the scene earlier than men's. If the date of the Oxford movement is put at that of Keble's assize sermon in July 1833, it is quite remarkable that it only took twelve years for the first order to come into existence. This was the Sisterhood of the Holy Cross, established in St John's Wood, London, largely due to the energies of Pusey and his followers. The sisterhood, which began with three sisters, was under the supervision of a local vicar. One of the sisters, a Miss Langston, was designated the superior. They had services at various times throughout the day and performed charitable work in the area: looking after destitute children, visiting hospitals and the poor, and assisting in the burial of the dead. The sisterhood in fact did not grow and in the end it was amalgamated with another similar society.

In 1841, some four years before the emergence of the Sisterhood of the Holy Cross, a woman called Marion Hughes took a vow of celibacy in the presence of Pusey and adopted a habit of her own choosing. For about eight years she was entirely alone, some say for fear of hostility from the anti-Catholic world. In 1849, she founded an institute of her own, the Community of the Holy and Undivided Trinity.

The year 1848 saw a considerable growth of women's communities. One notable example was the Nursing Sisters of St John the Divine, started under the encouragement and supervision of the Rev W. J. Butler, the vicar of Wantage. It later became one of the best known of all the institutes for women in the Anglican Communion, the Community of St Mary the Virgin, and to this day has its mother house in Wantage. It is an active order concerned with parish work and teaching. Also in 1848 there emerged in the Plymouth area a community known as the Devonport Sisters, who responded to a call by the bishop of Exeter to help the poor living around the docks. Priscilla Lydia Sellon, the daughter of a naval officer, founded schools and homes for orphans, soup kitchens, and lodging houses, and after the creation of the sisterhood the members became well known for their heroic work in dealing with the outbreaks of cholera in 1849 and 1853. They started the practice of a daily mass and it is thought that theirs was the first church or chapel where such a practice was established in the Church of England. The sisterhood grew and eventually helped in nursing soldiers during the Crimean War under the direction of Florence Nightingale. Later it established a sisterhood in Honolulu. As the community grew it absorbed the Sisterhood of the Holy Cross. After the death of Mother Lydia it changed the nature of its work and gradually declined. In 1851 the rector of Clewer, near Windsor, T. T. Carter, also concerned about the conditions of the poor in his parish, encouraged the development of a sisterhood and, after some difficulty in trying to formulate community life, the Community of St John the Baptist eventually came into existence. The Clewer Sisters turned out to be a very popular order in the Church of England and helped in parishes in and around London. Centres were established outside London in the south of England as well as in India and in the United States.

In the early days of Anglo-Catholicism the emergence of religious orders heaped on followers of the Catholic revival as much hostility from ardent Protestants as did the ritualization of Anglican services. The opposition was in part due to the fact that Anglo-Catholics, instead of trying to create specifically Anglican orders, just copied, with minor modifications, Roman Catholic orders (Pickering 1988a). It required much time for monks and nuns in the Church of England to become generally accepted but the notion of the religious life and religious communities of various forms has now spread to people of all shades of churchmanship. Today, individual members of orders may be found on synodical committees, or other national bodies, perhaps as ex-officio members. In 1935 the Church of England created a central administrative body, called the Advisory Council on Religious Communities.

At the present time (1986) the number of those in men's orders in England stands at 264, and those in women's orders number 1,085. There are ten communities for men and forty-three for women. (For issues raised by these statistics, see Pickering 1988a.)

6 Social and political theory

Catholicism, in contrast to Protestantism, is often seen as a religious system which attempts to embrace the whole of life. The Roman Catholic Church lays down general or particular moral, social, and economic principles which it sees as part of its Christian mandate. It does not accept the departmentalization of human life which is said to have come with the Reformation and which has been accelerated by bourgeois capitalism. Hardly surprising is the fact that Anglo-Catholics have attempted to wrestle with the social issues of the day and to develop a socio-political theory based on Christian or Catholic foundations. Two factors were influential. The first was a knowledge of the slum conditions to which poor people were subjected in England's cities and towns, which was brought home to them by the work of many Anglo-Catholic priests in such areas. The second was the tendency in Anglo-Catholic ideology to look to the middle ages as the highest phase in the history of mankind – the nearest to the manifestation of the Kingdom of God. Such a society was seen to be organic or holistic. In some ways it corresponded to the social thinking of the schoolmen. Anglo-Catholic clergy and intellectuals, where they spoke openly about social doctrine, sided with nineteenth century liberal humanism, and more particularly went further in supporting socialist doctrines. Some went to the limits in supporting Marxism or communism in one form or another. The most notable example was Conrad Noel (1869–1942), the vicar of Thaxted. He was followed as vicar by a lesser figure, although of a similar outlook, the Rev Jack Putterill. There have been many Anglo-Catholic priests who have been firm socialists or political radicals. Fr Stanton himself fervently supported the ideals of the French Revolution.

It must be recalled that in the second half of the nineteenth century there emerged in the Church of England a number of groups and societies dedicated to socialist thought. The father of all these groups is considered to be F. D. Maurice. They were often far from Anglo-Catholic in foundation but were generally supported by individuals of that persuasion (see Mayor 1967). The societies which were founded by Anglo-Catholics were often short-lived and had a chequered history. Such groups were: the Christian Socialist League, which began in 1906, the Catholic Crusade in 1916, and the League of the Kingdom of God in 1923. (For a history of these groups and other Anglican socialist societies, see Mayor 1967; Bocock 1973; Penhale 1986, chapter 8). The most theoretically inclined of all Anglo-Catholic societies concerned with social and economic matters was the Anglo-Catholic Summer School of Sociology, which first met in Oxford in 1925 and subsequently published a journal entitled *Christendom* in 1931. The Summer Schools were held almost yearly, except during the war, but they and the journal had ceased to exist by the early 1950s. The key figures were Maurice Reckitt, a wealthy layman, and V. A. Demant, a convert from Unitarianism, who became a canon professor in Christ Church, Oxford. Both of them wrote extensively on Christian social theory, which they and their followers called Christian sociology – a term coined by A. J. Penty in a book published in 1923 (see Lyon 1983). Other members of the group were Canon Widdrington, T. S. Eliot, and the philosopher and sociologist, Dr Langmead Casserley. Some of these were responsible for the famous Signpost series of books, published in 1940, which were an apologetic for Anglo-Catholicism and Catholic social theory. The aims of Christian sociology were far removed from those of the discipline of sociology, as it has been established in universities, where it is basically empirical and objective – at least it makes itself out to be so. Christian sociology, by contrast, is critical social philosophy. Much of the thinking of the Christendom group was close to Guild Socialism, whose most powerful advocate was a secular thinker, G. D. H. Cole.

Many of the groups concerned with social ideology and Christianity stood opposed to the prevailing political doctrines of the time. Capitalism, Fascism, and Nazism were all condemned. Only Christian and especially Catholic doctrine was right, not only for Christians but for all mankind. The world can never be saved, even in a worldly, cultural, or social sense, except by the Catholic religion. Full of optimism, Ross Williamson wrote: 'If she [the Church of England] returns to the Faith, she may yet save the world' (Williamson 1956:45). Similar sentiments appeared in a leader of the *Church Times* in 1933. But these words were also echoed by many Anglo-Catholics involved in the groups we have mentioned. Inevitably such thinking led back to the middle ages; and the Merrie Englanders supported by G. K. Chesterton, were the logical outcome. Most of the thinking of Anglo-Catholics in this respect was based on doctrines of the Incarnation and the Kingdom of God. It was argued that God's dwelling in the world as a man had a profound consequence for man in his social life. That life is to be realized in a kingdom on earth based on Christ's teaching (see Orens 1983).

Limited attention is given here to the social and economic thought which emerged in Anglo-Catholicism. This is largely because its influence outside smallish intellectual circles in England and perhaps on the Continent was not great. It has often been falsely exaggerated (Mayor 1967:351). As we have noted, it attracted virtually no followers from run-of-the-mill parishes and did not influence at all the thinking of the Labour Party, neither did it supply leaders who were Anglo-Catholics (ch. 4.5). Anglo-Catholic priests mostly worked in the poorest of parishes: such parishes did not produce men able to organize workers' for trade unions or the Labour party (Mayor 1967:336).

The most influential Anglican cleric in connection with the notion of social justice, but who was no Anglo-Catholic, was the greatly revered William Temple, archbishop of Canterbury, whose writings are said to have helped to create the Welfare State. His book, *Christianity and Social Order*, is said to have sold almost 150,000 copies.

Today, there is scarcely any interest amongst Anglo-Catholics in economic and social matters, at least at the level of theory and policy (but see Leech and Williams 1983). The high hopes of conjoining socialism with Anglo-Catholic principles upheld by a group of able Anglo-Catholic thinkers has now given place to a vacuum. But then Christian socialism as a whole is now in the same slough of despond as is the Labour Party itself. The fact remains that, throughout its entire history, Anglo-Catholicism has never been identified with one particular political party, despite its socialist vein. Unlike English Nonconformity its fortunes have not fluctuated with those of a particular parliamentary party.

7 Schools and colleges

Tractarians and Anglo-Catholics have always been much opposed to what is commonly called public school religion, not least because in their view it lacked sound doctrine and firm Anglican principles. With somewhat similar ideas Nathaniel Woodard (1811–91) founded the St Nicolas Society in 1848 (see *ODCC*; Kirk 1937; Heeney 1969). The result was that the society established the schools of Lancing (1848) and Hurstpierpoint (1850). Behind Woodard's great drive was the conviction that public schools were needed for the growing middle classes made up mainly of professionals: doctors, lawyers, and the like, who could not afford to send their sons to England's great public schools. At the same time, he wanted to establish schools which had uncompromising Anglican teaching based on a high church interpretation of the Prayer Book. Tractarians and Anglo-Catholics were attracted by the society and Woodard's ability in raising money. They gave weight to the movement and influenced it. As they have emerged the schools usually have a sung eucharist every Sunday morning in term-time and there is an opportunity for pupils to make their confession (Kirk 1937:106). Half a million pounds were raised by the founder (Clarke 1932:295–6). In the 1930s there were sixteen schools, some of them for girls. Other schools with an Anglo-Catholic ethos have also been created: St Peter's College, Radley; St Edward's School, Oxford; Bradfield College, St Swithun's, Winchester. In 1921 there were renewed pleas for Anglo-Catholics to bring 'to a knowledge and acceptance of the Catholic Faith . . . "the Public School class" of Englishmen'. This meant beginning with the boys and masters of public and preparatory schools (Gillett in ACPC 1921:193).

Anglo-Catholics were able to ensure that, as theological colleges were being established from the middle of the nineteenth century onwards, some of them were of their churchmanship – St Stephen's House, Oxford; Ely (now closed); Chichester Theological College; Kelham (also now closed): and Mirfield. Today, about a fifth of all those training for orders are at such colleges.

For a number of reasons Anglo-Catholics have not contributed to university education. The one notable exception has been the founding, in 1870, of Keble College, Oxford, which gained wide support from clergy and laity who stood generally within the Catholic revival wing of the Church of England. Its present ethos in a secular and pluralistic age is hardly in keeping with the intentions and ideals of its founders.

8 Simple and direct

It is not within the scope of this book to try to account for the development and success of Anglo-Catholicism. The subject is highly complex and requires placing the movement against the many social and religious changes of the nineteenth century. It calls for a detailed examination of a period of history which has not been the focus of this study. As we have proceeded we have drawn attention to a number of factors which have pointed to the strengthening of the movement, for example, the pastoral concern of the clergy, the appeal of the ritualistic services, mission services, the inadequacy of run-of-the-mill Anglican public worship, and so on. There is another factor which, although implicit in what has been said, needs emphasizing.

Without doubt one of the reasons why Anglo-Catholicism was

able to achieve what it did was because, once a person became acquainted with the intricacies of the rituals, it offered a simple, direct code for leading a satisfactory religious life. It had the advantage of appealing to the well educated and the not so well educated. Roughly following Roman Catholic teaching, Anglo-Catholic directives in, say, the 1930s might be as follows: 'Attend mass each Sunday; communicate at least three times a year; go to confession fairly frequently; obey the moral codes of the church.' A list of this kind has already been quoted in connection with one of the Anglo-Catholic congresses (see ch. 2.7). Such directions, clear and precise, if carried out bring with them self-confidence and reassurance. Obey these rules and one's guilt feelings about what ought to be done in matters of religion are at a minimum. And, if there is guilt at any time, this can be relieved immediately by going to confession. Having such means ready at hand, and accepting the fact that religious confidence can be obtained by the keeping of rules, then clearly Anglo-Catholicism had obvious attractions over and above other religious systems, especially where those systems left much to individual choice and where simple direct rules were absent. If rules in such systems were advocated, they were not thought to be of great value in achieving salvation. All this can be seen in contrast to middle-of-the-road Anglicanism. Anglo-Catholics pressed home their doctrine in day schools and Sunday schools. Charles Booth noted: 'it is the High Church which makes the most systematic and effective use of the opportunity that their schools offer for the the definite teaching of dogma' (Booth 1902,7:10).

Their priests realized the advantages of a simple approach and their clarion call, above all to their congregations, was expressed in such phrases as 'It's the mass that matters' or 'Everything turns on the mass and the box'. Such phrases were really summaries of what Anglo-Catholic priests were trying to do. Their goals made them carriers of a clear message. It was a practical message. Of course, there was much divergence amongst themselves as to what precisely was meant by catholicization. But at least in their own minds Anglo-Catholics felt that it was a realizable goal and one which had concrete tests of achievement. For the clergy it was not so much a question of introducing subtle, new doctrines, or paradoxical interpretations of dogmas but of doing something obvious to the eye – in having a sung mass every Sunday, by introducing benediction, by asking people to make their confessions, by introducing statues, by having incense, and so on. Do these things as a priest and one has done one's bit for catholicization. To be sure, there was the question of faith, of

Catholic doctrine, but by and large this was not a crucial issue although it was necessary to proclaim such a faith. Catholicism meant worship through ritual, and was not just a matter of listening to words, for example those dreadfully dreary sermons preached by Anglicans projecting their Oxford learning on to their congregations, whether they were educated or not. And the response of the man in the pew to Anglo-Catholicism was obvious. He could receive a certain amount of satisfaction in doing specific things, in obeying simple rules, in being assured that what he was doing was right and would gain him salvation. Further, it did not require a great deal of mental effort to work out what the religious life meant in practical terms, it was given to one on a plate and all one had to do was to pick it up. And if someone wanted more, wanted to go the further mile, to do something extraordinary, there, waiting for the individual, was the possibility of becoming a monk or a nun, of being a priest or a missionary. Further, some of these alternatives entailed being celibate.

II
Ambiguities

Chapter 6

Some inherent ambiguities

1 Ambiguity in religion itself

For the rest of the book an attempt will be made to take up and develop some of the ideas which were raised in the Introduction. There it was stated that all religions contain ambiguities. Such ambiguities arise initially out of the very nature of religion itself in trying to bridge two orders of reality – that of this world and that of the world beyond, a transcendental world. All religions have had to come face to face with such ambiguities or ambiguities dependent on their premises. They have either to accept them fairly and squarely and perhaps say they are irresolvable, or else to attempt to deal with them in such a way as to satisfy man's intellect but never completely gratify it. If ambiguity is resolved, religion itself disappears.

Neither Christianity nor Anglicanism nor Anglo-Catholicism can claim exemption from such analysis. Different systems contain different ambiguities, and perhaps it is true to say that each system has tried to solve ambiguities in various ways, often by introducing further ambiguities. It is to the ambiguities specific to Anglo-Catholicism that we now turn – ambiguities in which the movement was trapped from the very beginning.

Two lines of procedure will be adopted. One is to look specifically at those ambiguities which are unique to Anglo-Catholicism, but which may also be present in a less acute form in Anglicanism itself. The other takes up the problem from the standpoint of the individual and asks how it is that people can remain in systems of ambiguity; and, if they cannot, what are the paths open to them to try to solve the dilemma?

2 Catholic or not Catholic?

The problem *par excellence* for Anglo-Catholics is their claim to be Catholic within an institution which for several centuries has

141

generally been reckoned to stand in the Protestant camp, certainly not in the Roman Catholic camp. Some Protestants in the past, and still some today, have gone so far as to see in the Church of Rome the Antichrist. How can one be an Anglo-Catholic in a church in which only a proportion of the members openly claim they are Catholic and the rest say they are Protestant, or at least non-Catholic? Here is the ambiguity of using the self-designation Anglo-Catholic, or more simply, Catholic. Anglo-Catholics claim a loyalty to the 'One Holy Catholic Apostolic Church', which is

> their first and largest loyalty . . . and Catholics within the Church of England consist of those to whom this allegiance comes always and instinctively first, and for whom all other loyalties, to the Church of England, or to the Anglican Communion, are made to rank as subservient to this overriding, all-embracing, loyalty to the One Holy Church.
>
> (Hughes 1961:146)

The ambiguity is further seen in the tendency of those who would press the Catholic claims by emphasizing part of the name, Anglo-Catholic. So a true Anglo-Catholic would refer to himself as Anglo-*Catholic* whereas he would contend that the weak and woolly would stress the first, *Anglo*-Catholic.

It might be noted by way of introduction that the high church party, certainly in the nineteenth century, did not in common parlance use the term Catholic extensively and they may have had a number of reservations about using it widely. Tractarians indeed thought of themselves as being Catholic but they did not parade the term as one of identity.

Of course, it makes sense to refer to various Catholic churches. One speaks quite rightly about Polish Catholics but, in addition to pointing to the Roman Catholic Church in Poland, one can also legitimately refer to the National Polish Church which came into being at the turn of the century in the United States and which has a diocese in Poland. This Church and other Old Catholic churches like it split off from the Roman Catholic Church in 1870 over the question of papal infallibility. Members of these churches universally call themselves Catholic and no one for an instant would think of them as Protestant, although the Roman Catholic Church might refer to them as schismatic. The liturgical and cultural ethos of the groups is very close indeed to that of the Roman Catholic Church before the reforms of Vatican II. The difficulty over the term Anglo-Catholic is that it stands for a party in a church which does not as a whole, or at any authoritative level, accept the ideals projected by Anglo-Catholics. In the Roman Catholic Church (who can deny that is Catholic?), one does not say of two members, both fulfilling religious duties according to their consciences and the generally accepted requirements of the Church, that one is a Catholic and the other is not! But, in Anglo-Catholic terminology, it is common to refer to one member of the Church of England as 'Catholic' and another as 'just Anglican'. Indeed, to this very day it is not unknown for someone to say: 'I'm not Anglican; I'm Anglo-Catholic,' or even: 'I'm not Anglican; I'm Catholic.' It is clear from such statements that not all members can be called Catholic in the sense in which Anglo-Catholics use the word. Those who are Catholic are so by self-designation. The dilemma is this. The Church of England must be Catholic, since it adheres to the Scriptures, the creeds, and the ecclesiastical orders of bishops, priests, and deacons created by apostolic succession (ch. 1.2). Hence the Church is *Catholic* and all members must therefore be *Catholic*. Yet not all are Catholic! But numerically most are just 'ordinary C. of E. people'. What kind of Catholicism is it when in the one church some are held to be Catholic and some are not? Quite recently there was a letter in the *Church Times* which began: 'Sir, As a Catholic in the Church of England I find' (*CT*, 11 July 1986). The Federation of Catholic Priests composed a constitution in 1917 which started: 'The Federation is for Catholic Priests in communion with the See of Canterbury' (in Cross 1943:129; and see ch. 4.2).

To make matters more complicated there are held to be degrees of Catholicism amongst Anglo-Catholics. Thus, one person is 'fairly Catholic' and another is 'very Catholic'. Anglo-Catholics actually disagree amongst themselves as to who among them is 'truly' Catholic and who is not. A follower was heard to say in the presence of the author: 'I don't call *them* Catholic at all,' referring to some people who called themselves Catholic. When Fr Algy ʹRobertson, who was certainly an Anglo-Catholic was made vicar of St Ives in Huntingdonshire, the retiring incumbent was reported to have said: 'I am very much afraid that my successor, Father Robertson, is jeopardising the Catholic religion. I am credibly informed that he has already abandoned the Asperges' (quoted in Denis 1964:94).

One senses a feeling of arrogance on the part of those who delight in referring to themselves as being Catholic for they see themselves as being in an elite. In the competitive game of who can be the most Catholic, Anglo-Papalists obviously win (see ch. 1.2). Small wonder that they are referred to as 'more Roman than Rome'.

Anglo-Catholics, in their constant use of the word Catholic, want to suggest a meaning which is not accepted by society at large, and this fact alone demonstrates the assertion that Anglo-Catholicism as a movement has not influenced society sufficiently to convince it that Anglo-Catholics should generally be referred to as Catholics. Their identity remains firmly Anglican or Church of England, although they may want to pass as Catholics.

In their preaching and theological writing both Anglo-Catholics and Tractarians appealed to what they called 'the Catholic church'. By this they did not mean the Roman Catholic Church but a larger Catholic body in which the Roman Catholic Church was included. It is difficult to know, in sociological terms, what is meant by the Catholic church. Anglo-Catholics doubtless know. A few examples of how the term has been and still is employed by Anglo-Catholics may indicate some of the problems. 'The Catholic church teaches'; 'to preach not Roman Catholicism nor Anglo-Catholicism but a Catholicism complete and "unhyphenated"' (in ACPC 1921:195); 'fellow Catholics of the Roman obedience' [that is, we along with you are Catholics]; 'In spite of falsehoods, in spite of compromise, the catholic Church is still in every place the treasure house of all the grace and truth which is the legacy of Jesus Christ to His redeemed' (Gore 1889a/1905:184). What, then, is this Catholic church? Doubtless in the minds of the users of the term it is associated with the 'One Holy Catholic and Apostolic Church', reiterated every time the creeds are recited in public worship. Theologically the term could have some precise meaning, although exactly what is meant by it depends on the interpretation given by theologians. But in concrete social terms no such church exists, no institution can be found bearing the name One Holy Catholic and Apostolic Church. Anglo-Catholics might argue that, while it is not a sociological entity, it consists of those who hold to principles found in churches up to say the fifth century (see Simpson 1932:296). But this is a definition set up by Anglicans and Anglo-Catholics to their own advantage.

In the minds of many Anglicans who refer to the Catholic church there is the idea that it consists of a number of churches which have common characteristics, of which the chief is the Roman Catholic Church but to which other churches can be added according to some selected criteria. Such an attempt was enunciated in a book called *Northern Catholicism*, edited by Williams and Harris and published in 1933. Apart from the Roman Catholic Church and Anglican churches, the list included the Old Catholics and other small Catholic churches. The issue of the Orthodox was a problem. Should they be included in the Catholic church or not? On the whole Anglo-Catholics wanted them to be within the group. All these may be said to constitute the Catholic church, but none of them *is* the Catholic church and each of them contains variations in the matter of doctrine and liturgy. It is doubtful if they all would reach unanimity as to what constitutes the Catholic church. The Catholic church to which Anglo-Catholics so frequently refer does not in fact have any concrete, universally recognized existence. Anglo-Catholics and Tractarians indeed define Catholic in their own way. N. P. Williams, who had a great liking for Gallicanism, wanted to see emerge a northern Catholicism which suited Nordic and Anglo-Saxon races, somewhat differentiated from a southern Catholicism ideal for Latin races. Such a combination was based on socio-psychological criteria rather than theological doctrine.

One way of dealing with the notion of many Catholic churches at a theoretical level has been to put forward the notion of branching. Quite simply the theory is this. Christ founded the church, it continued through the disciples and apostles to the bishops, who, through apostolic succession, determined the basic structure of the church which in the course of time dominated all Europe up until the Reformation. The Reformation shattered Christendom and as a result some churches persisted in Catholic church order and others severed themselves from the tree by rejecting apostolic succession. One result was that two churches emerged out of the ecclesiastical holocaust, the Roman Catholic Church and the Church of England, which in the west are the two main branches of the Catholic church. They continued as separate churches and their divine nature was not profaned by the Reformation. The Orthodox churches had branched off earlier at the schism of 1054 but these had maintained Catholic concepts of the nature of the church. This theory of branching remains central to the thinking of Tractarians and most Anglo-Catholics. Sheila Kaye-Smith has written:

> It rests on a view of Christianity which is wider than that held either by Papal or Eastern Catholicism, since it holds that every part of Christendom which has maintained continuity with the past by a true succession of Apostolic Orders and

teaching is part of the visible organization of the Body of Christ on earth.

(Kaye-Smith 1925:169)

Although the theory is an attractive rationalization of the Tractarian position, it did not satisfy Newman, who became convinced that in social reality, as we would say today, there could not be more than one Catholic church. The logic of his position left him no alternative but to become a Roman Catholic. This theory, were it acceptable to the Roman Catholic Church and the Orthodox Churches, might have some validity in it, but as is well known, it is rejected by these bodies. They define the Catholic church in different ways.

So to another possibility. One generally accepted meaning of the word Catholic is universality. The Catholic faith – the Catholic religion – is intended for the world and for the world in its entirety and is held to be basically the same no matter where it has extended itself to. Catholicism attempts to transcend geographical, national, social, and racial lines of demarcation. St Paul himself speaks of the universality of the church (Romans 10.11ff.). So the Catholic religion is seen to be coextensive with a global church. All such adjectives as Roman, Latin, Polish, and Anglo- weaken the notion of the universality of Catholicism (see Pickering 1987). In practice the Catholic church, if it is to be found anywhere, is the Roman Catholic Church, for, on grounds of geographical universality, there can be no other contender. Roman Catholic theologians assert categorically that there is no Catholicism outside their Church. When Anglo-Catholics claim to be Catholic they are hardly adopting a universalist position but one which is essentially sectarian (see ch. 7).

Some Anglo-Catholics have realized the dilemma over their designation but have been unable to solve it by embracing another name which encapsulates their ideology and at the same time does not lead to ambiguity (see Mackenzie 1931:38–9). Without a great deal of success followers in the late 1960s tried to introduce the names Catholic Anglicans or Anglican Catholics. The effort did not really lessen the ambiguity. The old term, Anglo-Catholic, is best kept but inevitably it is misleading. Within Anglicanism the term has become acceptable and people know – at least many Anglicans know – what is implied by it. That does not, however, eliminate the inherent ambiguity of it.

Realizing their predicament some Anglo-Catholics have found another way out. They reject the notion that the Church of England is essentially 'a bridge church' or that its nature is comprehensive. This idea was strengthened by the thinking of Mandell Creighton (1843–1901), scholar and bishop of London, who encouraged the idea of the Church of England as a great national church which upheld a distinctive Anglican point of view (see Hughes 1961:35). Dean Stanley of Westminster Abbey was one who pointed to the many advantages of comprehensiveness (see Slesser 1952:13). But to admit to the comprehensiveness of the Church of England is to admit that it has Protestant elements and so weaken the argument for its Catholic characteristics (Slesser 1952:13). Further, it gives rise to a high church outlook in which 'Anglican' takes precedence over 'Catholic'. Any notion of compromise or uniqueness is not acceptable to the Anglo-Papalist. The Church is Catholic or it is Protestant: it is true or it is false. To maintain their position Anglo-Papalists have asserted the Church of England to be 'totally' Catholic. But then they are put in the extremely difficult position of explaining how it is that the Church has gathered unto itself so much that is not Catholic, i.e. that is Protestant. So one ambiguity is changed for another. Again, the firmly entrenched Protestants of the Church of England have had reservations about the Church being held to be comprehensive. The idea could be a cover for the Catholic-minded to introduce alien beliefs and practices. W. E. Bowen wrote in 1904 that comprehensiveness should not be confused with toleration whereby 'every clergyman was free to deprave its [the Church's] doctrine and discipline as he pleased' (Bowen 1904:vi).

In practical terms the patchiness of Catholicism in the Church of England comes out in the fact that Anglo-Catholics have to know where they can find a 'Catholic' church. As we have already observed, an individual has to rely on hearsay, his 'internal radar system', looking at the advertisements in the *Church Times*, or consulting an ecclesiastical guidebook. The English Church Union began to help people find churches which had 'Catholic privileges' from the late nineteenth century until the 1930s in the publication of *The English Church Union Church Guide for Tourists and Others* (see ch. 4.2). Such is the notion of Catholic universality.

The ambiguity which faces Anglo-Catholics is that they will not accept the fact that Anglo-Catholicism is a very different social entity from Roman Catholicism. To compare the two in a positive way can all too readily obscure their greatly divergent characteristics. A case might be made out for not comparing them or for denying that one is a better form of Catholicism than the other.

3 A bishop or not a bishop?

Anglo-Catholic priests have probably found no problem more difficult to deal with in the matter of ecclesiastical loyalty than that relating to bishops. The dilemma which they faced or, some would argue, brought upon themselves can be simply stated as follows. Church order rests on an organizational system based in the main on two types of functionaries – bishops and priests. Bishops are the chief pastors of an area, a diocese, for which they are responsible, ultimately to God. Priests have a similar responsibility in parishes as an extension of that of the bishop. A diocese consists of a number of parishes. Priests have to be ordained by bishops through the rite of the laying on of hands. On several occasions we have noted that in the eyes of Tractarians and Anglo-Catholics bishops are the *esse* of the church. To them it was something of a miracle that the Reformers in the Church of England kept what is held to be necessary for Catholic church order.

It seems legitimate to question whether Roman Catholic theologians see the essence of Catholicism in this way. Do they hold that the mere possession of valid orders makes a church Catholic? The question is whether Anglo-Catholics have it right. Do they define the situation in the same terms as Roman Catholics? In general the answer would seem to be no. J. W. Poynter, who was a Roman Catholic and became an Anglican, wrote in the 1930s that Anglo-Catholics were under a severe delusion and were cherishing a vain dream (Poynter 1932:503). Their hope for reunion with Rome was groundless because in the eyes of Roman Catholic theologians the Church of England was no church at all and 'her clergy are not clergy'. All Anglo-Catholics can do is to ape the one, true church. Of course Anglican orders were condemned by Leo XIII in 1896. But the question remains: do valid orders *ipso facto* give rise to a Catholic church? One imagines other factors are at stake to which Anglo-Catholics were blind. Since Vatican II there may have been some shift in the attitude of the *Curia* towards the Church of England, but it has not been one of making special overtures to those who feel they are so close to Roman Catholic Catholics. Recent events would seem to confirm the fact that Anglo-Catholics have not seen the situation correctly. Archbishop Marcel Lefebvre and his followers in France and elsewhere, who wish to keep the ethos of the Roman Catholic Church as it was before Vatican II, have found themselves on the point of being excommunicated. The reason is not because they have invalid orders but because they refuse to accept the final authority of the pope. Thus, in the last analysis, it is not a question of church order but obedience which determines whether people are Catholic, or a church is Catholic – at least according to Rome. This point will be raised again in connection with other issues (see ch. 11.6).

From a complementary angle, a Free church theologian writing at the turn of the century was apperceptive enough to question the fixation of many Anglicans on a valid ministry. He claimed that their position was 'a calamity' for the Church of England because its claim to be Catholic was made to turn on one question, that of orders. The result had been to disturb 'the whole balance of the Anglican system'. Thus, the ministry was no longer a means to an end but was the Church's 'pillar and ground of truth' (Fairbairn 1899:xix). Every priest stands convinced that he has apostolic authority and this inevitably gives rise to the notion of a priest who has independence derived from valid ordination (Fairbairn 1899:xx). He thus has his own power! All that is necessary according to this reasoning is that the priest be validly ordained. Where he is there is the Catholic church! Once again, one wonders whether Roman Catholic theologians would accept this position. For Tractarians and Anglo-Catholics the burning issue over ministry was validity, not order; power, not obedience. The position is clearly stated in Gore's book on Roman Catholicism:

> Every Church which claims her following in the catholic fraternity must be prepared not only to show that she is not wilfully schismatical, but also, and before that, to meet two legitimate challenges – to vindicate her orthodoxy and to vindicate her orders, that is, her claim to be within the historical succession of the Church's life.
>
> (Gore 1889a/1905:141).

Bishops were, therefore, necessary for ordination but beyond that in the 'Catholic' Church of England they had little else about them that was Catholic. Spiritual authority and power these bishops might have, but all could see that they did not exercise their ministry in ways in keeping with Roman Catholic bishops, or bishops in other Catholic churches. Anglican bishops do not act as bishops for the simple reason that they do not support Catholic teaching and practice. The result has been that Anglo-Catholics have found themselves in an extremely difficult position. Are bishops bishops in the Catholic sense or are they Protestant leaders? The issue turns on the problem of canonical obedience. Bishops certainly have the power to ordain but within the service of ordination vows have to be taken and in those vows the person ordained promises to be obedient to the bishop. Should Anglo-Catholic clergy be obedient to the bishops whom they think are not sympathetic to Catholic ritual and belief? What if bishops told them not to use incense or have reservation? Would they accept the ruling? The many court cases which took place in the early days of Anglo-Catholicism occurred where in fact the priest had refused to accept the decision of his bishop. Anglo-Catholics became notorious in their refusal to accede to episcopal injunctions they felt were contrary to their particular conception of what it was to be Catholic. Many of the controversies with bishops concerned loyalty to the Prayer Book (see ch. 1.5). Where Anglo-Catholic priests professed such loyalty, their actions and intransigence made it clear to bishops that their words of loyalty were negated by their actions. Thus, Fr Ommanney, very much an Anglo-Papalist, complained that despite his obedience to the Book of Common Prayer he was constantly subject to episcopal censure (Belton 1936:148). What in fact was at stake was a hermeneutical problem of interpreting the meaning and legality of the Prayer Book.

A further issue which affected both priests and bishops was that no up-to-date canon law existed which bound them both in the upholding of standards and in the management of the Church. Neither side could appeal to codified norms. It meant that in the long run bishops could enforce no sanctions. Arguments about what was right or wrong rested, as we have just seen, on tradition and an appeal to the Prayer Book, which was never intended to be a legal code (Fairbairn 1899:xx). So it was that Anglo-Catholic priests found themselves face to face with bishops who at one and the same time were both Catholic and not Catholic. In practical terms bishops were divided between those who were sympathetic to Catholic ideology and those who were opposed to it. The naming of names was a necessary procedure. Thus, Frank Weston, himself a bishop but, more importantly, an overseas bishop, could say at the 1923 Anglo-Catholic congress: 'I am not asking for obedience to a bishop. I ask for obedience to the bishops in so far as they themselves obey the Catholic Church' (quoted in Wilson 1940:118; see also ch. 2.4). As Ronald Knox was to say after he had become a Roman Catholic, Anglo-Catholics treated bishops as '"confirming and ordaining machines," not as *de jure* custodians of the deposit of faith', and we would add, figures of authority (Knox 1918:130). Obedience, therefore, depends not on the office of a bishop but on individual attitudes of priests, who, in a subjective way, consider a bishop to be either a Catholic or not a Catholic. Hardly a Catholic position! This is not to say that there have never been priests who have defied their bishops in the Roman Catholic Church; but they have not defied them on the grounds that the bishops were not thought to be Catholic! Would Anglo-Catholics have wanted English bishops to have the role Roman Catholic bishops had, as, for example, when Cardinal Bonnechose, who was converted to Catholicism in 1830, said: 'My clergy is a regiment; when I say *march*, it marches' (quoted in Martin 1878a:131).

So here is the ambiguity for Anglo-Catholic priests: bishops are necessary functionaries for their very existence, yet vows of obedience made to them may be ignored. Bishops were thus seen as functionaries – as impersonal machines making valid priests. All they did and said was of no consequence. They were near to being a necessary thorn in the flesh. As Fairbairn ironically said the clergy who most pleaded for 'an apostolic episcopate as the condition of Catholic unity, defer least to the episcopal voice' (Fairbairn 1899:xxi). The Anglo-Catholic outlook in this respect was more individualistic than Congregational independency (Fairbairn 1899:xxii). Such ambiguity was also to be found amongst Anglo-Catholic laity who trusted their own clergy more than their bishops. And this was precisely what Anglo-Catholic priests asked of their parishioners – 'follow us and disregard what bishops say'. Given their basic premises, priests had no other position to take. One of the more personal ways of dealing with the dilemma was to joke about it; indeed, sarcastic asides and quips by spiky priests about bishops are unending. Let one example suffice. The learned Gregory Dix said to someone worried about the Church of South India, 'I really don't see why you should be surprised at the conduct of your fathers-in-God. After all, the sign of a Bishop is a crook and of an Archbishop a double-cross' (quoted in Williamson 1956:144).

In many respects and quite rightly, Anglo-Catholic priests saw themselves as a powerless minority. They carried no weight in the appointment of bishops and had no one to represent them in the corridors of power. They could find virtually no bishops with whom they could identify and therefore were nearly always in opposition to bishops.

We have already noted that Anglo-Catholics were very disappointed that only a few bishops supported the congresses between the wars (see ch. 2.6). In the nineteenth century, and indeed later than that, Anglo-Catholics had little to thank bishops for – bishops who were often goaded into action against them by aggressive Protestants or perhaps worse were unable to prevent Protestants embarking on court actions: Fr Mackonochie was forced to leave St Alban's, Holborn, after several years of a successful ministry: Fr Dolling likewise, after ten years in Landport, Portsmouth, was evicted and had to go to another parish. Admittedly in days gone by – and still today – there were some bishops with Tractarian leanings and others who were fairly well disposed towards Anglo-Catholics, if they were not liberal Anglo-Catholics themselves. One might mention E. Benson, archbishop of Canterbury, Winnington-Ingram of London, Gore of Oxford, Wand of London, Frere of Truro, Talbot of Rochester, Underhill of Bath and Wells, and, the most controversial of all, the saintly Edward King of Lincoln. Nevertheless, ardent Anglo-Catholics in the past felt themselves betrayed when bishops refused to allow them to hold services of benediction and adoration and demanded that they did not use the Roman missal or hold devotions to the Blessed Virgin Mary. 'Could these really be Catholic bishops?' Lord Halifax wrote in 1899 to Edward Talbot, bishop of Rochester who was on the edge of Anglo-Catholicism and who, Lord Halifax felt, in some degree betrayed its ideals when he became bishop. Lord Halifax said:

> The rulers of the Church of England will not face what belief in the *Catholic Church* involves, and shrink from such a defence of unpopular men and unpopular practices, as will be given by the heads of any other body of men in the world . . . what people are saying is this: 'there is not a Bishop who stands up for the Catholic truth and practice. . . . Even the bishop of Rochester'.
>
> (quoted in Stephenson 1936:154)

Other bishops disappointed Anglo-Catholics after they had been appointed for the same reason, that they no longer stood by the unequivocal Catholicism they once professed.

The critical attitude of Anglo-Catholics, both clerical and lay, towards bishops on fundamental issues remains almost as strong today as ever it was, although bishops are far more tolerant of Anglo-Catholicism than they used to be, and sometimes were and are Anglo-Catholic, though not Anglo-Papalist. In recent times one should mention Kenneth Kirk, bishop of Oxford. Furthermore, Michael Ramsey, archbishop of Canterbury from 1961 to 1974, was the most Anglo-Catholic Primate there had ever been. The present archbishop, Robert Runcie, is very much within the camp of moderate Anglo-Catholicism. But neither of them led the movement. One who might appear to have this role is the present bishop of London, Graham Leonard, who is by far the most 'Catholic' of the senior bishops there has ever been. But to show the leanings of bishops in recent times one only has to look at the gatherings at the Anglican shrine of our Lady of Walsingham in Norfolk, itself created by an Anglo-Papalist priest, Hope Patten. In 1986 at the pilgrimage in May, when it was reckoned that 7,000 were present, there were four diocesan bishops (London, Wakefield, Norwich, and Chichester), four suffragan bishops, several retired bishops, and two Roman Catholic bishops (*CT*, 30 May 1986).

Yet it is ironical that, just at the time when bona fide Anglo-Catholics were becoming bishops, the movement was showing marked signs of diminution (see ch. 11.1–3). Simultaneously hardline clergy and laity continued to be dissatisfied with bishops, not so much because they prohibited Roman practices in parishes but because of their liberal and compromising views assumed when they rose to the episcopacy. The sorest point at the moment relates to the ordination of women (see ch. 11.9). But there are other sources of controversy, for example, the remarriage of divorced people in church. Thus, one incumbent, a former Oxford don, wrote recently:

> Furthermore, the bishops have shown themselves in this matter to be right out of touch with the ordinary rank-and-file of the clergy. The only hope of the Church of England maintaining its Catholic heritage, humanly speaking, seems to lie outside the House of Clergy [of the General Synod].
>
> (*CT*, 3 February 1984).

We have already had occasion to touch on the controversy between clergy and bishops over the reserved Sacrament, and how parish priests applied for the right to take it to the sick and dying but at the same time wanted to use it for cultic purposes at weekday or Sunday services for perfectly fit people (ch. 2.7). With permission given for the reserved Sacrament, bishops usually found themselves caught when they discovered that such extra-liturgical services were introduced. Once the practice had started, it was extremely difficult to make priests give it up. Possession is nine-tenths of the law. The argument put forward by priests against abandoning these extra-liturgical practices was that such a removal would cause spiritual impoverishment amongst parishioners (Mackenzie 1931:89; see also Mackenzie 1924:190). Bishops sensitive to the arguments probably found it difficult to deny the possibility of such 'spiritual advantages' to

153

devout Anglo-Catholics used to services involving the reserved Sacrament.

But what should the attitude of Anglo-Catholic priests have been? They were placed in a very difficult position in which it was virtually impossible to resolve the ambiguity. If they accepted the decision of a bishop against the implementation of their policy for catholicization, they were conscious of either denying Catholic 'truth' or of watering it down. If they rejected the decision, they could be accused of denying a fundamental Catholic principle of canonical obedience to the bishop, and therefore acting in an individual manner, contrary to church discipline. With the latter solution the priest does exactly what he wants to: he is his own measure of what is Catholic. Every parish priest is thus his own pope! One practical way of dealing with the ambiguity was for priests to seek parishes in dioceses which they knew were controlled by bishops sympathetic to things Catholic. In the early days this was by no means easy. Further, for the sake of a parish church it might be necessary for an Anglo-Catholic priest to accept an appointment to that church although it was in a diocese where the bishop was hostile to Catholic ideals.

One of the reasons why Anglo-Catholicism was able to grow and flourish within the Church of England was because, as has been noted, despite the attitudes and ruling of many bishops against Anglo-Catholic practices, the bishops were powerless to take any disciplinary measures against offenders. In a power struggle with a bishop a clergyman was well aware that, on account of his freehold, it was extremely difficult for him to be removed from his living. Clergy were given tenure in their livings and could not be ejected legally save for a serious moral offence or for failing to see that services were held in the parish church. Over the years bishops have experienced frustration and fury, which, as is so often the case, are derived from impotence. To exert discipline they could do little but exhort Anglo-Catholic clergy to be less extreme. Efforts by bishops to refuse to license undesirable Anglo-Catholic priests were gradually abandoned. A sense of defeat sprang up amongst bishops which gave way to a reluctant acceptance. In the matter of frustration experienced by bishops, we offer an old example, that in the charge of Bishop Blomfield of London given in 1842:

> It is a subject, my brethren, of still deeper concern, that any of our body, though but few, should evince a desire and longing to revert, not merely to some of the outward ceremonies, but to the devotional formularies of the Church of Rome; that they

should speak disparagingly and disrespectfully of our Liturgy, and prepare men of ardent feelings and warm imaginations for a return to the Romish mass-book, by publishing for daily use devotions and homilies taken from authors of that Church, and embodying not a few of its superstitious and unscriptural doctrines and practices; that they should recommend, or justify, under any qualification, prayers or addresses to saints, which began in poetry and ended in idolatry; intercessions for the dead, which our Church, by her formal discontinuance of them, has implicitly forbidden, and which tend directly to the notion of purgatory; and auricular confession, a practice utterly unknown to the Primitive Church, one of the most fearful abuses of that of Rome, and the source of unspeakable abominations.

(quoted in Kelway 1914:64–5)

In many respects the position today is the same as it was when Bishop Blomfield proclaimed this indictment. Anglo-Papalists still go their own way and in many cases do not accept the liturgy and rubrics of the Prayer Book, or now the Alternative Service Book, which was intended in many respects to legitimize services in the Church of England and to introduce some level of conformity which could be enforced. Many Anglo-Papalist churches are to be found in the London diocese and one can go into such a church, for example that of the parish of Holy Cross, Cromer Street, near King's Cross station, and find that the mass is that prescribed by Vatican II (see ch. 11.8). On entering the church the worshipper is given a Parish Mass Book together with a hymn book, the *Celebration Hymnal*, both of which are Roman Catholic. There is nothing in the service or in the furnishings which would identify the church as being Anglican, save in one prayer where the name of the bishop of London is mentioned. There stands this extraordinary ambiguity that prayers are offered for 'John Paul, our Pope, and Graham, our bishop, and David, our area-bishop'. In another Anglo-Papalist church, St Magnus the Martyr, in the city of London, a similar liturgy can be found, where the readings are those according to the new Roman rite and the liturgical calendar that of Rome, and where in fact the parish bulletin is printed by the Redemptorist order and local notices are inserted as a supplement to other printed material. Whether the bishop of London wants to change the situation may be open to question but one thing is quite certain, that, canon law or no canon law, he has no way of effectively disciplining his clergy so as to make them abandon their

Anglo-Papalist ideas and practices. (For an earlier example see the Hoxton parish of Fr Kilburn in ch. 1.3.)

The long history of Anglo-Catholic criticism of bishops and disloyalty to their rulings has in recent years been extended to the thorny issue of the ordination of women, which has created a near crisis and which will be considered briefly at the end of the book (see ch. 11.10). But this, like so many other questions, raises a much deeper one, that of the possibility and nature of change. How do Anglo-Catholics deal with it? And change is at the heart of their movement.

Much of what has been said about Anglo-Catholic attitudes towards bishops could be used to support another ambiguity, that of ecclesiastical authority. Is it to be found in a person (a bishop or Primate) or in a collective body (synod)? In the light of the evidence in this section, there seems little virtue in repeating what has been said. It is clear that authority in the church is a problem Anglo-Catholics cannot unambiguously solve.

4 To change or not to change?

The Anglo-Catholic, and perhaps the Anglican, concept of Catholic and catholicity is inevitably static and backward-looking. What is Catholic is basically what the church formulated in matters of doctrine and practice in some earlier period. Precisely when is beside the point. Of course all the churches of the Christian world face the problem since Christianity is based on a historical figure. The Tractarian and Anglo-Catholic position is more often than not encapsulated in the canon of St Vincent de Lerins: *Quod semper, quod ubique, quod ab omnibus creditum est*. It can be paraphrased as: What is to be believed is what has always been believed, everywhere, and by all. This formula was supported by St Thomas Aquinas and according to the Anglo-Catholic theologian, N. P. Williams, can never be superseded. He said: 'for the Anglo-Catholic Priest, whose whole *raison d'être* as a teacher is to recall men to the faith of the Undivided Church' (ACPC 1921:18).

Not surprisingly the statement of St Vincent has been the subject of a great deal of comment by nineteenth- and twentieth-century writers. Williams, a prominent Anglo-Catholic thinker, admitted that 'this is the static system of Catholic doctrine' (ACPC 1921:19). By contrast, Fairbairn (1838–1912), a Congregational theologian, questioned the value of the principle for deciding what doctrine was to be accepted and what rejected, since it was difficult to apply in specific cases and in the last analysis could only be used in deciding what was *not* Catholic (Fairbairn 1899:310ff.). Most of the more learned Anglo-Catholic theologians were inevitably conservative. The patristic scholar Darwell Stone (1859–1941), who became principal of Pusey House, had a firm conviction about the doctrine of revelation in the Scriptures and the church. It was a supernatural deposit which could not be changed by intellectual apprehension (see Cross 1943:39ff.). He was therefore opposed to notions of development, for example, that of Newman, and not surprisingly disliked the liberal interpretation of Catholicism as put forward by Charles Gore, E. G. Selwyn, and others, whose work has already been mentioned (see ch. 5.2). But deep down Gore was conservative when he maintained that in essence the Church had a finality 'expressed in the once for all delivered faith, in the fulness of the once for all given grace, in the Visible Society once for all instituted . . . and in a once for all empowered and commissioned ministry' (quoted in Fairbairn 1899:344). But Stone was the more conservative and his influence in the 1920s and 1930s on Anglo-Catholicism and Anglo-Papalism was very considerable. Gore was always suspect in such circles.

That Anglo-Catholics have been forced to adopt a virtually fixed position with regard to basic doctrine largely stems from the fact that they are not governed by an authoritative body which has the right and power to make changes or to introduce official interpretations of doctrine. The highest level of government in the Church of England is either mistrusted or held to lack any right to make such changes. Anglo-Catholics admit that it is possible to change certain minor matters but not major ones. If these greater issues are at stake, they say they will be willing to accept changes, even, for example, the ordination of women to the priesthood or schemes of church union with Protestants, if such changes are sanctioned not only by the Church of England but by the whole church. By the whole church they usually mean what they call the Catholic church. As we have noted before, this implies that Anglo-Catholics would accept the decisions of a meeting of bishops of the Anglican Communion, together with those of the Roman Catholic Church and those of the Orthodox Churches, along with the other bodies which might be designated Catholic. Heads of Protestant churches would, by definition, be excluded, although today some Anglo-Catholics might admit them. As the churches stand at the moment, such a meeting in the near future is beyond man's wildest dreams. Since no assembly of this kind is practically possible it means that no modifications of an important nature can be made. There is, therefore, nothing left to do but to fall back on the past and to adhere rigidly to it. It leaves Anglo-Catholics standing still while many churches are able to make modifications, where required, without being unduly influenced by other denominations. The Roman Catholic Church, which is so much idolized, acts unilaterally and unequivocally. Since all other Christian bodies are by definition not Catholic, there is no need to consult them, although in these more liberal days observers from other churches have been asked to attend important gatherings, notably Vatican II. Anglo-Catholics as such were not invited.

Roman Catholicism, therefore, is not encased in the rigid mould which surrounds Anglo-Catholicism. To the outsider it would seem that Roman Catholicism has been subject to a great deal of change over the past century. The most obvious alterations came with Vatican II (1962–5). But more fundamental issues concerning doctrine occurred in the past. One might point to that of the Immaculate Conception of the Blessed Virgin Mary (1854) and to the controversial first Vatican Council of 1869–70 where papal infallibility became part of official Roman Catholic doctrine. In 1950 there was the promulgation of the doctrine of the Assumption of the Blessed Virgin Mary. Whilst no earlier doctrines have been repudiated, others have been raised to the status of dogma. Changes in the future cannot be ruled out. No one has more persuasively dealt with this issue than Cardinal Newman in his concept of the development of Christian doctrine. A book of that name appeared just after he was received into the Roman Catholic Church and it is quite clear from what he wrote that it was this rigidity, precluding the possibility of change or modification within the Church of England, that was one of the reasons for his leaving it. He put forward the view that Christian faith (or basic doctrine) does not change but the church's understanding of it deepens and grows with the passing of time and it is therefore open to change and development. Here is an almost evolutionary approach to doctrine – and evolution was very much a term of the times – which, in marked contrast to the outlook of Tractarians, allows for reformulation. The mammoth task before Newman was to prove that modern Roman Catholic doctrine 'was substantially the same as that of the Apostles, only more explicitly defined and amplified' (Knox 1933:328).

Needless to say, some theologians have seen various weaknesses in Newman's position. First, what constitutes a new understanding of the faith has to be decided by an authoritative body which has the right and power to make the necessary modification or reformulation. For Roman Catholics the right and power obviously reside in the pope or councils called by him. In the Anglican Church no such parallel body exists. Second, there is the danger that one part of the Catholic church will proceed on its own path without taking into consideration the tradition or wisdom of other parts of the church. It comes back to the old Anglo-Catholic position that decisions can only be taken by the whole church. The third issue is a theoretical one. What constitutes a new understanding of the faith? Obviously the formulation of faith is influenced by historical, social, and cultural processes, but how does one distinguish between basic faith and developing expressions of it? Can the two really be separated? And is all growth genuine growth? It may mean retrogression or morbidity. What are the criteria of 'natural' growth? This is a relatively simple question when one examines certain organic phenomena. But what of institutions which have a social component? How is a conflict resolved between what appears essential and a later development of it? Fourth, on evolutionary principles one would have to allow for all heresies and orthodoxies to be implicit or contained in the original seed (see Knox 1933:328). These and other questions have to be answered by those who would support a developmental or evolutionary approach to doctrine. Doubtless, on account of such difficulties, the Roman Catholic Church at its most official level has never supported these ideas. That does not, however, alter the fact that the Church does decide for various reasons to introduce new doctrines which, some would argue, have always been held by the Church but have never been officially promulgated before.

The Catholic and apostolic faith is 'impossible to modify'; so said some Anglo-Catholic bishops who met recently in Fairfield, Connecticut (*CT*, 21 March 1986). If so, Anglo-Catholics have to nail their colours to the status quo mast. To other churches and to the outsider, such an attitude gives the impression that this religious group will make no concessions to change and has adopted a policy which is little short of fossilization. In the past Anglo-Catholics have made concerted efforts to prevent certain proposed changes introduced by the most authoritative bodies of the Church of England. All possibilities of modernization were automatically ruled out: in one simple practical way, by opposing any change in the parish system (Kent 1987:96). Naïvely it was thought that all attempts to modernize the Church would be frowned upon by the Roman Catholic Church. The conservatism of Anglo-Catholics revealed itself in their rallying opposition so as to outvote intended measures for change. They were thus successful in preventing a reform of the 1662 Prayer Book in 1928, thanks not least to the learning and leadership of Darwell Stone (see Hughes 1961, chapter 8). They were antagonistic to the Church of South India reunion scheme of the 1950s, which the Church of England then had to decide whether or not to accept. They tumbled the Anglican–Methodist reunion scheme of 1969, which had taken years to prepare. John Kent is right in stating that the Protestant movement for unity, very much the province of church bureaucrats, would have made much more progress had it not been for the stubbornness of the Anglo-Catholics, along with that of some Evangelicals (Kent 1987:215). Further, many Catholic-minded clergy and laity stood opposed in the mid-1980s to various suggestions for remarrying divorced people in church. They failed, however, in 1987 to prevent initial steps being taken towards the ordination of women to the priesthood. Anglo-Catholics must be praised for their logic in opposing changes which modify the details of what Catholicism means for them.

When one looks at the official pronouncements of the Vatican, it is interesting to observe that Anglo-Catholic clergy today make little reference to the issue of birth-control. Moral matters of this kind do not seem to be of importance to them (see ch. 11.8; Wilkinson 1988). In the face of changing social attitudes, ideals, and mores, they have little or nothing to offer of a positive kind. They negate any attempt at compromise or radical change on matters of belief or church order and it is this negation which gives rise to criticism or indifference from the world outside. Stephenson, himself an Anglo-Catholic, wrote in the 1970s, somewhat condemningly: 'So much of the Catholic Movement in the Church of England has been a turning backwards and a holding on to certain positions with a fanaticism bred from a sense of insecurity' (Stephenson 1972:186). In the Church of England itself Anglo-Catholics have few friends or allies, save Evangelicals on occasion. The extremists, the Anglo-Papalists, have one simple solution to the problem of change. They merely accept all the changes made at Vatican II on the principle that whatever Rome does is right. They therefore have no independent position of their own. For them the ambiguity of change is resolved. But this produces the more fundamental ambiguity of being a papalist group which is not recognized by the papacy. But then why overlook the Roman teaching on birth-control? In the end the imitation of Rome means just doing your own thing.

5 Ritual: important or not?

Anglo-Catholics, in being called ritualists, a name popular and used mainly by their opponents in the early days of the movement, could be seen to be those who stressed the importance of ritual. That they introduced into the Church of England rituals which many, if not most, outside the movement saw as alien to the Church demonstrated their concern for religious action and ceremony within the church building. They held that such rituals were important, demonstrated not least by the fact that their clergy were willing to oppose bishops, withstand riots, and, if necessary, go to prison. That they were prepared to forgo preferment was but a minor cost. Society after society, congress after congress, aimed at trying to secure adequate and correct ritual in Anglican churches. And it cannot be denied that it was the rituals and services, so new to the Church of England, which were the centre of interest to people of all kinds. The attention of most was clouded with curiosity and quite often hostility. To the faithful the rituals were connected with new experiences of worship and devotion which were seen to be spiritually exciting and uplifting.

Yet there were Anglo-Catholic priests, especially in the early days of the movement, who were indifferent to ritual in so far as they saw it as no more than a means to an end. What were more important were doctrine and attitude. Some Anglo-Papalists tried to argue that they had less ritual and were less concerned with it than high-church ritualists (for example, Maughan 1916). It was something which had to be introduced and then taken for granted. There were much greater tasks afoot than arguing about ceremonial. There were people to convert to Christianity; there were the faithful who had to improve their inner spiritual lives. Behind all ritual existed a reality which transcended outward forms, Catholic though they might be. Fr Ommanney, when he went to Sheffield in 1882, made it his aim 'to get people to help me in working for the good of souls instead of fighting over some trifling matters of ceremonial' (Belton 1936:47). Two points arise from this quotation. The first is that the clergy were rigid and utterly convinced that they and they alone made decisions about the policy and practice of ritual. Lay people might be interested in it and many were but it was from the point of view of the spectator. The second is that the laity were encouraged to be interested in liturgy. Many servers became highly knowledgeable about vestments and ceremonies of all kinds. Hardly surprisingly they became much involved in what they did and saw. To them it was of supreme importance. And how often did they get the message that 'it's the mass that matters'? Clearly Anglo-Catholic priests could not blame their devotees for seeing the essential place which ritual had in the Anglican thrust towards Catholicism. What the priests did was more important to such lay people than what they said. 'Sermons are so Protestant anyway!' What is seen is what matters.

6 Conclusion

Faced with ambiguities, Anglo-Catholics have adopted a number of ways of dealing with them. Some will be considered in the pages ahead (see chs 9, 10, 11). At this point, passing reference is made to that kind of intellectual juggling which somehow justifies accepting the ambiguities. In some measure this is the work of theologians and clergy in rationalizing the antinomies. How this has been done is apparent in the presentation of the ambiguities themselves. Twenty years ago, John Gunstone, a member of a group of modern Anglo-Catholics who described themselves as Catholic Anglicans, openly admitted that in the past the movement 'brought with it an extreme form of casuistry in matters of worship and discipline which attempted to justifiy almost any innovation or policy' (Gunstone 1968:187).

Chapter 7

The ambiguity of Catholic sectarianism

1 A church or a sect?

As the words are commonly used, a church stands in marked contrast to a sect. The characteristics which may be said to differentiate a church from a sect began to be enunciated systematically by the theologian and sociologist, Ernst Troeltsch (1865–1923), in *The Social Teaching of the Christian Churches* (t.1931), and have subsequently been the subject of very considerable study. To open up this highly complex, extensive, and, in the last analysis, probably infertile debate is of doubtful value in the context of Anglo-Catholicism. Nevertheless, using rather loose definitions, the terms church and sect can be usefully applied to typify attitudes towards ecclesiastical positions and organizations. A church orientation is one which is associated with a religious organization which has an extensive following, is well established in society, and is usually highly regarded by that society. A church tends to accept most of the mores and morals of the society in which it is located. In contrast, a sectarian attitude of the church-oriented groups, where rigid boundaries where beliefs and attitudes often run counter to, or are distant from, those of society at large. They may also be antagonistic towards those of major religious groups. A sectarian society tends to draw rigid boundaries between those who are members of the group and those who are not. Quite different is the attitude of the church-oriented groups, where rigid boundaries may be disregarded and degrees of membership accepted.

There is nothing new in asserting that Anglo-Catholicism is sectarian. This has been stated not only by those outside the party but even by those in it. As an example of the second category one might cite T. A. Lacey, canon of Worcester, who was a leading writer and spokesman for the movement in the 1920s. At the beginning of his book, *The Anglo-Catholic Faith* (Lacey 1926), he said that Anglo-Catholicism was in fact a sect and he stressed the point again in the conclusion. Strangely enough what he wrote was an apologia for the sectarian status of Anglo-Catholicism. Lacey, perhaps ignorant of the work of German sociologists on the church–sect typology, held that a sect is nothing more than a movement or a school of thought within, say, a religion or an academic discipline (Lacey 1926:1ff.) Its distinguishing mark is a group of followers around a leader – a group which exists within a larger body. But to make such a group equivalent to a sect, especially as Lacey refers to the origin of the word, the Latin verb *secare*, to cut, is to miss the point. To be sure, there is the notion of cutting, of being different, in the word sect but there have always existed groups within any church which have emphasized particular doctrines, cults, or policies, but which may not have engendered a sectarian outlook. They may have worked for some simple, direct, practical goals – goals which are not related to basic doctrines or practices, for example, the cult of the Sacred Heart or societies for helping the poor. The sectarian spirit, on the other hand, exudes a sense of superiority, a sense that it possesses 'truth' which is not owned by the larger group. In other words, what is sectarian turns on important matters of faith and practice. In this respect Anglo-Catholicism is sectarian, in a way Lacey did not imply, for it is concerned with the very nature of the church, and in particular with its Catholic reality. It might seem strange that Anglo-Catholics should want to be thought of as being sectarian. Did Lacey and those who thought like him realize that in speaking of a Catholic movement as sectarian they were in many respects using contradictory language? After all, as we have noted, Catholic in one sense means universal: sectarian means the very opposite (see ch. 6.2).

We turn to those aspects of Anglo-Catholicism which would support the contention that the movement has much about it that is sectarian in spirit. What has already been written has shown that Anglo-Catholicism has many characteristics which are to a large extent sectarian. It is a movement with a limited following, standing in a larger group, having notions of truth and ritual which it thinks are superior to those of the main body. In many fundamental doctrines Anglo-Catholics think they are right and the attitude they take, as with their opposition to bishops, speaks not only of arrogance but of veiled hostility. In more theological language the movement is an *ecclesiola in ecclesia*, and further sectarian characteristics of the movement must now be briefly examined.

2 Language

One of the most effective ways a group secures its identity and separates itself from another group is by the employment of a language in some ways different from that of adjacent groups. In all religions there is a great deal of technical or theological language. But within a religious group there may be different levels at which technical language is used. The first is amongst professional theologians and intellectuals, where rather sophisticated terms are employed, such as transcendence, eschatology, baptismal regeneration, grace, and so on. The other level is amongst rank-and-file members who develop their own religious language based on theological terms but which may be more practical and less sophisticated than that of theologians.

An in-language has a number of merits which are closely related. The first is that of giving unity and strength to the group which uses the language. Those who use an in-language know that they have common bonds. The use of the language gives confidence and strength. Again, a language decisively marks the speakers off from others who do not know the language. An in-language used in a mixed group provides a means of discovering whether there are others of one's own religious persuasion. Someone tries out a few words and sees if others respond positively: if so, a relationship may be established. In such a situation there is also the possibility that the language produces a self-conscious sense of superiority: 'You are not one of us; we don't speak the same language.'

Anglo-Catholics have introduced into the Church of England a language which did not exist in the Church before. It is a kind of Anglican–Roman Catholic patois, quite distinct from the main language used in the Established Church. Although it is the language of Anglo-Catholics, some of the words, not surprisingly, have crept into the wider Church, although others are used strictly within their own ranks. Because of their ideology, Anglo-Catholics hold – and with some justification – that they possess the same language – the same terms and phrases – as that employed by Roman Catholics. Indeed, Anglo-Catholics delight in aping the language of that church – at least they used to until recent times and Anglo-Papalists still do. It may be generally said that admiration frequently leads to assimilation of language. Here Anglo-Catholic language both unites followers and at the same time separates them from other sections of the Church to which they belong. Further, it helps them to pass for Roman Catholics. Over and above all this stands the wish to break away and be

removed from conventional Anglican marks of identification – its
language and symbols.

Needless to say, the most important word of the in-language is
Catholic which is used on every possible occasion. So one hears:
'We Catholics', 'Does your church have Catholic privileges?', 'In
every school the Catholic faith was taught and practised'
(Donovan 1933:94), 'They teach sound Catholic doctrine in our
church' (but would Roman Catholics use the word sound?), 'Is
there a Catholic church near by?' (i.e. an Anglican parish church
which is Anglo-Catholic). And in a more academic vein, when
the 1928 Prayer Book revision was being debated, a prominent
Anglo-Catholic said that a certain idea being considered 'need
not trouble any Catholic in the English Church', and 'it is not to
be supposed that the objections of Catholics to the Deposited
Book refer only to the rubrics about reservation' (Stone 1928:13,
but see the note on the use of the word Catholic on p. 7).

As important as any other word is mass. Up to the time of the
Catholic revival the word which was commonly used in the
Church of England for such a service was and still is holy
communion, perhaps the Lord's Supper. Anglo-Catholics identify
themselves by deliberately not using the word communion,
except in such phrases as making one's communion. Mass is the
word which gives identity. On notice boards outside Anglo-
Catholic parish churches there are phrases such as low mass, sung
mass, high mass, mass with hymns, parish mass, and so forth.
And on special occasions when a bishop is present the service
might be pontifical high mass. But there are other phrases
borrowed from Roman Catholicism which use the word mass.
Parishioners 'hear mass' and priests 'say mass'. A newly ordained
priest declares that he is going to 'say his first mass'. 'Where will
you say your mass, Father?' (note the use of the possessive
adjective). In connection with this some priests 'need an altar',
when for example they are on vacation or are not directly
associated with a parish church. There is the story of the wife of a
central Anglican priest, a chaplain of a Cambridge college, who
was phoned up by a local Anglo-Catholic priest and asked: 'Does
your husband want an altar for Christmas?' Her immediate
reaction was to think, 'What on earth will he do with such a
Christmas present?' Anglo-Catholic ideology, as we have already
noted, is often summed up in the phrase 'it's the mass that
matters'. Said one priest:

> Experience has proved again and again that the Mass will hold
> people, once they have learned how to use it, when everything

else fails . . . it is the Catholic belief about the Mass which makes it the intensely satisfying method of worship, which it is.

(Mackenzie 1931:57)

The language implies that when the Anglo-Catholic talks about mass he means something different from what Anglicans generally mean by holy communion. Of course, scholars and educated laymen know that the mass, holy communion, eucharist, liturgy, and so on all refer to the same service and that the term eucharist, often adopted by Prayer Book Catholics, is widely used throughout the Church of England. But as we have suggested, the way Anglo-Catholics have used the word mass implies something different from holy communion as used by Anglicans. Perhaps Anglo-Catholics would argue that what they mean is first of all definite dogmatic teaching about the service and its importance for the Christian. Here they would emphasize the doctrine of the sacrifice of the mass which states that in some real yet mysterious way the priest in celebrating the mass performs a sacrificial act in the offering of Christ himself on the altar. This creates an ambiguity since not all Anglican clergy celebrate with such an intention. So there is the implication that the efficacy of the rite depends on the belief or worthiness of the priest, which is very close to a popular Protestant position, namely, that the reception of religious virtue is dependent on the faith of the individual.

'Father' is the proper and popular mode of addressing an Anglo-Catholic priest. Indeed, Anglo-Catholic priests can be identified by the way they are addressed. Anglo-Catholic lay people seldom call their priests 'Mr', for that is 'very Protestant'. Nor do they often refer to them as vicar or rector, names which are commonly used by the general run of Anglicans. So, in parishes and at gatherings of priests, one hears people delight in saying 'Father Smith or Father Gordon', and 'Father says this' and 'Father says that'. It is an infallible way of letting people know that the speaker and the person who is addressed are different from the rest of the Church of England. By and large, calling each other Father in public seems to be the recognized practice amongst Anglo-Catholic priests, but privately they will use Christian names amongst themselves. Today, Anglicans frequently call their clergy by their Christian names: such familiarity is not accepted by many Anglo-Catholics, who think, quite rightly, that that mode of address undermines the status of the priest. This is not an occasion to recall the historical development of the use of the word Father amongst Anglo-Catholics. Let

167

it be said that in the early days of Anglo-Catholicism, whilst Father was frequently used amongst the laity, the word Mister was also held to be quite acceptable and there did not appear to be a reaction of disapproval on the part of clergy if they were referred to as Mr. The standardized procedure of referring to priests as Father seems to have been firmly established in the inter-war period (see ch. 2.2).

Inevitably Anglo-Catholics had to employ new words because the services and forms of devotion they introduced were new. We have referred to some of these words before – benediction, adoration, the rosary, the angelus – but there are numerous others such as asperges, holy water stoup, acolyte, and thurifer. In one respect they might be acceptable to non-Anglo-Catholics since there is simply no alternative word. What probably has caused more offence is the discarding of quite satisfactory words which existed in the Church of England but which were deliberately rejected in order to adopt Roman Catholic equivalents. It might be true that there are subtle differences in meaning but Anglo-Catholics seemed to delight in referring to as many Roman Catholic terms as they could. We present a list of some of these terms with the common Anglican equivalent, or near equivalents:

clergy house, presbytery	rectory, vicarage, parsonage
parish priest (abbreviated PP)	rector, vicar, priest in charge, curate
cotta and cassock	surplice and cassock
fulfilling one's religious obligations	going to church
vespers	evensong
missal	Prayer Book
mass	holy communion, eucharist

In the *Church Times*, one can read church notices and advertisements which in themselves are very difficult to distinguish from those which might appear in a Roman Catholic newspaper. We pick one out at random:

IN MEMORIAM
CROWTHER-ALWYN. – Vivian Crowther-
Alwyn, Priest, obit. St. Luke's Day.
1967. Requiescat in Pace, Jesu Mercy,
Mary Pray.

Finally, within the context of language, one should mention that, while Anglo-Catholics adopted an in-language which they felt identified them with Roman Catholic Catholics, they developed a form of humour that was theirs and theirs alone. Most of their jesting related to various aspects of ritual, to bishops whom they delighted to torment, and to Protestants. As we have mentioned before, double-breasted cassocks were called maternity dresses and Sarum albs night-shirts. A lot of the jokes are connected with gossip about 'Fr X' and 'Bishop Y'. Evelyn Waugh noted the peculiar genre of Anglo-Catholic humour and that it was very different from the jokes which are to be found amongst Roman Catholic priests (Waugh 1959:115).

The Society of St Peter and St Paul, the foremost Anglo-Papalist society of its day, bated bishops in its publications, and sold Ridley and Latimer votive candle stands, as well as Lambeth frankincense. Ronald Knox, whom we have already mentioned, was renowned for his wit and was one of the leading lights of the Society (see ch. 1.3). Moreover, it has a kind of naughtiness and sourness mixed in with it – something one expects in adolescent boys (see Waugh 1959:97; Pinnington 1983:111). But it should be noted that some of that kind of humour can be found in clerical groups of less extreme churchmanship. And to the credit of Anglo-Catholics they are prepared to laugh at themselves. Some have been good writers of humorous verse, for example, E. L. Mascall in *Pi in the High* (1959). Although ecclesiastical jokes can relieve psychological tensions and aggression, such jocularity amongst Anglo-Catholics may seem to the outsider to be in poor taste and are one of the least attractive elements of such clerical life (for further examples, see Williams 1982:116ff.).

3 'Against the stream'

It was not only in using certain words – particular ecclesiastical words – that Anglo-Catholics deliberately marked themselves off from their fellow Anglicans but in many other ways they tried to demonstrate that they were different from the rest of the Church to which they belonged. There was something which told people at large quite simply that Anglo-Catholics were not ordinary 'Church of England' people. In various ways they stood over against much that the Ecclesia Anglicana stood for. They were not only *contra mundam* but seemed to desire to be so. Perhaps they felt themselves to be heirs to Athanasius.

Some Anglo-Catholic clergy have been politically to the left. They were staunch followers of socialism or liberalism, for example, of those in the early period, Fr Stanton was an anti-royalist. In a later period there were a few who were Communists, the most notable being Conrad Noel (see ch. 5.6). They were frequently opposed to the establishment, defined in the widest terms, socially and religiously. They were not on the whole critical of a Church of England in and for England but there were some who disliked it being established. Indeed, their concept of Catholicism was that every country should have its own Catholic church. Quite obviously they were opposed to Erastianism, as were the Oxford Fathers, and any interference by the state in matters religious was abhorrent to them. It was this issue which after all sparked off the Oxford movement. Some Anglo-Catholic priests, however, such as Fr Stanton, have always favoured disestablishment. But, provided the Church could be guaranteed a certain amount of independence from the State, many priests saw little reason to push for disestablishment. The more cautious, concerned with holding on to the positions already gained, saw the advantages of being in a church which was established. They argued that if the Church were disestab-lished, power would pass automatically into the hands of bishops or synods and that this would not necessarily be of advantage to Anglo-Catholics. The Anglo-Catholic position had been preserved in the face of the opposition of bishops and, thanks to their limited powers, by allying themselves on occasion with secular powers, as in the case of their rejection of the revised Prayer Books of 1927 and 1928 (see ch. 6.4). The more radically minded, especially those of a socialist outlook, advocated a complete severance of the Church of England from the State in order that its independence would be guaranteed for ever.

Attitudes towards the establishment did not only relate to the status of the Church of England but also to the establishment viewed as a social concept involving the well-to-do, those with a public-school and Oxbridge education, the middle classes, the economically and socially secure. Against these groups there tended to be some opposition. The reasoning was that in the eyes of Anglo-Catholics the establishment was associated with a particular form of religious life found in the Church of England. Anglo-Catholics strongly disliked the comfortable, traditional 'nothingness' which they saw as characterizing so many of the middle-of-the-road Anglicans, both lay and clerical, who were so much associated with the middle classses. It was a watered-down Protestantism, which made few demands on its followers either by way of belief or in terms of action. It was conventional religion which contained nothing unpleasant, nothing which called for sacrifice, nothing which savoured of asceticism, nothing which went against the comfortable living of the times. In social terms it always played for safety. It treated with extreme scepticism anything which approached religious enthusiasm, such as might be seen in Roman Catholicism, amongst Evangelicals, or even in themselves. It was epitomized by liberalism and evident in a rational approach to Christianity. Above all it had no cutting edge. Public-school religion demonstrated it best of all. Dom Anselm Hughes, an Anglican Benedictine, who was born of Anglo-Catholic parents, wrote that the public-school religion to which he was subjected 'was merely a temporary necessary evil with no real impact on life' (Hughes 1961:5). By contrast, Anglo-Catholics could point to the demands of their religion – attending mass every Sunday, receiving holy communion early in the morning, going to mass on a weekday, going to confession, having to subscribe to doctrines difficult to stomach – doctrines which run-of-the-mill Anglicans knew nothing about. To these demands were added those of fasting, abstinence from meat on Fridays, the possibility of entering the religious life to be a monk or nun, the call for celibacy amongst the clergy. Here was no sitting at ease in Zion. Just because conventional Anglicanism was identified with the English way of life, it was suspect. Wilkinson has written: 'The Catholic [Anglo-Catholic] reacts with distaste and scepticism to those who admire the Church of England as the quintessence of all Englishness' (Wilkinson 1978b:44). He goes on to say, quite rightly, that Anglo-Catholics can probably understand better than run-of-the-mill Anglicans the mentality of dissenters and Roman Catholics, because of their outside status.

There is also among certain Anglo-Catholics, especially of previous generations, an adolescent desire to shock, to do what is illicit in the matter of minor legal offences. Behaving in this way creates a kind of excitement, even pleasure. It is like young boys doing what they know they ought not to do according to their parents' standards but who delight in doing it. Ronald Knox, when he was an Anglo-Papalist, was very conscious that he was behaving in such a manner. After he had seceded, he grew out of what he considered was a schoolboy attitude, one of defiant contest (Knox 1918:203). And of course it could be argued that, once Anglo-Catholicism became accepted by the Church, such defiance had its ground cut from under its feet. This is not to say that it can no longer be found in the movement.

It often used to be said amongst Anglo-Catholics that they would have preferred to have worked in France where people

were either staunch, devout Catholics who practised their religion
or else anticlerical or atheist. At least one knew where one was
with them! In England everything was wishy-washy: people were
neither devout nor anticlerical; they knew nothing about religion
and they were prepared neither to commit themselves whole-
heartedly to it nor to reject it publicly. Anglo-Catholics would
have liked to have worked within well-marked boundaries. In a
similar vein, Hugh Ross Williamson, at the time when he was an
Anglo-Catholic, wrote: 'Protestantism is a half-way house where
one takes refuge because of a disinclination to think the matter
out to a conclusion. Only the Catholic and the agnostic are to
reach the end of their journeys' (Williamson 1956:45). Similar
sentiments were often echoed in the nineteenth century. For
example, in dealing with the forces of secularization and
agnosticism, Roman Catholic thinkers felt that Protestantism was
of no account. Thus, Abbé Martin, writing in the 1870s, could say
that: 'Rationalism on the one hand, and Catholicism on the
other, – these are the two systems on which to devolve the future
of our race' (Martin 1878a:116). Anglicanism and Protestantism
were not integrated systems, or, if they were systems, they were
not powerful and logical enough to deal with the prevailing
hostile ideologies (see Introduction). Anglo-Catholics have
yearned for precise boundaries. They imagined that such was the
situation in France, and it may well have been in the nineteenth
century, but in the decades following the Second World War
social changes have occurred which make it not dissimilar to that
which Anglo-Catholics held existed in England between the wars
and which still exists today.

In the attempt to create a distinctive religious way of life,
Anglo-Catholics fashioned a counter-culture which tended to
unite them and which provided values, language, and actions that
marked them off from the rest of the church and society. At the
same time it gave them a certain sense of superiority. They had
knowledge others did not have. They claimed to have logic on
their side and they certainly had a number of able thinkers and
scholars. In a mocking way they often said of others: 'Poor dears,
the Prots are so ignorant.'

4 Clergy marginality

That Anglo-Catholicism, an essentially clerical movement, has
sectarian characteristics is in part attributed to the thinking and
energy of priests who have led it. It is therefore apposite to focus
briefly on the clerical leadership of the movement and to be

aware of the fact that the clergy have not only been responsible for the spread of the sectarian spirit but in various ways have exemplified it in their own lives.

C. C. J. Webb, certainly a high church layman, if not an Anglo-Catholic, who was an Oxford professor of philosophy in the 1920s, wrote that one result of the Oxford movement was that it 'unquestionably created a new ideal of the Church's ministry and a new type of clergyman' (Webb 1928:9). Anglo-Catholicism did this and went further, but by so doing it gave rise to aims and ambitions which in many respects removed the priest from the general run of Anglican clergy. We shall raise the matter in connection with marriage and celibacy later on (see ch. 8.2). For the moment the issue is seen in other terms. Many Anglo-Catholic clergy have seen and still do see themselves as a 'peculiar' group amongst the clergy of the Church of England. Hugh Ross Williamson said of himself in the 1950s: 'I decided to become not, indeed, an Anglican parson but a Catholic priest in the Church of England' (Williamson 1956:112). Priests had standards and ideals which marked them off from others. Their ideals, in practical terms, were those of the Roman Catholic priest rather than those associated with a Protestant minister. Anglican clergy were seen to be amateurs, gentlemanly, easygoing in their approach to the ministry, given to a relatively comfortable mode of existence, which was epitomized by the ethos of a rural town or cathedral city. Some characters in Trollope's novels spring instantly to mind. In contrast, Anglo-Catholic priests strove to be professionals, totally dedicated to their task. Apart from the issue of celibacy, the ideal had one definite consequence: that priests should be better trained in their craft, and therefore that they should have a more thorough theological education, especially in pastoral theology. In the late nineteenth century, and even up until the time of the First World War, not every ordinand had to go to a theological college (see ch. 5.7). The implementation of a full seminary training such as that in the Roman Catholic Church was not seen to be possible. One way of achieving better training was to learn from other parish clergy who were thoroughly experienced priests themselves. The other method was through the publication of books on pastoral theology, and there can be no doubt that the development of this method of pastoral training in the Church at large was strongly influenced by Anglo-Catholic publications. Another outcome of adopting a professional approach to the priesthood was the call for celibacy. The celibate was the true professional. The arguments for this are set out in the next chapter.

Nevertheless, despite the attempt to be professional, most Anglo-Catholic clergy could not escape their Anglican background and the fact that their training was not as rigorous as that of the seminary formation through which all Roman Catholic clergy had to go. Anglican clergy were essentially self-taught. But even in later times, when nearly every ordinand was expected to go to a theological college, training was still amateurish compared with that of the Catholic seminary, which demanded that a student be under instruction for at least seven years. In an English theological college the expected time was between one and three years, dependent on whether the ordinand was a graduate of a university or not.

Another factor had an important bearing on the matter of professionalization, or lack of it. Because Anglican clergy possessed the freehold of their livings, they had great liberty in pastoral ministry and this encouraged some to be eccentric.

When one examines the lives of certain Anglo-Catholic clergy, it is evident that they were marginal people and yet at the same time very sure of themselves and their ideas, doubtless in part due to their social background (see ch. 4.3). Although slum priests worked long hours under very bad conditions, some of them had well-tried escape routes. They would spend holidays on the Continent, particularly in Switzerland or France, and many, even into the 1930s, were members of London clubs. During the week, and perhaps after strenuous work on a Sunday, a priest might go from his slum parish and have a meal and a good bottle of claret in the congenial surroundings of some exclusively male institution in St James or Piccadilly (see ch. 4.5).

Apart from this 'living in two worlds at once' some priests behaved eccentrically in other ways. There was an ostentation about certain Anglo-Catholic clergy which made them far removed from the conventional, middle-of-the-road Anglican priest. When Fr Lawson celebrated his first mass at St Paul's, Oxford, he carried a bouquet of flowers. At the same church, when Fr Stephenson said his first mass, the altar was covered in Madonna lilies and a professional singer was hired to sing during the offertory. There was also a rose on the altar which he gave to his mother after the mass (Stephenson 1972:95). A Fr de Waal, who was curate in a certain church, performed sung mass and vespers in one part of the church, while the vicar said matins and evensong in another (Stephenson 1972:99). The same priest said: 'I can't think why people would join in when one is saying Mass . . . if they try it on with me I go first fast and then slow and they don't keep it up'; he had another peculiarity: 'he hated all things Sarum but particularly Gothic vestments and, if he went into a church where they were used, he would produce a card of safety pins and turn them into the Latin shape' (Stephenson 1972:99; many other examples of Anglo-Papalist eccentricities are to be found in this book).

At a more sober level, Anglo-Catholic clergy were nearly always dressed in cassocks, not only in church and vicarage, but as they went round their parishes. They frequently wore birettas as well. Some parishioners have been known to say jokingly that they thought their priest wore a cassock in bed and, one might add, the biretta as a night cap! Anglo-Catholic clergy scorned all other forms of clerical dress and in this respect, as in so many other matters, they turned their eyes towards the Continent. In wearing a cassock all the time they modelled themselves on priests in France and elsewhere, whose 'professional uniform' was a soutane. Certainly they adopted clerical collars when they came into fashion. These were commonly called Roman or dog-collars. For Anglo-Catholics they had to be narrow, simply because Protestant-minded ministers were thought to favour a broad collar. Similarly, as we have noted, moustaches – the sign of being a Protestant minister – were out, and, although beards with moustaches were acceptable, by and large Anglo-Catholic clergy were clean-shaven, once again following the pattern found on the Continent. Uniformity in clerical dress was fairly well maintained up until the Second World War. After that, variations were to be seen, not least due to the relative freedom in many matters which came in the wake of Vatican II. Today there is enormous variety in dress, not only in the Church of England but also amongst Anglo-Catholics. Eccentricities have in no way disappeared. The writer quite recently had occasion to observe a priest travelling on the London underground, obviously an Anglican, wearing a soutane with cape and on his head not a biretta but a grey pork-pie hat of Donegal tweed! Nevertheless, very many die-hard Anglo-Catholic and Anglo-Papalist priests still prefer to wear a Latin cassock when on duty. And more so. At a meeting in connection with the 1988 Lambeth conference a well-known leader of Anglo-Catholics, a canon and a member of the General Synod of the Church of England, was seen to be dressed like a cardinal, 'though he said that he was attired as a Spanish canon: wide-brimmed canon's hat, scarlet-trimmed soutane and a cummerbund . . . in "true Roman purple"' (*CT*, 29 July 1988).

There is one kind of eccentricity which is associated with rather nondescript personalities, but another which is carried off by those who exert considerable influence on others – it is part of a flamboyant personality which transcends social and ecclesiastical conventions. Anglo-Catholics have had a full share of such people. One who comes immediately to mind is Bernard Walke, the vicar of St Hilary in Cornwall, who has already been mentioned (see ch. 4.4). He was a person of great imagination. He initiated parish plays which were broadcast as early as the late 1920s. He opened a home for children who were refugees from Austria. He attempted to deal with the problems of unemployment amongst tin-miners after the First World War by starting the co-operative ownership of a mine, which never got off the ground. He was constantly in the company of well-known artists and writers – his wife was an artist – and he was much devoted to horses and, more particularly, donkeys. He always used to travel around the neighbourhood in a chaise drawn by a donkey. Moreover, he was a pacifist and he defied official charges to change his ritualistic services. Someone said of him: 'Ber was a pure nonconformist' (in Walke 1935:iii); but, one might add, an animated nonconformist. But even religious orders were not free of unusual members. Adrian Hastings has written of the Oratory of the Good Shepherd, which was based in Cambridge and recruited mainly dons, that 'it was a society with few rules [and] many eccentrics' (Hastings 1986:196).

To cite further examples of priestly eccentricity is pointless. It is impossible to know whether Anglo-Catholic clergy have had more than their share. The Church of England, certainly in the past and perhaps still today, is unique amongst the major denominations in producing an abundance of eccentric clergy, nor does it appear to regret the fact. That English clergy can behave in eccentric ways is largely due to the parson's freehold, as we have noted, and to their training based on an ideology of individualism found in Oxford and Cambridge and, above all, in Anglican theological colleges. Anglo-Catholic clergy might be thought to be marginal because, although they are priests in the Church of England, they behave in ways peculiar to a minority standing against conventional religion. Over and above their sectarian qualities there are those of English eccentricity. Let Fr Stanton have the last word. He wrote to an undergraduate: 'I am politically socialistic, in faith papistical, in Church policy a thorough-going Nonconformist' (Russell 1917:138). Only in the Church of England could one find such a priest. It might be commonly upheld that Catholicism inculcates uniformity. The ambiguity of Anglo-Catholicism has been that it has not.

5 A one-sided affair: sectarian unreality over reunion

It has been stated frequently enough that the object of Anglo-Catholicism from the outset was the catholicization of the Church of England. The question that was always raised, even from the beginning of the movement, was whether in fact that was the true aim of the movement. Was there not something deeper, more important? Some have argued that to say that Anglo-Catholics would be satisfied if the Church of England were catholicized would not be to tell the whole truth. It was only the first step of a longer process. That process had as its finishing point the reunion of the Church of England with the Church of Rome. Critics and some Anglo-Catholics alike maintained that that was precisely what Anglo-Catholicism was all about. The dream of the Catholic-minded was to draw together the two Churches so as to eliminate the effects of the Reformation and thus to restore the situation to what it was in the middle ages. The achievement of the goal could be hastened by changing English parish life so that it resembled what could be found in Roman Catholicism. Thus, when the act of reunion came about, English parish churches would be found practising what was required. Indeed, to get things ready now would be nothing more than a declaration of intent. Two groups took this position very seriously: Anglo-Papalists and Protestant extremists.

It was the Protestants, outraged by Anglo-Catholic policy, who made most fuss and feared that all the achievements of the Reformation would be lost if England became a country subservient to the pope. In their minds they linked the possibility with the fear of the inquisition and persecution. They publicly proclaimed their fears on every possible occasion. Anglo-Papalists, on the other hand, kept a lower profile and wrote on the subject without too much flourish. But what they did write was fuel for Protestant extremists, who, supporting a conspiratorial thesis, saw the work of Anglo-Catholic priests as that of Jesuits and other Roman agents (Walsh 1900:35; and see ch. 9.4). The argument ran something like this: since the Reformation, Catholic countries had failed to invade England; further, the Roman Catholic Church was unable to convert the country by preaching and missions; so now it was doing it by infiltrating into the Church of England through the disguised agency of Anglo-Catholics. Confusion and radical changes would then give rise to internal capitulation. Roger Lloyd in *The Church of England 1900–1965* did not hesitate to say that Anglo-Catholics were often accused of being the Holy Father's fifth column in the Anglican citadel (Lloyd 1966:123). (Did the critics actually use the words fifth column?) Lloyd, who was sympathetic towards Anglo-Catholicism, said 'The accusation was silly but believed' (Lloyd 1966:123). Nevertheless, one wonders how far people as a whole believed that Anglo-Catholics were directed and manipulated by the pope or, more specifically, by the Jesuits (see Munson 1975:386).

In a somewhat more serious approach, Walter Walsh around the turn of the century brought home to the English public what he held to be the subversive nature of Anglo-Catholicism as a movement of betrayal of the Reformation. After his much publicized *The Secret History of the Oxford Movement* (1897), he specifically charged Anglo-Catholics and their associates with aiming to bring about the 'Corporate Reunion with Rome' and, needless to say, pointed out their unswerving admiration of the Roman Catholic Church, with even some cases of priests accepting papal infallibility. Walsh, who became a Fellow of the Royal Historical Society, presented his case in a short book, *The Ritualists: Their Romanizing Objects and Work*, published in 1900. In it he was able to show how the Oxford Fathers, let alone Anglo-Catholic extremists, deeply desired reunion with the papacy, and that it was therefore something which emerged in the Oxford movement at its very beginning. One of the most outspoken groups which worked specifically for such an aim was the Association for Promoting the Unity of Christendom, which was founded in 1857 by Ambrose Phillipps de Lisle and the bishop of Brechin, A. P. Forbes. The concept of the unity of Christendom by definition excluded all reference to Protestant bodies of any kind. However, the Anglo-Catholic apologist of the day, and a member of the Association, R. F. Littledale, admitted that, once unity had been achieved amongst Catholics, Protestant bodies which held to the creeds would then be invited to enter a larger union (Littledale 1878:796). The Association, along with the Society of the Holy Cross, the Alcuin Club, the English Church Union, and especially Lord Halifax, were all roundly condemned by Walsh for their admiration of the Church of Rome and their wish to see the Church of England united to it.

The evidence that Walsh used in extracting passages from the writings of the Oxford Fathers appeared later in the works of Anglo-Papalists in the 1930s, published by the Council for Promoting Catholic Unity. In a series of nine Tractates, whose symbol at first sight looked like the crossed keys of the papacy, an effort was made to show how all through history Rome had a unique place and that theologians, and especially Anglican theologians, exalted it as the centre of Catholic Christianity (the *Tractates* are to be found under Harris *et al.* 1933; see also Harris 1934). The early Oxford Fathers, for example, Froude, Ward, and Pusey, were far more pro-Roman than most people have realized; so wrote the Rev Silas M. Harris, who largely organized the Tractates (Harris 1934). To those who promoted Catholic unity, the Holy See (as it was always called) was virtually without error (see ch. 9.9). The group grew out of a centenary manifesto, which appeared in 1932 and was signed by 350 priests, among them Fynes-Clinton (see ch. 1.3). This was an open declaration at the time of the centenary of the Oxford movement that the Catholic revival was at its heart concerned with reunification with the Holy See and that any other position was contrary to the goal of the movement. The Council for Promoting Catholic Unity had another object – to counteract modernism and liberalism in the Church of England, not least to oppose certain Anglo-Catholic leaders who were suspect, such as Charles Gore, E. G. Selwyn, and Wilfrid Knox. Doubtless such a move could be interpreted as the desire of Anglo-Papalists to follow the line taken by the *Curia* in fighting and suppressing doctrinal error. There seemed to be a spate of books around the 1930s by Anglo-Papalists calling for reunion. Another example was *The Oxford Movement* by the writer, J. Lewis May. For him the object of Tractarianism was clear:

> This great union [with Rome] I hold to be the end implicit in the theory of the Tractarians (though some of them would have strenuously denied it – as many of their successors do to this day) – this great union, and not the establishment of any rival to the Church of Rome, which would adopt her rites and appropriate her doctrines in all things save her allegiance to the See of St. Peter.
>
> (May 1933:v)

Some twenty years before the appearance of the Tractates, Fr Fynes-Clinton (1876–1959) had started the Catholic League which had similar aims to those of these other groups and which has aleady been commented on in connection with Anglo-Papalism (see ch. 1.3).

It cannot be denied that the strivings of Anglo-Papalists towards unity, together with more moderate trends in Tractarianism, were largely responsible for Anglican leaders as a whole spearheading efforts at reunion amongst all churches. This movement began to gather considerable impetus in the 1920s and continued to grow thereafter. Over against that, however, stands the sectarian ambiguity of Anglo-Papalists, which is to be seen most clearly in 1864 when, through the efforts of Cardinal Manning, the Association for Promoting the Unity of Christendom was condemned in Rome. Such a threatening reaction did not deter the Association, which sent a letter of protest to the pope. Nor did the movement generally abandon its goal, despite the condemnation of Anglican orders by Pope Leo XIII in 1896, when the Malines Conversations were terminated by papal intervention in the 1920s, and when there was not the slightest sign of initiative coming from the Vatican for reunion with the Church of England. There was always the vain hope that the pope would turn a kindly eye towards them. Thus, Anglo-Papalists and Anglo-Catholics, openly seeking a reunion, were in the peculiar position of a person who wants to marry someone who does not love him and rejects his overtures. It places Anglo-Catholics in an extraordinarily narrow and isolated position and one where 'reality' does not seem to impinge upon them. And, when eventually, and totally unexpectedly, moves were made towards church *rapprochement* as a result of Vatican II, Anglo-Catholics were not sought out as a recognized church body. Any possible marriage now would have to be with someone else (see ch. 11.5).

6 Conclusion

Some intellectually inclined Anglo-Catholics had no desire to be considered sectarian, to be branded as insular, or even to be thought of as characteristically British. Nor did they wish to be viewed as being members of an ecclesiastical party. Just as the Roman Catholic Church was thoroughly international and global, so Anglo-Catholics would see themselves in the same mould. Frank Weston, in a circular letter sent out before the 1923 Anglo-Catholic congress, wrote:

> We now stand for the Catholic Faith common to the East and West. We are not concerned with the shibboleths of low Church, high Church, broad Church, liberal, modernist, or even the new 'non-party' party. We stand or fall with Christ's Church, catholic and apostolic. And we wait patiently till the Holy Father and the Orthodox Patriarchs recognize us as of their own stock. We are not a party: we are those in the Anglican Communion who refuse to be limited by party rules

and party creeds. Our appeal is to the Catholic Creed, to
Catholic worship, and to Catholic practice.

(quoted in Wilson 1940:108–9)

The great desire that Anglo-Catholics should be seen as part of a
universal church was not matched by realistic thinking. They
might not want to be thought of as being ultra-British, belonging
to a religious party, even being sectarian, but if ever there was a
uniquely English product it was Anglo-Catholicism. Set in a
particular socio-religious culture, it was unique to Anglicanism
and that meant it was unique within a church already unique.
Extremism in Anglo-Catholicism in aping the Church of Rome
has, as we have shown in this chapter, given rise to its sectarian
characteristics. The coterie of extremists remained so, claiming
more than their share of the truth – Catholic principles as they
saw them were confined to a corner. Their sectarianism, their
attack on things British, not least the Established Church, made
them many enemies, not least in high places and in the political
world. Their actions were sometimes seen to be 'anti-religious' in
hindering a wider acceptance of Christianity. So C. T. Longley,
who became archbishop of Canterbury in 1862, in his charge as
bishop of Ripon in 1850, could say:

> It is the follies and extravagances of those who would mimic
> the Roman Catholic Church . . . that have so materially
> hindered the progress of our own, and entailed upon us many
> of the evils which we now have reason to deplore.
>
> (quoted in Yates 1975:13).

Perhaps Anglo-Catholics had no alternative. That many went
so near to Roman Catholic practice inevitably meant rejection by
the authorities. Therefore, despite their good leadership and
their able thinkers, they always found themselves in opposition,
removed from centres of power, and with little hope of becoming
the majority. Admittedly, as we have demonstrated, they grew in
numbers to quite a remarkable extent, but although they
commanded a largish following they were inevitably viewed with
suspicion. Having found themselves in this position, either by
adopting it or being forced to assume it, they quickly realized its
advantages and what was adversity was turned into gain. In many
cases they received compensations in having gained psychological
satisfactions, not least in the notion that the truth of the minority
was more important than the ignorance of the majority.
W. L. Knox lamented the fact that he found in Cambridge 'how
many of the young really like a clerical sect'. This wish to be in a

minority appeared in a recent letter to the *Church Times* from
two Anglo-Catholic correspondents, in which they supported
what they knew were unpopular attitudes. They wrote: 'We
would all do well to note carefully George Bernard Shaw's
words: "The majority is always wrong; the minority is sometimes
right"' (*CT*, 24 April 1982). What kind of Catholic thinking is
this? Hardly a Catholicism reigning supreme: it is nothing short
of individualism. As we have seen, one Anglo-Catholic writer,
T. A. Lacey, admitted that the movement was sectarian but said
that there was nothing to be ashamed of. A sect, as a school of
thought around a leader, could be for good or ill: it could be for
development or for fossilization (Lacey 1926:181). The intrinsic
goodness of Anglo-Catholicism was that it stood for 'a focus of
Catholicity within the Catholic Church of England'. He held that,
'when the temper of Catholicity has permeated the whole
Church', Anglo-Catholicism would have fulfilled its sectarian
function, that is, it would have ceased to be a sect by becoming a
church (Lacey 1926:182). In one way that position has probably
already been reached. As Troeltsch has observed, a sect can
indeed become a larger body, a church, for that is what happened
to Christianity in its early days. In that case, however, the sect
was an independent body, not a movement within the body.
Wriggle as one may out of the situation, the ambiguity still
remains – Anglo-Catholicism is a social entity which claims to be
something of the universal but yet has the status of a sect.

It seems strange, in the light of its ideology and its constant
looking towards Rome, that Anglo-Catholics should either be
branded as sectarian or even acknowledge themselves to be
sectarian in spirit. Surely the notion of a Catholic sect or Catholic
sectarianism is a contradiction in terms? What Catholic wants to
be called sectarian? To speak of a Catholic sect can only mean
one thing, a small group of people who were originally Roman
Catholic but who have cut themselves off from the Church, or
who have been expelled from it. Such a group of people might
consider themselves to be Catholic in so far as they subscribe to
the creeds and rituals of the Roman Catholic Church, along with
the valid ordination of their clergy. We have already mentioned
one such group, the Polish National Church, and there have been
other similar bodies in the history of Christendom. The same
argument applies to sects which emerged in the middle ages, such
as the Waldensians and Albigensians. Today, there is a group,
actually within the Roman Catholic Church, which has characteristics in some ways not far removed from those of Anglo-
Catholicism. It is the movement of Archbishop Lefebvre in

France which upholds the ethos of the Roman Catholic Church in its Ultramontane mode, that is, the Church as it had established itself up to the time of Vatican II. One thing is certain: the Lefebvre movement faces the same ambiguities as Anglo-Catholicism in so far as they are both sectarian in outlook and make their reference point Catholicism.

Anglo-Catholicism has parallels with other religious movements which exhibit sectarian qualities. The most obvious example is Methodism in its early phase. Like Anglo-Catholicism it began its life in the Church of England and it, too, was suspected of being a popish plot by weakening the Church from within, of propagating popish doctrines, and of influencing dissatisfied social classes. This is not the place to explore the parallels further, but simply to note that Anglo-Catholicism has not been the only movement in Anglicanism which has had sectarian characteristics. But one point is important: unlike Methodism, it has not become an independent ecclesiastical body.

Chapter 8

Ambiguity over sexuality

1 Introduction

'There are three sexes: male, female, and priests.' So runs the well-known French saying. What precisely is implied by the sexuality of the clergy in this connection has never been clear. Were they celibate in the strict sense of the word and, true to their implied standards, did they never embark on sexual activity? Or were they completely indifferent to sexual drives and could they therefore be called asexual? Were they homosexual by orientation and practice? Or were they bisexual, going through phases of sexual attraction to both sexes? The notion of the third sex is difficult to interpret. What is important is to see that the saying applies only to a priesthood where celibacy is demanded. It would not have the same force if applied to clergy of the Church of England, where today over 80 per cent are married – a figure that has probably not changed much over the past century. Its lack of relevance to that church is all the more strengthened by the fact that some observers would point to the particular contribution to society which Anglican clergy are said to have made, at least in the nineteenth century, by creating examples of warm family life to which everyone might aspire. And all this is quite apart from the fact that sons from clerical homes have consistently helped to swell the ranks of the professions.

In any church where the clergy are allowed to marry, question marks are often placed against those who, with the passing of years, do not marry. Have they no interest in sexuality, in children, in family life? Are they afraid of such ventures? And, with our current knowledge of psychiatry and the workings of the human psyche, the question arises, are they homosexuals? Or, are they bisexual? Are they afraid of their sexuality and so remain celibate? Does a religious vocation to celibacy transcend all sexuality? The curious mind wants to know. And the curiosity

184

is particularly pertinent when the subjects are people who are prominent in local or national affairs. Within Anglicanism at least, there was during the nineteenth century, and still is today, an ideological justification for a parson's marital status according to some acknowledged vocation. He has a vocation to the priesthood and perhaps a vocation to celibacy as well.

2 Vocation and ambiguity

The question of whether a priest has been called to marriage or celibacy has been debated far more extensively in high-church and Anglo-Catholic circles than amongst those of central or Evangelical persuasion. It was of considerable importance to the Catholic-minded because, although it was often couched in terms of vocation, it contained certain theological overtones. Nor was it a question of marriage and celibacy being options of equal merit. There was a strong normative streak, which maintained that it was better to be unmarried for the goal of dedicated service to Christ. Those who advocated celibacy often appealed to the example of Christ himself and to the writings of the early fathers. And what more telling evidence could be mustered than the fact that the Catholic church has always extolled virginity and celibacy? It was a requirement for joining a religious community and also, during most of its history, it made celibacy obligatory for those entering the priesthood. Traditionally celibacy was linked with asceticism and in embracing celibacy monks, nuns, and priests identified themselves with the spirit of self-sacrifice which was called for by Christ and exhibited in his life (see the plea for celibacy in *CT*, 11 January 1933, p. 163). The argument was that each priest could view himself as an *alter Christus*.

Most of the debate in high-church and Anglo-Catholic circles has centred as much on the theological arguments for celibacy as on utilitarian ones. It was held that the unmarried priest could give more time to his professional work than could the married priest. He could go into certain situations, for example into slum parishes or into missions overseas, which the married man would inevitably enter with some trepidation, being anxious for the well-being of his wife and family. The unmarried man would need a smaller salary than the married priest and could employ a curate, if necessary, to be paid out of his own income. Indeed, an unmarried priest could remain a curate all his life. But there was also the argument that the unmarried man would be more popular and effective amongst the poor since he could spend more time with his parishioners than a priest with a wife and family. Charles Booth, in his survey of London, made much of this point. To live a life of voluntary poverty seemed a good way to gain the ear of the poor of London (Booth 1902,7:23ff.). The utilitarian arguments for celibacy could be undergirded by citing the fact that much of the success of the Roman Catholic Church in evangelizing large parts of the world in the past, and in the maintenance of its parish system and its bureaucratic, centralized power, has been due to the devoted work and loyalty of unmarried priests who have needed minimal economic rewards for their services. To Anglican clergy dedicated to the catholicization of their church, a largely celibate priesthood was held to be highly desirable, not least as a means of effecting the various aims of the movement. The ideal was to some degree realized, for many Anglo-Catholic priests from the mid-nineteenth century onwards embraced celibacy. And so powerful has been the acceptance of the ideal amongst some of the laity that in one Anglo-Catholic parish where the priest took a wife in middle age a parishioner remarked that he thought it was illegal for clergy to marry! The strong, ideological norm that Catholic-minded clergy should not marry is expressed in the phrase 'committing matrimony', suggesting an act not far short of adultery (Stephenson 1972:62). Another way of putting it was in the absurd formula: a priest is celibate, a clergyman married: when a man marries he ceases to be a priest! For 'established' celibate priests to cross the divide was something of a shock to parishioners with deep-seated beliefs that their clergy must be celibate. Something of this comes out in the novels of Barbara Pym (for example, Pym 1952). And *Punch* in 1929 captures the Anglo-Catholic attitude towards married clergy:

Fiancée: 'After we're married, dear, you won't mind if I don't come to your church much, will you?'
Curate: 'But why ever not, precious?'
Fiancée: 'Well, you see, I don't really approve of married clergymen.'

(Punch, 6 November 1929)

'One priest writing of another said he was 'a dear man with a large humorous face and, surprisingly enough, a wife' (Stephenson 1972:69). The person who wrote those words also referred to a 'Fr. Bristowe of Bagborough, one of the great parish priests, [who] even went so far as to try and persuade clergy-wives to leave their husbands and boasted as a virtue of the separations he had caused' (Stephenson 1972:77).

Many Anglo-Catholic parishes, and certainly the majority of the famous ones, have been able to ensure that incumbents and curates were always unmarried. And if anyone crossed the Rubicon he would have to leave. Thus, in the well-known church of St Alban's, Holborn, a vicar, H. C. Frith, 'caused something of a flutter in Anglo-Catholic circles by resigning in order to get married' (Reynolds 1965:282). In the past and still in many cases today Anglo-Catholic priests who are married are barred from becoming incumbents of well known Catholic parishes. In a similar vein, the story is told of an ordinand who recently wanted to join a parish staff as curate where all the clergy were unmarried. He was told he would be accepted only if he terminated his engagement.

Anglo-Catholic ideals concerning the celibacy of the clergy contain considerable ambiguity. If the issues were those merely of personal choice, in the way in which doctors or carpenters choose to be married or single, there would be little need to consider it in a theological light. But, if the celibate priesthood is seen as an ideal, then an ambiguous situation arises. The ambiguity does not occur in the Roman Catholic Church, where to be a priest automatically means embracing a life of celibacy; the one implies the other. But, since the Church of England has always allowed its clergy to be married, the possibility of choice is ever present. Anglo-Catholics knew they could not impose a celibate priesthood on the entire Church. Their only hope was to continue to argue for increasing numbers of those who would accept celibacy rather than matrimony. A persuasive advocate for the celibacy of the priesthood was Vernon Stuckey Coles (1845–1929), formerly a principal of Pusey House, Oxford, who was influential amongst undergraduates around the turn of the century. He asserted that 'as a layman ought to have some special reason for not marrying, so a priest ought to have a special one for marrying' (Borlase 1930:18). Here is the desire to uphold a dual standard for laity and clergy, something, if one includes the religious life, deep in the heart of Roman Catholicism.

The utilitarian argument used by Anglo-Catholics can be justified only by results. Do celibate priests in fact give more time to their ministry than married priests? Is their ministry more effective? Such questions are crucial but impossible to answer in an objective way. Inevitably one falls back on personal experience and limited observation. Not all celibates have embraced tough jobs, not all sought low salaries, and not all devoted long hours to the ministry. And one has to compare the achievements of married clergy, both Anglo-Catholic and non-Anglo-Catholic. Looking at Anglo-Catholicism today, one might well ask where are the celibate heroes of the 1880s, the 1900s, the 1920s? It is very difficult to discern them. One of the last 'great men' whose lives have appeared in print was Fr Joe Williamson, who was himself born in the slums of the East End, did not go to a university, and was married with several children (Williamson 1963).

3 The charge of ho:nosexuality

As soon as some Tractarians and Anglo-Catholics began to advocate celibacy for the clergy, Protestant extremists, and even some of the less extreme, began to question the rightness of the policy and to doubt the motives of those who pressed the claims for and practised such a life. One charge was that celibacy would lead to fornication, in the same way as it was rumoured to exist amongst certain Roman Catholic priests who, it was said, cohabited with young girls and nuns (see Hill 1971). Perhaps reflecting on the writings of the founding fathers of classical Protestantism, such as Luther, Calvin, and Bucer, the Protestant apologists felt that enforced celibacy, or deliberately embraced celibacy, was unnatural and that it was impossible for men in such a state to contain morally their sexual drives (see Biot t.1963:7ff.). The danger of celibate priests committing acts of fornication at least implied 'normal' or heterosexual drives and attitudes. Where Roman Catholic priests were the targets of hostility, immorality committed with women and young girls was the object of attack. That might have been the charge levelled against Anglo-Catholic celibate priests, but fairly early on hostile critics of the high-church movement were quick to hint, and sometimes more than hint, that many of the advocates of celibacy had inclinations towards homosexuality. Naturally in the nineteenth century the charges were discreetly made, not least because it was difficult to substantiate them and because of their very serious nature. Right up to the years which preceded the Second World War, homosexuality was a taboo subject very seldom, if ever, given a public hearing. The only occasions were those such as the trial of Oscar Wilde (see Symonds 1984). Within the churches the taboos were even stronger. Nevertheless, in the course of time homosexuality has commonly been called 'the Anglo-Catholic disease', and, in the early days of the movement, hostile Protestants referred to Anglo-Catholicism as a sexual aberration. In his well known novel, *Brideshead Revisited*, the convert to Roman Catholicism, Evelyn Waugh, wrote about the crude advice given to a young man in the early 1920s, shortly to go to Oxford, 'Beware of the Anglo-Catholics – they're all sodomites with unpleasant accents' (Waugh 1945:35).

4 Problems of definition and identification

In trying to deal with the subject of homosexuality in an objective and scientific way, the crucial question is to discern what is meant by homosexual behaviour and attitudes.

Such is the complex nature of homosexuality that some argue that it does not exist in any homogeneous form and is therefore beyond definition. This is no occasion to enter into the controversy. The purpose on hand is to relate male homosexuality to Anglo-Catholicism and in order to do that some kind of initial definition is required.

At the heart of homosexuality is the disposition of the sexual desires of an individual towards someone of the same sex, which may or may not be accompanied by an emotional attachment. The French priest and doctor, Marc Oraison, has put forward the definition that a homosexual is 'a person beyond puberty who feels sexually attracted, exclusively or otherwise, to people of the same sex' (Oraison t.1977:13). With such a starting-point we would not disagree.

In trying to establish a framework based on such a fundamental disposition amongst adult men who are potentially or actively homosexual, something wider than a bare definition is required. It is necessary because Anglo-Catholicism is being examined where 'hard data' are difficult to come by and where much of the evidence in the past appears to relate to latent homosexuality. Based on a cluster of attitudes around the definition of homosexuality just stated, the framework posits three levels.

The first level relates to the general preference that individual adult men have to be in the company of other males, whether boys or adults, or both. Such individuals feel more relaxed, joyful, intellectually stimulated, and generally happier in such company. They prefer to be in 'a man's world', not only for purposes of work, but also for mental and cultural stimulation and interchange. They obviously find some such company emotionally stimulating. The preference may be undergirded by negative attitudes towards women, who may frighten them and who are often labelled as 'emotional', 'irrational', 'stupid'. Such men as a rule do not feel attracted by the sexual and biological functions unique to women. The extreme position is that of the misogynist. This level is called the social level.

The second level relates to those who as individuals become strongly attached in an exclusive way to one particular male. The relationship might be said to be approaching a love relationship where the one has an emotional fixation on the other. The attachments are often high-minded, noble, and tender, especially where one person is deeply concerned for the well-being of the other. This level is called the emotional level.

Finally, there exists the level of homosexuality which involves physical contact between individuals, such as handling, fondling, and kissing, and which may issue in such forms of physical satisfaction as are possible between two males. Since this level involves men who are sexually active, it refers to those who are commonly called practising homosexuals. In today's parlance the homosexual is located at this level. It may be held that such physical activity is an expression of the emotional level and may be associated, but is not always, with notions of fidelity. On the other hand, it may be confined to seeking male prostitutes or to very transient acts involving an anonymous partner. Emotional considerations may not be involved as they are at the second level. The goal is physical satisfaction, though it may also be accompanied by emotional involvement. This level is referred to as the physical level.

The terms homophile or homophiliac could aptly be used, and indeed are, for the first two levels, the social and the emotional. These terms are now widely accepted. They are to be contrasted with the general use of the word homosexual which is associated with the physical level. Yet it must be firmly asserted that the three levels are by no means mutually exclusive. A homosexual's life may include all three or it may involve only one level. Any combination is possible. Nor can it be maintained that there is a natural progression from the first to the third level, although that often is the case. Nor, again, do the levels in any way negate, nor are they negated by, the notion of bisexuality. The levels constitute nothing more than a framework to analyse the many possibilities that are associated with the term homosexuality.

5 Application to Anglo-Catholicism

In relating these three levels of homosexuality to Anglo-Catholicism, practical difficulties are immediately encountered. Only one or two studies have been made on the subject. In dealing with the early days of the Oxford movement and Anglo-Catholicism, the historian, David Hilliard, has marshalled considerable material in his article, 'Unenglish and unmanly: Anglo-Catholicism and homosexuality', to show that from the very beginning of the Catholic revival homosexuals, or those inclined towards homosexuality, have been associated with it (Hilliard 1982). But some fifty years before, at the time of the centenary of the Oxford movement, Geoffrey Faber, a fellow of All Souls, Oxford, who had become much influenced by Freudian analysis, published what some saw as a despicable book, *Oxford Apostles* (Faber 1933). In it he attempted to show that Newman had homosexual proclivities.

Until the late 1960s the main evidence about homosexuality and Anglo-Catholicism related to the first two levels, the social and emotional. This was very much the case in the approach of Faber and Hilliard. All references to homosexuality or homosexual tendencies were heavily veiled or obliquely hinted at. Christian and Victorian decorum called for silence, and the confessional was the only really legitimate place for the matter to be raised. But the evidence there is sealed by a vow of absolute silence. All public evidence of homosexuality had to be deduced from biographies and autobiographies, where hints or accidental references may have been dropped. This paucity or uncertainty of evidence has led to disputation about the interpretation of evidence. The rumours that homosexuality was closely correlated with Anglo-Catholicism, especially at the physical level, could never be proved. To offer further oblique evidence is possible. Quite a lot of material can be marshalled to show how amongst clergy in particular there has been a strongly misogynist outlook (see Penhale 1986:147–8). In the light of current events and homosexuals 'coming out', this kind of information is of limited value.

Today in society at large homosexuality is there for all to see. It is a subject which frequently appears in the mass media, in novels, in surveys, and in various churches. The issue is not so much whether homosexuality exists at the social and emotional levels or even at the physical level, but the extent of it and its ramifications.

The Wolfenden Report of 1957 was instrumental in removing legal sanctions against certain forms of homosexuality, which were enacted ten years later. As a result homosexuals 'came out' – declared themselves to be what they were – often without any feelings of guilt or embarrassment. Their proclivities were catered for by gay associations, gay pubs, gay clubs. They pressed their case by furthering their rights in demanding no discrimination on account of their sexual orientation, particularly in the matter of being allowed to live their own life style and in seeking employment. Subsequently the situation has been made more explicit and more complicated by the advent of AIDS, where, at the moment, on grounds of probability sufferers from the virus are likely to be homosexuals or drug addicts or both. To be diagnosed as having AIDS immediately makes the person suspect of belonging to one or other of those categories. And, yet again, a new vista has been opened up, together with a number of complications, through public investigations into child abuse, which has both homosexual and heterosexual connotations.

One would have thought that the churches, which have always supported traditional sexual morality, namely, that all sexual acts outside marriage are sinful, would have stood firm, at least in the matter of doctrine and in the face of a fast-accelerating acceptance of the permissive society. That has not been the case. Certain churches, those with a powerful liberal component, have shown themselves to be in sympathy with those who would attack the traditional Christian ethic on sexuality. Others have stood firm, notably the Roman Catholic Church and Evangelical groups in and outside the Church of England. In 1979 an official Anglican report on homosexuality, commonly referred to as the Gloucester Report, was produced and then debated in 1981 with the result that an open, liberal position began to be favoured. Under certain conditions, it was argued, such as those of a stable, loving relation, genital homosexual relations could be seen to be moral and have the same status as those of a married hetereosexual couple. One effect of the changes of attitude which have occurred in the Church is that those who have physical homosexual relationships are open and frank about them. In 1981 in the General Synod, a clerical member publicly said he was a homosexual. He has maintained, however, that such practices are immoral (*Daily Telegraph*, 31 December 1987). Of course the churches have not in recent times condemned homosexual dispositions as being sinful. What is open to debate and censure is whether homosexual physical acts are.

What has been most surprising has been that Anglo-Catholics did not as a group stand firm and follow the ideal they have always respected, the Roman Catholic Church. And so it was that traditional attitudes towards homosexuality in the physical mode, fornication, and other sexual irregularities were not condemned by Anglo-Catholics. The moral barriers which had operated for so long and which spoke of potential tension between sexual desire and serving Christ seemed to disappear or were thought to be unnecessary. It cannot be overstressed that the issues over homosexuality in the churches must be seen as part of changes generally in morality concerning sexual relations outside marriage and the possibility of remarriage of divorced persons.

From personal observation, the moral controls concerning clergy indulging in homosexual activity appeared to be effective until the advent of the permissive society. With legal sanctions removed and a greater acceptance of homosexuality, Anglo-Catholic clergy tended to declare their sexual orientation and sometimes openly acknowledged their homosexual activity. The clergy were prepared to accept the basic argument of homosexuals that their life style is a legitimate and moral alternative to a heterosexual one.

It was not, however, only Anglo-Catholic clergy who accepted the new situation but those of other churchmanship as well. It is often, therefore, very difficult to discover from press-cuttings the churchmanship of those clergy who openly declare their homosexuality or who are put on trial for soliciting or for seducing the young or are charged with child abuse.

When, towards the end of 1987, the Rev Tony Higton, an Evangelical incumbent, challenged the General Synod of the Church of England over the presence of homosexual clergy in the Church and called on the Synod to reaffirm traditional Biblical teaching in matters of sexuality, he did not specifically refer to Anglo-Catholics. He was not concerned with types of churchmanship, except that he was opposed to those who might be labelled liberal. He pointed to the fact that homosexuality *per se* was no bar to ordination and to the existence of the Gay Christian Movement (see *The Times*, 13 July 1987; Higton *et al.* 1987:76). The Gay Christian Movement is at present located in St Botolph's church, Aldgate, where, it is alleged, undesirable publications are sold (*Independent*, 30 April 1987; and see Higton *et al.* 1987). The Lesbian and Gay Christian Movement has today (1987) about 4,000 members, of whom 1,000 are said to be clergy (*The Times*, 31 December 1987). Of course, not all these are necessarily Anglican or Anglo-Catholic.

Yet the problem remains of the long-standing association of Anglo-Catholicism with homosexuality. It has in no way been negated by the changes in the social and ecclesiastical scenes (see Penhale 1986:148). And it is remarkable that some of the first clergy to declare publicly that they were homosexuals were Anglo-Catholics. In a Gallup poll taken at the end of 1987 amongst 300 Anglican clergy, to the statement 'The church can never approve of homosexual acts', 28 per cent of the high-church group disagreed, while only 1 per cent of the low church group took the same stance. Overall three-quarters of the clergy supported the proposition (*Daily Telegraph*, 23 December 1987). Indeed, it was deduced from the survey that the high-church group was traditional in everything except this moral issue. Amongst the single clergy, 35 per cent disagreed with the proposition that homosexual acts can never be approved (*Daily Telegraph*, 23 December 1987).

Probably one of the most moving and honest accounts of the private life of a homosexual priest is the autobiography of Harry Williams, a traditional Anglo-Catholic in his early days and formerly a dean of Trinity College, Cambridge (Williams 1982). Another example, which was taken up by the national press, is that of the self-declaration made by the Rev Peter Elers when he was vicar of the famous Anglo-Catholic church at Thaxted. Although a married man with four adopted children, he openly declared from the pulpit that he was a homosexual and later, in 1976, he became the first president of the Gay Christian Movement. He performed a service of blessing for two lesbian couples. In 1986 he died and money was later raised to perpetuate his name. Of other well-known Anglo-Catholics one might recall Fr Hugh Bishop, who was for a number of years a much respected superior of the Community of the Resurrection and who was popular amongst undergraduates, not least in Oxford university. In the 1970s he left the order and set up house with another man. Amongst prominent lay Anglo-Catholics of recent times, one might mention Tom Driberg. In 1977 he published his autobiography, *Ruling Passions*. He was a journalist, traveller, and member of Parliament. In the book he confessed that from adolescence he had been a promiscuous homosexual (Driberg 1977:143). As a result of rebellion against home values, he confessed to '"deviant" sex, "exotic" religion – and Left-wing politics' (Driberg 1977:16). The exotic religion, needless to say, was Anglo-Catholicism: for many years he was a staunch member of St Mary's, Bourne Street, in the West End (see ch. 1.4). He delivered the University Sermon in Oxford in 1965 (Driberg 1977:59). More recently in the public eye has been Sir Maurice Oldfield. He was head of MI6 from 1973–8, was said to be an active homosexual and seen as a potential security risk (*The Times*, 23 April 1987). St Matthew's, Westminster, was the church he attended regularly.

6 Some recent evidence

In one respect it is hardly surprising that homosexuality is found in Anglo-Catholicism, since according to any general distribution one would expect to find it in every religious group. On a priori grounds Anglo-Catholicism would be no exception. But in the light of so much evidence this does not seem to be the case. To try to substantiate the position we present some more facts, disjointed though they are (see note on p. 205).

When it is said, as sometimes it is by psychologists, that between 7 and 10 per cent of the population is homosexual, there is the implication that the proportion refers to practising homosexuals or to those who have practised as such. Kinsey and his colleagues held, admittedly in their researches in the United States, that 37 per cent of their very considerable sample of males had had some homosexual experience during their lives, that 10 per cent were 'more or less exclusively' homosexual for at least three years, and that 4 per cent had been 'exclusively homosexual' from adolescence (Kinsey *et al.* 1948:610). This was a study carried out as early as the 1940s. As a rule such evidence is derived from asking people a direct question as to whether or not they are homosexual. No comparable figures for clergy, irrespective of their denomination, have ever been compiled, at least in this country. One small contribution to the issue comes from research, carried out by Paul Appleton, amongst Anglican clergy in the Bristol area. He found that a sixth (17 per cent) of the respondents declared themselves to be homosexual and this was without reference to churchmanship (Paul Appleton, personal communication: see his forthcoming Ph.D. thesis, Bristol university). Elsewhere there are only pointers or indicators which are based on certain assumptions. Since clergy who have contracted AIDS are more likely to have become infected through homosexual relations than through using drugs, incidents of AIDS amongst clergy have a particular poignancy. The first person to die of AIDS in Britain was an Anglican prison chaplain (see Higton *et al.* 1987:59). In July 1987 it was reported in the General Synod that over twenty clergy were suffering from AIDS, but *The Times* reported that 'the total of those [clergy] who are known to be HIV positive is believed to be climbing towards three figures' (13 July 1987). The diocese of London is generally regarded as one of the most Anglo-Catholic dioceses at the present time and a recent report by the religious correspondent of *The Times* states that:

There is said to be at least one Anglican deanery in London where more than a third of the clergy are homosexual. Those who know the scene well could name half a dozen nationally prominent churchmen who are, at least by long-standing repute and good evidence, the same. And 'homosexuality' in this context means not just a disposition of character, but an activity.

(*The Times*, 23 October 1987)

In a survey carried out in the 1950s amongst 127 male homosexuals, a self-confessed homosexual said: 'I was once High Anglican, that's *the* homosexual religion. Then I had a dispute with my confessor about homosexuality and left in high dudgeon' (Westwood 1960:55, Westwood's emphasis). Incidentally, one man said that he had learned about homosexuality when he was 16 years of age 'from the vicar who was preparing me for confirmation. Both theory and practice' (Westwood 1960:23). Gordon Westwood, the director of the survey, said that 'some of the contacts maintained that the highest proportion of homosexuals who are regular churchgoers favoured the Anglo-Catholic churches' (Westwood 1960:54–5). Similar evidence comes from a case history used by F. Musgrove, formerly professor of education in Manchester university. His book, *Margins of the Mind*, was written later than that of Westwood and in the period which followed that of the permissive society. He recorded the story of a homosexual, a Cambridge graduate, who later became a social worker (Musgrove 1977:31ff.). This man was brought up an Anglican, broke off an engagement, and finally 'came out'. Of his experience in Cambridge he said:

But first I became High Church. I went to a very High Church college at Cambridge, and it was quite noticeable that the chapel crowd were homosexuals. I became scared to death, because the whole of my life was bent towards cloaking this and denying it to myself. So I began to find it intolerable to be an Anglo-Catholic, because it tarred you with the suspicion of being a homosexual, which was the one thing I was most at pains to avoid.

(Musgrove 1977:32)

Then he became a Roman Catholic, although he later abandoned his faith, and was delighted to find that the social mix in the Catholic Church was very much broader and healthier than in Anglo-Catholic churches. He observed: 'A very large percentage of Catholic converts are gay – that's something that you notice, and of course a large number of High Churchmen also' (Musgrove 1977:31). This observation about Catholic converts has frequently been made (see ch. 9.6).

In a similar vein Jeffrey Weeks in a much praised book, *Coming Out*, stated that: 'Anglo-Catholicism seems to have been a particular breeding-ground for elevated passions, but it is highly unlikely that anything improper happened in most cases' (Weeks 1977:34). He implies that until recent times Anglo-Catholicism contained a great deal of latent homosexuality, such as we have suggested in positing the first two levels, and that it was contained within moral parameters.

Tom Sutcliffe, who has been much associated with Anglican church choirs from the inside, has stated that homosexuality – and here he seems to imply physical relations – was more likely to be found amongst churchmen of the 'smells and bells' variety than amongst Evangelicals. Referring to a homosexual church in the United States, he wryly commented: 'though mass at St Alban's Holborn was supposed to be the next best thing' (Sutcliffe 1973:553).

In recent years Anglo-Catholic and high-church theological colleges in and around Oxford have been centres of homosexual troubles and scandals. A. N. Wilson in his novel, *Unguarded Hours* (1978), portrayed life in one such college in the wake of the moral openness of the 1970s. Students were characterized as homosexuals of the female type. They were given or adopted female names and used endearing language: 'Still as Father said to us on our last Walsingham pilgrimage, "Grin and bear it, darlings, till opening time"'(Wilson 1978:100). And in another vein, 'I knew Felicity Fogg [a member of the staff] would get her knickers in a twist over those cottas' (Wilson 1978:109). How far Wilson's novel can be said to be in any way an accurate account of the ethos of an Anglo-Catholic theological college at the time might be debated. It must not be forgotten that he was himself an ordinand in such a college. What is most interesting is that when the book was published it did not cause an outrage, nor, so far as is known, did the author create such an effect that he was in danger of being taken to court. It has been tacitly accepted (see reference to Wilson in the *Independent*, 30 April 1987; and the debate in the General Synod on 11 November 1987 as reported in *The Times*, 12 November 1987). Penhale, writing in the mid-1980s, stated: 'As is well known within the Anglo-Catholic sub-culture, certain theological colleges, societies and churches have the reputation of being homosexual enclaves' (Penhale 1986:148). He admits that the evidence rests on hearsay but, it might be added, hearsay which has not been contradicted.

Some interesting figures emerge from a recent survey of theological colleges (the following statistics have been provided by the Advisory Council for the Church's Ministry, Church House, Westminster, and cover the years 1980–4). In three Anglo-Catholic theological colleges, the percentages of unmarried students over the age of 30 were 50, 40, and 35. By contrast Evangelical colleges had very small percentages indeed, and one college of that persuasion had no one who was unmarried and over 30 years of age. The conclusion would therefore be that men of mature years who are training for the ministry and who are unmarried are mainly found in Anglo-Catholic theological colleges. It is amongst such people that one might expect to find a number of homosexuals. In a similar way one might note the findings of a recent survey amongst Anglican clergy for the country as a whole. Of all single clergy 42 per cent described themselves as high church. But of single clergy in city areas, the percentage rose to 61 (Gallup 1986:25). It is generally held that homosexuals tend to gather in cities.

Some Anglo-Catholics themselves have been apologetically aware of the charges that can be levelled against the movement in the matter of homosexuality defined in the widest terms, for at certain periods of its history it was obvious that it projected a form of religion particularly attractive to pious sanctuary boys (see quotation in Bocock 1973:40). Anglo-Catholicism, especially in its early days, was definitely thought to be a man's religion, primarily a religion for young men (Hilliard 1982:190; and see ch. 4.3). It still seems more male-orientated than most sections of the Anglican Church.

All this is fragmented evidence but fragments keep on being found and the evidence is becoming increasingly strong that the level of homosexuality in Anglo-Catholicism, especially amongst clergy, is above the general level. As we have said there is the need for scientific enquiry, but, until it has been carried out, individual observations and the results of limited surveys all add up to the one conclusion. And nothing has come to light which negates it.

7 Why the association?

The question which the enquiring mind will not abandon is why is there such an alleged high proportion of Anglo-Catholics, priests and lay people, who have homosexual proclivities? Although, as we have seen, the characteristic has been noted for a long time, very seldom has anyone tried to find an answer to the question. Before attempting to fill the gap, one or two caveats need to be made at the outset. Despite the ever-continuing research undertaken in medicine, psychiatry, and sociology, the cause or causes of homosexuality have still not been determined. There is no intention of rehearsing here, even in summary form, the state of play amongst scientists working on the problem. Nevertheless some general observations are not out of place.

No one has yet demonstrated that biological factors have an exclusive bearing on homosexual attitudes and practices. Some who emphasize psychological factors often make their starting-point Freud's theory. They argue that homosexuality is brought about by failure on the part of a man to go through the recognized developmental stages of a human male, from the early years to maturity and marriage. The homosexual gets fixed at an early stage when his libido remains focused on males, be they boys or a particular boy, men or a particular man. He fails to move to a stage where his erotic fantasies and emotions centre on women. He thus becomes fixed and unable to take the necessary step of entering into a heterosexual relationship. A more socio-psychological approach bypasses the concept of developmental stages and holds that 'human sexual behaviour is controlled and directed primarily by learning and experience' (Ford and Beach 1952:253; and see Plummer 1975:56–7). This means that at a very early stage erotic fantasy and practice centre, perhaps for a short time, perhaps all one's life, on males, females, or some inanimate object. It is true, of course, that changes do take place in the object of erotic fantasy but the initial stimulus never completely disappears and may continue to be dominant.

Assuming that psychological factors are, if not entirely then to a very large extent, crucial in the sexual orientation of men (and perhaps also of women, where the libido configuration is more complex), it is legitimate to argue that such psychological factors are modified by social forces. As Marcel Mauss has convincingly demonstrated, psychological behaviour is influenced by social determinants, since very few actions are 'natural' and nearly all one's activities, including sexual action, are in some measure determined by cultural or social influences (Mauss 1935).

Amongst those who have demonstrated the influence of cultural or social factors on homosexuality are Ford and Beach (1952), who carried out a survey of a large number of societies around the world. Much was made of attitudes and practices in preliterate societies in connection with homosexuality, and great variation was observed. Because the research had not then been published, the authors were unable to point to the fact that homosexuality was not detected in a survey made amongst the Hutterites. They are members of an Anabaptist sect who live in tightly bounded communities situated in North America (see Eaton and Weil 1955:143).

If variations can be seen to exist between society and society in the matter of homosexuality, then in any one society, especially if it is a large society, one would expect to find variations between social groups where factors which might affect sexual norms and practices are at work. Thus, in British society, coeducational schools, whether boarding- or day-schools, do not appear to be as troubled with homosexuality as are single sex schools, especially boys' schools (see Westwood 1960:26). In the past homosexuality amongst boys in English public schools has been frequently commented on. It has also been observed that, on ships making fairly long voyages, heterosexual men often indulge in homosexual practices whilst at sea but revert to 'normality' when they get on land. As is well known, however, there are some sailors who do not make the change. Again, certain occupations seem to attract homosexuals, notably the theatrical world in its many aspects, the world of musicians, travel agencies, the catering trade and so forth. If the underlying factors operating in such groups could be scientifically determined, one might be in a better position to understand the problem of homosexuality amongst Anglo-Catholics.

In the absence of established influences known to be at work in Anglo-Catholicism, all one can do is to point to possible social factors inherent in the ethos of the movement which encourage, evoke, or sustain homosexuality.

We have already suggested that there exist ambiguities in Anglo-Catholicism which relate to the ideal of celibacy for the clergy. Might it not be possible that the adulation of celibacy is seen as a legitimate rationalization of actual or latent homosexuality? Someone might be drawn to be an Anglo-Catholic priest by reason of the fact that he can give some kind of publicly acceptable doctrinal and moral backing to his homosexual proclivity.

The role of the parish church in society is often overlooked in connection with homosexuality. Because of the ethics of the Gospel and because of pastoral concern, the local church often, but not always, extends a welcome to the lonely. There is no shortage of people with whom one can come into contact. Indeed, Newman once preached a sermon on the subject of the lonely and the church. Many who do not have friends, men and women, find a chance of friendship in churches and it is not surprising, therefore, that homosexuals, on account of their loneliness, certainly in the past, and in their hope of creating friendships with others, gravitate to places where they may have some kind of friendship. The places may be of two kinds: where people can be found generally, as in a parish, or where homosexuals know they can find others of a similar disposition. Of the latter in particular, large towns and cities, as we have just hinted, are better bets than villages. Today, London has become very much a centre for homosexuals, and certain Anglo-Catholic parishes, both in London and in other cities, are well known for the fact that their congregations contain a relatively high level of homosexuals. This points to the simple sociological observation that like-minded people collect in groups in order to meet others similarly disposed, and to express and give satisfaction to their particular inclinations and interests.

These observations relate primarily to priests but also to lay people. It might also be argued that lay people with homosexual inclinations, who are worried about them and who want to receive sympathetic help, might decide that their best policy would be to join a church where they knew the clergy would be sympathetic and offer them assistance. There can be no doubt that in the past, but to a lesser extent today, young men who are both Christians and homosexuals find it difficult to square the two issues. Further, they may look to the church for guidance and decide that they may well get it in a church where they know the vicar would not be censoriously critical of them. They believe, perhaps with good reason, that guidance is more likely to come in Anglo-Catholic churches than in those of a strong Evangelical persuasion. Through auricular confession, through the advice of wise pastors, who perhaps themselves are troubled with the same problem, more help can be found in this form of Anglicanism than elsewhere. Yet, on the other hand, there is always the danger of playing with fire and many who might be drawn to Anglo-Catholic churches because they want help find that it is soon forgotten in the presence of self-confessed homosexuals, namely, the clergy themselves. Some of the quotations previously given point to this.

A number of other factors which have direct bearing on the subject have already been raised: the predominantly male atmosphere of theological colleges; a mildly anti-woman ethos amongst some clergy; clergy houses where unmarried priests are forced to live together; the existence of a number of male organizations such as religious orders, or specific parish groups, for example the Guild of the Servants of the Sanctuary. The last has, in very recent times and, some say, reluctantly, admitted women and girls to its membership. The consequence of such factors on potential homosexual life does not need to be further elucidated.

But other social influences should be mentioned. On the assumption that there are certain types of homosexuals who adopt an effeminate role, which involves dressing up, the ritual and ceremony in Anglo-Catholicism gives them opportunities which are emotionally attractive. Something of the female dress, or certainly male dress of an exotic kind, is to be seen in eucharistic vestments, lace cottas, cassocks, especially those which fit tightly to the body, buckled shoes, the wearing of medals or crosses, birettas, to name but a few. All these can have a sexual 'thing' for both priests and servers. Such clothes are in stark contrast to the drabness of the minister's clothing used in Protestant churches. In the Catholic world there is colour, perhaps ostentation, excitement; and some homosexuals derive much pleasure in searching through the wardrobes of the sacristry or vestry. Vestments of various kinds, their cut or colour, and the way people wear them are often the source of much pleasure and at the same time of jokes amongst the 'boys'. In 1865 *Punch* had the caption: 'Parsons in Petticoats' (10 June 1865). It was a *double entendre*, whether intended or not. Were Anglo-Catholic clergy accused of dressing up in peculiar ecclesiastical garments or of being effeminate? Perhaps both.

It is not only dressing up but acting itself which appeals to a large number of homosexuals. We have mentioned that a high level of homosexuality is to be found amongst actors. The acting out of religion in ritual has its obvious attractions for some homosexuals. Moving around the sanctuary, standing at the high altar, using a censer, carrying candles, taking part in processions of the Blessed Sacrament, all give the impression of being on the stage, of being in a play, of performing before an audience. It applies to servers and priests alike. A self-conscious concern with the carrying out of ritual, where the actor is at the centre of things, is obviously attractive to prima donna figures.

A point made by Hilliard is that the ethos of nineteenth century Anglo-Catholicism stood in stark contrast to that of the rest of the Church of England. The movement contained aesthetically attractive ideals and practices (Hilliard 1982:197). Anglo-Catholicism was ready to impart religious truth through colourful symbols and actions, by the decoration of churches with pictures and statues, by the use of poetry and literature (see May

1933:249ff.). To a very large extent the projected ideals were those found in the middle ages. They were embedded in the novels of Sir Walter Scott and Charles Reade. Unconsciously these authors did much to make Anglo-Catholicism acceptable and indeed attractive to those of the intellectual classes. The search for beauty and for the aesthetic was also associated with and fostered by many of the undergraduates and dons of the universities of Oxford and Cambridge. It was also associated with homosexual ideals. There was a not uncommon tendency to see the aesthetic in terms of superior beings who had refined tastes, far removed from the pedestrian ordinariness of marriage and family life. What was required was something distinct from the mundane, and from the repugnant aspects of birth and the nurture of children. There can be no doubt that some of these attitudes stemmed from the study of the classics, which were dominant in Oxford and Cambridge in the nineteenth and early twentieth centuries. Hence, an undergraduate seeking the beautiful, who at the same time had some religious inclination, would find himself more disposed to Anglo-Catholicism and Roman Catholicism than to Evangelical and Nonconformist expressions of Christianity. One aspect of the Greek ideal is to some degree evident in attitudes that certain early Anglo-Catholics and high-church enthusiasts held towards their close friends, where the masculine figure was seen as the highest form of beauty. The triad was: the aesthetic/Catholicism/homosexuality.

The weakness of this association in any general application is that it is restricted to time and class. It might be quite valid in the early days of Anglo-Catholicism when concepts of beauty were dominant in the outlook of many undergraduates in Oxford and Cambridge. Today, it is probable that Anglo-Catholicism is more openly associated with homosexuality than it was a hundred years ago. Yet the quest for the beautiful no longer predominates and the exaltation of the middle ages and Pre-Raphaelite art forms have ceased to be generally attractive.

Another problem of making a generalization from the triad stated above is that it applies mainly to upper- and middle-class intellectuals, or at least used to do so. Yet, amongst Anglo-Catholic lay people, amongst, for example, those cases we have already mentioned earlier on, there are some of working-class background who have become associated with homosexuality. Today, the notion that homosexuality is a middle-class affair is simply not true.

What needs to be emphasized is that all the associations which have just been made constitute legitimate actions within the

203

church itself. Individuals who participate in such activities are behaving in ways acceptable to and indeed advocated by the church. They can therefore be indulged in without people generally knowing what is going on in the minds of those who for 'sexual' reasons find the actions particularly satisfying. Clergy and laity might happily and joyfully indulge in 'transvestite' activities in the church, aware that such activities are perfectly 'normal', whereas to don women's clothes or extraordinary suits and dresses in the privacy of the bedroom might smack of sin or perversion and, if publicly known, would be seen as reprehensible. Thus, within the ritual there exists a good and totally acceptable outlet for indulging in desires which otherwise might be guilt-ridden. Activities, then, of various kinds exist in Anglo-Catholicism which are legal but which at the same time give some satisfaction to those of homosexual inclination.

The factors just mentioned relate particularly to the social and emotional levels which we have associated with homosexuality and which are particularly obvious in Anglo-Catholicism. But what of homosexuality at the physical level, which is not necessarily associated with transvestitism? About this a little more will be said. The factors at work at the other levels might well draw individuals directly or indirectly to the physical plane in their homosexual proclivities. Some people move steadily from one level to another when once the homosexual fire has been lit. One thing would appear to be a very important factor at the present time. The practice of homosexuality has become more open and moral sanctions have been lifted against such actions, not only in society at large but in the Church itself. The withdrawal of moral sanctions is undoubtedly associated with increased homosexual activity.

We have delineated several factors which on grounds of logical connection would appear to be significant in trying to understand how it is that Anglo-Catholicism is positively associated with homosexuality. It has been impossible to expedite empirical research to attempt to determine if the connections between the factors and homosexuality are in fact real connections or whether they are merely accidental and have no bearing on the phenomenon. There may well be other factors which have not been raised here. Further, if any factors can be positively correlated with homosexuality, this does not in itself imply some form of determinism. The factors indicate probability. There is no question of inevitability and it would be utterly foolish to imagine that every male Anglo-Catholic is an actual, latent, or cryptic homosexual. One must also be sceptical about making everything turn on a single factor within Anglo-Catholicism, even if it is positively correlated with homosexuality.

It would also be totally wrong to imagine that the participation in ritual is universally a kind of homosexual activity. If it were, how is it that, according to common observation, the level of homosexuality in the Roman Catholic Church is not as high per capita amongst priests as it is in the priestly world of Anglo-Catholicism. Yet once more there is a lack of scientific evidence. Of course, it can be argued that sexual misdemeanours committed by Roman Catholic priests are usually covered up and swift action is taken by higher authorities to deal with them. Cases do not usually find their way into the media. Roman Catholic bishops exert far more power in dealing with these issues than do Anglican bishops. However, cases are increasingly coming to light, as, for example, that of a Roman Catholic priest charged with homosexuality in the United States (*The Times*, 8 February 1986). Of course, it would be totally absurd to assert that homosexuality amongst Roman Catholic priests or young men who are Roman Catholic is absent. But it is true that Roman Catholic clergy have not earned for themselves, certainly by way of hearsay, the charge of homosexuality. The sorts of temptations to which they appear to be vulnerable are those of a heterosexual kind, as early Protestants noted. One recalls in this respect the moving novel by Bernanos, *The Diary of a Country Priest*.

Also, from what knowledge one has of the situation in the Roman Catholic Church, there is, relatively speaking, less concern with 'dressing up' and having a fastidious attitude towards clerical attire. It is often said that known homosexuals in the Roman Catholic Church are refused ordination. The subject cannot be pursued further; but what has been said is sufficient to indicate that participating in some well-defined role in ritual is not universally correlated with homosexual attitudes and practices. If anything, it is the other way around, that is, some of those with homosexual inclinations find certain satisfactions in ritual be-haviour. Similarly, it is fundamentally wrong to imagine that Anglo-Catholicism 'creates' homosexuality. What can be said is that there is a positive association between certain social organizations, structures, and occupations and homosexuality. Amongst these stands Anglo-Catholicism, for reasons we have suggested.

Note

It is not intended to consider evidence regarding the relation of homosexuality to the churches in countries outside England. This is largely because attention is focused on cultural factors which relate to Anglo-Catholicism. It should be noted, nevertheless, that the issue of homosexuality and the churches has been much more prominent in the United States than in England. It would appear that the question was brought before the public much earlier than in this country. Laud Humphreys has given a very sympathetic account of what happened in the United States in the late 1960s and very early 1970s (Humphreys 1972). He himself was a minister and married man. He noted that many ministers and priests were leaders and rank-and-file members of homophile organizations, both radical and reformist (Humphreys 1972:144). He said: 'My impression is that most religious leaders are aware that many of the nation's sanctuaries, choir stalls and pews are filled with homosexuals' (Humphreys 1972:151). Many clergy have been defrocked because they confessed to being 'gay' (Humphreys 1972:152). He went so far as to assert that in about 20 per cent of sacristy closets in America there are 'gay' priests (Humphreys 1972:151). We are unable to say anything about a possible connection between homosexuality and Anglo-Catholicism in the States.

III
Responding to ambiguity

Chapter 9

A popular escape route

1 Escaping from ambiguity

Some people when they are faced with ambiguity in religion find that its presence is threatening and too much to bear. This awareness may come to individuals quite suddenly, perhaps through some historic event or an unexpected general change in the religious scene. Such a change produces great unease and distress and the mental turmoil is intolerable. One logical resolution of the ambiguity is to escape. The prerequisite of an escape must be that one is able to flee from the situation without, as a consequence, having to face greater suffering of one kind or another. Each individual has to weigh up the possibilities and chances of being happier in a new group. The religious pluralism of modern western society allows freedom of movement from one religion to another, or from one religion to none at all, without let or hindrance.

For those who cannot accept the peculiar position of Anglo-Catholicism with the many ambiguities of its ideals and practices, one path of escape has been, and still is, into the obvious haven of Roman Catholicism.

2 The path described

To read the lives of Anglo-Catholics or Tractarians from the mid-nineteenth century onwards is to be made immediately aware of the well-worn path many have trodden and which was first taken by members of the Oxford movement, such as John Henry Newman, W. G. Ward, F. W. Faber, Hugh Benson, and others. The path can be picked up at various stages but its religious geography is something like this. It has as its starting-point an Evangelical or low-church base in the Church of England, it moves to the high and dry position established by the Oxford movement, then onwards to Anglo-Catholicism, and finally ends in Roman Catholicism. A symbol of the path has been found in the village of Thame in Oxfordshire where there may be still a signpost pointing from the main road to the 'Catholic Church'. The words beneath read, 'No Through Road'.

There is no shortage of names of those who have become famous in ecclesiastical and other circles who have followed this path during the past century and a half (see early publicized lists, Gorman 1884, 1899, 1910; Church Association 1903, 1908). Amongst the well-known names which come readily to mind, apart from those who have just been mentioned, are Ronald Knox, G. K. Chesterton, Compton Mackenzie, C. C. Martindale, Sir Henry Slesser, and Christopher Butler. In some periods of its history the path has been crowded; at other times less busy. Today, despite the changing social and religious circumstances, not least a much more 'Protestant' face to Roman Catholicism, it has once again become more popular as tensions, threatening to Anglo-Catholics, grow within the Church of England (see ch. 11.10). From 1983 onwards there have been a considerable number of conversions of parish priests, some of them prominent, such as one of Newman's successors at the church of St Mary the Virgin, Oxford, Peter Cornwell, and a former vicar of St Mary Magdalene, Oxford, Fr Smith, who was considered a prominent leader of the Anglo-Catholic movement. There is also the case of an incumbent, the Rev Leslie Hamlett, together with his flock of about forty, in the area of Stoke-on-Trent, who have become Roman Catholic (*Times*, 22 September 1983). The path has had about it a certain inevitability. Once a person is on it and proceeds vigorously, there is little or no turning off. This is implied in the phrase 'Roman fever'. Of course, not everyone goes the whole way, not all Anglo-Catholics become Roman Catholics, very far from it! Most – the vast majority – do not proceed to the end of the road. But there are, generally speaking, no side-roads along the way, no crossroads which might encourage the serious-minded Anglo-Catholic to turn in a different direction, become a Baptist, a Quaker, or a Methodist. The flow is very largely unidirectional. One does not often meet many who are going in the opposite direction, that is, leaving Roman Catholicism and becoming Anglican. It is true that there are more converts to Anglicanism from Roman Catholicism than is sometimes realized. The number of ex-Roman Catholics who have become Anglo-Catholic is microscopic. Those who do embrace Anglicanism tend to avoid 'imitations' – after all they deliberately left the 'real thing' – and opt for central or Evangelical churchmanship. Further, unlike converts to Roman

Catholicism, virtually no one has reached a high position in the Church of England who was formerly a Roman Catholic.

The existence of the path to Rome is testified to not only by the many thousands who have trodden it but by the many phrases which have described it. In addition to Roman fever, just mentioned, there are others such as 'going to Auntie', 'going over', 'verting', 'seceding', 'crossing over', 'poping', 'becoming a Catholic' (in the proper sense of the word!), 'making one's submission', 'submitting', 'being received'.

3 A clerical path

When one recalls the well-known people who have taken the path, it is usually the names of clergy which most readily come to mind. Shane Leslie, a lay convert, estimated that, in the hundred years that followed the Oxford movement, 1,000 clergy had crossed the divide. Over against the overall average for the period of ten priests a year, one has the fact that in the early years there were relatively few converts. In recalling the names of the more recent converts who were formerly Anglican priests, Shane Leslie held that it was difficult to cite men of stature. He was referring to the 1930s (Leslie 1933:154). Many of the early converts were either formidable intellectuals, for example Newman, or men of devotion such as Faber, or leaders, such as Manning. Leslie is quite right. Compared with the mid-nineteenth century clutch of great men who became Roman Catholic, those of more recent times have not been of the same calibre. This may not be the case for lay people, for example, G. K. Chesterton and Graham Greene were received into the Church in the 1930s. But amongst clergy of the same period one might note George Tomlinson, who was received in 1932. He became headmaster of the Oratory School and subsequently administrator of Westminster cathedral. In 1933 W. T. Stead, a fellow and chaplain of Worcester College, Oxford, became a Catholic. Probably the most notable convert to have risen in the Roman Catholic Church recently is B. C. Butler, who was a Benedictine and an eminent theologian: he was also bishop auxiliary to the archbishop of Westminster from 1966 to 1980.

By and large the lay people who have followed the path have been well versed in theological issues and liturgical niceties. The path in many respects might be called un-English. The reason is that it was incomprehensible to ordinary 'C. of E.' folk who made up the bulk of the Church in the late nineteenth and early twentieth centuries. Theological controversies, apart from crude anti-Catholic feelings, were far removed from 'ordinary' Anglicans. The relationship of Church of England clergy to their people, both in the past and in the present, is basically a pastoral one. What Anglo-Catholic priests were able to do was to bring to the attention of their congregations rituals and theological doctrines heretofore unknown. This underlines a most important characteristic common to the Oxford movement and Anglo-Catholicism, namely, the fact that they were basically clerical. By this it is meant that the movements were led by clerics, that the theological issues at stake were of direct interest to the clergy, and that the values and practices projected by the movement came from the clergy to the laity and not vice versa. The movements were not lay because they never became popular amongst rank-and-file Anglicans. Some movements may be started by the clergy and then may quickly be espoused by lay people, who take over their leadership. Church leaders may subsequently have to restrain such movements or at least firmly control them. Examples of lay movements which come readily to mind are the creation of certain religious orders, local cults of saints, the Waldensians, the Flagellants, the Methodists, and more recently the charismatic movement. The Church of England itself has for most of its history been essentially a clerical church, controlled and dominated by 'inferior clergy' over whom bishops have wielded little or no power. Even today the laity exercises very little control, despite the measures designed to encourage them to participate in the life and structure of the church. By contrast the Roman Catholic Church is basically an episcopal or papal dominated church.

The clericalism of the path is borne out by the fact that certainly in the past when clergy converted to Roman Catholicism, even in parishes which were strongly Anglo-Catholic, the laity did not as a general rule follow them. This was particularly the case in working-class parishes (see Ellsworth 1982:43). The charge that romanizing clergy directly encouraged their flocks to become Roman Catholic, that is, by asking them or suggesting to them that they should 'go over', is not generally borne out by the facts, although at St Saviour's, Leeds, convert clergy tried to entice members away from their church (Yates 1975:15). Of course it might be said that most Anglican clergy, even when they become Roman Catholic, are too polite for that kind of manipulation!

4 The effect on the Church of England and on Anglo-Catholicism

The loss to the Church of England at large of the many clergy who forsook their Anglican heritage cannot be overemphasized. Their departure occurred at a period of the Church's history when it could ill afford such losses. The weakness has to be seen against the background of growing secularization, of a widespread indifference to Christian belief and practice centred on the churches. Whereas the numbers of those who left the Anglican priesthood by going to Rome would not have turned the enormous tide, their departure exacerbated rather than helped solve the major problem which faced the Church of England. Further, it might be argued by some that the disagreement over the Catholicity of the Church of England and the problem of valid orders and sacraments diverted intellectual, emotional, and spiritual energy from the greater issue – that of dealing with secularizing influences.

The withdrawal of so many Anglo-Catholics enormously weakened the movement to which they had belonged. Sparrow Simpson, himself a devoted supporter, described the continual losses as 'a deplorable calamity' (Simpson 1932:289). As the path became increasingly popular, so were seeds of uncertainty and doubt multiplied amongst those who had not embarked upon it. Some saw the exit of their close friends and colleagues from the Church of England as an act of betrayal. With them they had struggled to propagate the Catholic faith and its sacramental system within Anglicanism and now their fellow workers had fled. No religious movement in the Church of England has experienced a comparable threat within its ranks or seen such a large number of disaffected members moving away, and all in the same direction. Only the most hard-hearted could fail to see the sadness caused in some situations by clergy becoming Roman Catholic. One of the most moving examples occurred in Fr Lowder's parish in 1866. The following is Ellsworth's description of what happened to three of his curates:

> One day in February 1868, Windham took a morning off to visit a sick relative in Kensington. He did not return for dinner at mid-day, and by the afternoon it was known that he had seceded to Rome. He reappeared the next day, when he and Akers spent several hours in conversation and left the house together. Akers, too, was then received into the Roman Church. When on the following day Lowder heard what had happened, he hurried to Wellclose Square in a vain search for

Akers, and then sent for Shapcote, away on holiday at the time, to return at once. But Shapcote never got further than the railway station waiting room, where Windham and Akers met him and persuaded him to follow their example. We have Lowder's word for it that at least in the cases of Akers and Windham secession was 'totally unexpected'. Windham had given no sign of his intention, while Akers had preached a sermon on the preceding Sunday in which he contrasted the benefits of the Church of England with the defects of the medieval Church. Only Shapcote's secession was foreseeable. Lowder knew that he was not a strong-minded man and that he was under pressure from his Roman Catholic wife. Nevertheless, he was supposed to be happy in his work at Wellclose Square, and he was not, after all, the first to secede.

(Ellsworth 1982:86)

The effect of these events meant a serious set-back to the development of the parish, for Akers had promised £4,000 for the formation of a district church. Indeed, one of the ways in which Anglo-Catholicism, generally, suffered was through the loss of money destined for an Anglican church of Catholic outlook being taken to their new church by converts to Rome. One notable example was St Saviour's, Leeds, in the conversion of a wealthy merchant by the name of Haigh (Yates 1975:8n.34).

In religious houses for monks and nuns established by the Oxford and Anglo-Catholic movements, secessions to Rome were often devastating. In some cases an entire house would embrace the Roman faith. That which caused most stir was when the Anglican Benedictine nuns of Milford Haven seceded virtually en masse on 18 February 1913 and the Benedictine monks of Caldey Island made their submission the next day (see Anson 1955:427–8, 164–81). No such large migration has happened since, although individual members of religious orders have become converts. During the past few years George Every of the Society of the Sacred Mission, a scholar and writer of some distinction, was received into the Roman Catholic Church. The religious life in Anglicanism has never been as strong as it has been in the Roman Catholic Church despite the efforts of Anglo-Catholics (see ch. 5.5). Those who embraced the religious life in the Church of England and then defected to Rome obviously weakened what was already a weak component of Anglo-Catholicism (see Pickering 1988a).

Some places and certain periods were notorious catalysts for Catholic conversions. One such breeding-ground was St Saviour's,

Leeds, built with Pusey's money and in memory of his wife. The early history of the church caused much controversy and sadness to Pusey, not least the fact that during the 1840s and 1850s ten clergy associated with the parish made their submission to Rome. Their exit and subsequent behaviour caused much unhappiness (see Yates 1975:32). Another case occurred later, in 1910, in Brighton when the bishop of Chichester banned benediction in the church of the Annunciation and as a result the vicar of St Bartholomew's, plus two curates, crossed over the divide (Hennock 1981:187). Converts have also departed in waves at various periods of time. One recalls the number who left just before and just after Newman's reception into the Church of Rome. Another important period was around 1930 when people like Chesterton, Sheila Kaye-Smith and Fr Vernon of the Society of the Divine Compassion, left the ranks of Anglo-Catholicism for 'Mother Church'. This occurred about the time of the centenary of the Oxford movement and caused great misery amongst those they had left behind (Morse-Boycott 1947:291ff.). Again, around 1960, as a result of developments in connection with the Church of South India, some Anglo-Papalists associated with the Annunciation Group, including Hugh Ross Williamson, along with Patrick McLaughlin, 'moved over'.

A sense of uncertainty and betrayal was engendered in Anglo-Catholic ranks by the 'poping' not only of giants such as Newman, Chesterton, and Knox, but also of lesser lights. One catches this in some of the novels of Barbara Pym, where the vicar of a small parish, or a curate, causes considerable disturbance when it seems that he will 'turn'. In the examples of Leeds and Brighton just given, a great amount of effort was required by clergy who took over to try to restore equilibrium after the converts had left. Today, the fears remain. They are often roused by the pronouncements of a liberal bishop, the possibility of women being ordained to the priesthood, or a sudden realization that the Church of England is not Catholic. The feeling of betrayal and being misled by those who 'go over' is apparent in Dr Orchard's account of his conversion. He was not an Anglo-Catholic but an eccentric Congregationalist minister with charismatic tendencies who turned a congregation in London into a 'Catholic temple' (Orchard 1933). Acts of betrayal have been more difficult to accept than other burdens which have weighed upon Anglo-Catholics, for example, the mob riots in the early days of the movement. Such suffering is accepted for the sake of truth and is in the same league as martyrdom.

The fact that so many Anglo-Catholics, and clergy in

particular, walked the path to Rome gave Evangelicals and staunch Protestants just the sort of ammunition they needed. It was now quite clear for all to see that through the agency of Anglo-Catholicism the Established Church was indeed being radically changed. All that Walsh said in his book, *The Secret History of the Oxford Movement* (1897) was in fact coming true (see ch. 7.5).

5 The effect on Roman Catholicism

It is often trite to say that one man's loss is another man's gain, but it was certainly the case for the Roman Catholic Church in England in the converts it received from Anglicanism. Shane Leslie, one himself, wrote in the 1930s on the occasion of the centenary of the Oxford movement:

> The Oxford Movement had acted as a feeder to the remnant of the old Church. No branch of the Catholic Church in a missionary country had ever received such a ready-made assistance or such unhoped for encouragement.
>
> (Leslie 1933:153)

And another convert praised the church from which he had departed in so far as it had led him to Catholicism and indeed had been for him 'the gangway of the ship of St. Peter' (Fry 1938:32). Ronald Knox, who was a convinced Anglo-Papalist from the time he was ordained as an Anglican, spoke of the Church of England with gratitude as 'a schoolmaster to bring me to Christ' (Knox 1918:221). Such was the role of Anglo-Catholicism in the eyes of enthusiastic, newly converted Roman Catholics. Nowhere else in the world did the Roman Catholic Church gain such a cache of academic and clerical converts, and that without making any great effort. The fruit did not have to be picked off the trees: it had fallen on the ground and was there for the gathering. The Anglican Church did what no Roman Catholic apologist could have done in preparing an extremely fertile ground. Effortlessly the Catholic Church in England grew in a way it had never expected to do. This is not to say that the Roman Catholic Church had clergy who to a man were passive in the matter of conversions. From the early days up to the present, many Catholic priests have laboured to accelerate the flow.

In the period 1845 to 1848, fifty-six priests of the Church of England seceded to Rome (see Ellsworth 1982:5).[1] This path, which became so well travelled after the secession of Newman, has changed the face of Roman Catholicism in Britain. Without it there would have been a very different Catholic Church from the one we see today. Converts have constituted a group of potential leaders of upper- and middle-class background, men born in this country and so often educated in public schools and at Oxford and Cambridge. When they were reordained in the Roman Catholic Church, as so many of them were, they provided priests, bishops, even a cardinal or two, monks, and nuns, and contributed greatly to the lay intelligentsia. Certainly, converts helped to bridge the social gap, present in early nineteenth century Catholicism, between the recusants and aristocracy on the one hand, and a fast-growing, semi-literate population of Irish immigrants on the other. But the aristocratic sector of Roman Catholicism was also strengthened by converts from the Church of England. The Catholic apologist, W. G. Gorman, claimed that a cursory inspection of the list of names of converts which he compiled around the turn of the century showed that 'there is hardly an English noble family which has not given one or more members to the Roman Catholic Church' (Gorman 1910:x).

It cannot be denied that the class structure of Catholicism has grown nearer to that of the population at large, due to factors related to social, occupational, and geographical mobility. The move, however, was initiated by Anglican converts, who found themselves very much in the middle and so helped to bridge the extremes. Much can be said of the influence of converts on the internal policy of the Catholic Church with regard to its relation to the State, education, universities, and so on (see Archer 1986, chapter 1). It seems quite extraordinary that matters of policy were to a large extent determined by one or two converts, for example Manning and Newman, who rose to great heights, rather than by ex-Anglicans viewed as a group and influencing the Roman Church at large. This is but a reflection of the hierarchical structure of that church.

English converts not only gave the Roman Catholic Church a more English ethos, which in itself made it more attractive to other converts, but it also meant that advocates of Catholicism who were converts were able to speak as those knowing the Anglican Church from the inside. In this respect, Newman's policies, often frustrated, were dictated by such experience. In a certain way, Newman was able to function in both camps. It was said of him: 'For polemical purposes he is all the better a Catholic for having been an Anglican; and, indeed, in a very real sense, he did not cease to be an Anglican when he became Roman Catholic' (Fairbairn 1899:79). What applied to Newman applied, in a lesser degree, to many Anglican priests who seceded.

Nevertheless, it should be noted that conversions to Catholicism over the past century or more, which might have seemed numerous to Anglo-Catholics who saw their friends depart from their ranks, have not contributed as much as other sources to the growth of Catholicism in England. More important has been the natural increase in Catholic families and the influx of immigrants from Catholic countries on the Continent. The question of the growth of Catholicism in Britain is complicated and outside the scope of this book.[2] The contribution of converts from Anglo-Catholicism was not so much a matter of numbers but of the type of convert and the contribution that many, although by no means all, made to the development of that church.

6 Searching for explanations

If ever a movement contained seeds of its own self-destruction, it was Anglo-Catholicism. It has experienced success, triumph, and many achievements, yet running through them all has been a vein which was opened and which has led to a severe weakening of the system through the draining away of its life-blood. If the converts had remained in Anglo-Catholicism, it would have been a much greater movement than it turned out to be. But why was it that so many Anglo-Catholic priests, who in many cases were devoted and ardent in their faith, who laboured assiduously for the cause, took, sometimes with extreme reluctance, sometimes with some degree of enthusiasm, the path which led them directly out of the Church of England and into the Roman Church?

Where can an answer be found? One method of finding it is to search through the biographies and autobiographies of those who have taken the final step. Here obviously interest is focused on the motivation of individuals themselves. One might readily point to Newman, to Manning, to Chesterton, and show from their accounts the reason they went to Rome. But what sorts of reasons will one find? The desire to be under some form of absolute authority exemplified by the pope? The wish to embrace clear-cut and precisely formulated doctrine? The search for a deep spirituality? The wish to be in a church that is truly universal? The fear that the Church of England was not really Catholic? These are some of the possibilities which may emerge in reading biographies and autobiographies of converts. Sometimes there are many reasons put forward by the one person. There is, of course, considerable merit in such an approach but it is limited as it relies only on published material. Such writers were those who felt compelled to give an account of themselves and at the same time possessed the ability to write. Much depends on the willingness of publishers to publish the manuscripts of converts. What of the countless life-histories which have never been written? The danger of using printed biographies and autobiographies is that one has no means of determining whether the ideas can in any way be generalized. And there is also the difficulty of unconscious motivation. If the details of biographies and autobiographies are made the basis of analysis, one may wonder whether those who wrote about their journeys did not declare or were not aware of the reasons for their travels. In connection with this, one might refer to authority figures, to the need some individuals have for firm psychological props in dealing with everyday life, or to a search for ways of overcoming some traumatic childhood experience, or, as we have already noted, at a more conscious level, to the possibility of finding in Roman Catholicism a way of dealing with homosexuality through its social structures and moral teaching. Again, it is sometimes infuriating to read a biography or autobiography and never be told why the person became a convert.

While not denying the value of approaches which rely on biographical material, and indeed making some use of them, we shall adopt a different method which might loosely be called a structural or positional approach. It is related to the ambiguities of Anglo-Catholicism already referred to. In other words, an attempt will be made to see how conversion to Roman Catholicism is a direct response to a realization of the ambiguities within Anglo-Catholicism. This, of course, is not to deny that Roman Catholicism has a number of strong attractions for people imbued with Anglo-Catholic ideals. But in any theory of conversion one has to look at both sides of the coin: to negative factors which suggest that the present position is undesirable; and also to positive factors which indicate that a better position is possible. The ambiguities of Anglo-Catholicism cause one to do both. They demonstrate the intellectually unsatisfactory position of Anglo-Catholicism and at the same time suggest that there is only one direction to go, the path that leads to Rome.

In addition to the ambiguities that have already been mentioned we raise some more which have a more immediate bearing on taking the decision to be received into the Roman Catholic Church.

7 'The Catholic Church is the True Church'

'Those who become Anglo-Catholics or who are born into Anglo-Catholicism can be said to have a doctrinal *raison d'être* which is something like this. If it be agreed that Christianity is the true religion, that Christ is the Son of God, that he founded a church to carry on his work, then that church is the Catholic church as it has existed throughout history. The Catholic church is therefore the true church. Protestantism denies this and is therefore a false form of Christianity. A more liberal interpretation of the Anglo-Catholic position would be that Catholicism is the one true development of the teaching and the work of Christ and that the Catholic church is a fuller, more worthy, more meritorious, more human, wiser, and older expression of the Christian ideal than that found in Protestant churches. So much for basic assumptions. What follows is the contention that the Church of England is part of this Catholic church. The Tractarians emphasized the idea and tried to demonstrate theologically that the Church of England is as much part of the Catholic church as is the Church of Rome (see ch. 1.2) The Catholic foundation of the Church of England is theologically sound because of the fact that through the grace of God the Church has retained valid orders of bishops, priests, and deacons guaranteed by apostolic succession. Further, the Church has never promulgated any doctrine which repudiates fundamental Catholic doctrine. Although the Church has been through dark days in forgetting its Catholic characteristics, all that is now needed is the revival of a Catholic consciousness and the presence of Catholic-minded clergy who could put into practice the sacramental system latent in the Church.

Yet Anglo-Catholics have seen that despite their ideals and achievements there has been an enormous hiatus between what was sought and what has been achieved. As 'part of the one true Church', Anglicanism has remained remarkably insular, tied to the English-speaking areas of the world alone, and with little influence beyond the 'parochial' (see Pickering 1988b). Anglo-Catholicism, although it has made enormous strides within the Church of England, remains a minority movement whose influence, diffused as it has been, is severely limited in the life of the Church. It has not been successful in catholicizing the Church in the way followers dreamed of. Few bishops have embraced 'full Catholic doctrine and practice'. Even those Anglo-Catholics who have been made bishops appeared to dilute their zeal for things Catholic when once they had ascended an episcopal throne (see ch. 6.3). To the outsider it seemed that, despite gains made by Anglo-Catholics, the Church of England remained Protestant, i.e. it was not Catholic (see ch. 6.2). One might proclaim the Catholic heritage of the Church of England but in practice the Catholic marks were not clear for all to see and the public still thinks of the Church of England as being 'vaguely Protestant'. Those who have not been Anglo-Catholic, theologians and bishops in particular, have continued to put forward ideas, some of them liberal, some of them Evangelical, which were very far removed from those which Anglo-Catholics have proclaimed and which they have believed were essential in upholding the Catholic character of the Church of England. 'It is the true church', yet the facts seem to belie the words. Was not the proclamation of the Catholic-minded a vain proclamation which could not really be sustained? In the confrontation of the ideal with the real, where is one to place one's bet? Anyone can have ideals, the test comes with putting them into practice. And it was here that Anglo-Catholicism within the Church of England seemed to fail so lamentably.

8 The eternal presence of the Roman Catholic Church

It is, therefore, not an exaggeration to say that Anglo-Catholics inculcated doctrines, ideals, and practices which have only been partially carried out or accepted in the church to which they belong. But over against the way Anglo-Catholics have seen themselves in the Church of England has stood the ever-growing Roman Catholic Church. Here was the ideal, not found in the recesses of the mind or in the imagination, but as a reality around the corner, as it were, with its cathedrals, especially Westminster cathedral, with its new abbeys and convents, with its well-disciplined schools which taught the Catholic faith, and with its direct links with the church in Europe and indeed all around the world. In this form of Catholicism there was a uniformity of ritual and belief – we speak of the period before Vatican II. What a contrast with the Church of England! Moreover, there was what some Anglo-Catholics saw as real leadership in the Roman Catholic Church, which was absent in their own church. So Sheila Kaye-Smith could write in the 1920s:

> The rank and file of the Catholic Movement follows Rome because it is the only leadership they have. If Anglican authority would speak with a clear and Catholic voice they would be only too glad of its direction.
>
> (Kaye-Smith 1925:158)

221

But how could Anglican bishops speak like Roman Catholic bishops? To hope that they would is to live in a world of fantasy. Yet the same writer asked Anglo-Catholics to transcend what they were doing and to perform an act of magic: 'They must never turn to Rome so as to lose sight of Constantinople; their vision must always be large enough to hold both the East and the West' (Kaye-Smith 1925:160). But she herself was soon to 'go over'.

Being brought face to face with the Roman Catholic Church in this country, as well as perhaps seeing it in action on the Continent, is to be made acutely aware of the fact that Anglo-Catholicism, like Anglicanism itself, is essentially a British phenomenon, and tied to things British. Yet the Gospel and the church up until the time of the Reformation were firmly transnational. Whether it was possible to maintain the church as a universal institution as the western society grew and developed is to be contested. But, if universality is held to be desirable, Anglicanism and Anglo-Catholicism are no match for the Roman Catholic Church (see ch. 6.2; Pickering 1988b).

That the Catholic Church stood on the doorstep was not always consciously held to be a threat by many Anglo-Catholics, despite the fact that it represented a goal which they themselves could never achieve. They might, sometimes seriously, at other times in jest, talk about the 'Italian [or Roman] mission' to England, implying that Catholicism was already in the country, a genuinely English Catholicism. The Church of England, through the efforts of Anglo-Catholics, had the responsibility for the nurture of Catholicism in England. The Roman Catholic Church was intrusive. The quip about the 'Italian mission' made those who used the phrase a laughing-stock rather than those whom they ridiculed. The phrase could never be taken seriously and, although it pointed to a love–hate relationship, the amount of hate on the part of Anglo-Catholics was minimal. Rather, it indicated a love–jealousy relationship. Interestingly enough, the term Italian mission is attributed to E. W. Benson, archbishop of Canterbury, whose son, R. H. Benson, as an Anglo-Catholic, converted to Roman Catholicism (see Benson 1913:52). The other side of this coin has another extraordinary claim. C. B. Moss, the Anglo-Catholic theologian, held that the Episcopal Church in Scotland (numerically very small) was 'in its own eyes the only genuine Church' in the country and 'claims to be the proper home of all Scottish Christians', and, further, 'The Roman Communion in Scotland, apart from Highland districts, which never accepted the Reformation, is the Church of the Irish immigrants after the famine of 1847' (in Wand 1948:256). Only on grounds of a peculiar kind of logic can such claims also be taken seriously.

It is obvious that when an ideal is achieved in practice, and at the same time is of easy access, people who share that ideal are magnetically drawn to its realization.

9 To criticize or not to criticize?

The continued growth in numbers of Roman Catholics in Britain during the nineteenth and twentieth centuries was an embarrassment to Anglo-Catholics. Hardly surprisingly, they seldom criticized the Roman Catholic Church at all vigorously. How could they, since the Catholic Church embodied nearly all the ideals of Anglo-Catholicism? That Church was as much part of the Catholic tree as was their own. Does one branch radically criticize another? Intoxicated by their discovery of the Catholic heritage of the Church of England, they felt that as a whole there was relatively little wrong with the Roman Catholic Church. It was admittedly a rival but one which had to be admired.

This attitude was particularly evident in the 1920s and 1930s when a spate of books appeared on the controversy of Anglo- versus Roman Catholicism. At that time a convert wrote: 'the story of the passing from some form of Protestant belief to full Catholic faith has been so often told of late that it is surely becoming a monotonous recital' (Orchard 1933:4). The period between the wars was a seed-bed for controversy about conversions. The result was the appearance of many apologetic books about the two forms of Catholicism. A period of triumphalism it might have been for Anglo-Catholics in their congresses, but it was also a period of great growth and triumphalism for the Catholic Church in England, helped as it had been by Anglican converts both before the 1920s and 1930s and particularly during that period. After all, 1933 was the centenary of the Oxford movement. Given the interests of the times, energetic Roman Catholics wanted to have more people take the path of conversion; Anglo-Catholic leaders, for obvious reason, wanted to halt them.

Roman Catholics who had formerly been Anglicans were enthusiastic to tell the story of their conversions. There were those who turned out to be very scathing, as was Compton Mackenzie in his trilogy of novels, beginning with *The Altar Steps*, published in 1922. This, and the other continuing novels, *The Parson's Progress* (1923), and *The Heavenly Ladder* (1924), did little to enhance Mackenzie's status as a novelist but they turned out to be a lively account of a young, Anglo-Papalist priest, who eventually and inevitably became a Roman Catholic.

The Dominicans, based in Blackfriars, Oxford, strengthened by Anglican converts, as they still are today, were particularly enthusiastic in 1933 to hasten the flow into the Roman fold (see *New Blackfriars* 1987:307–8). The editor of *Blackfriars* at that time wrote:

> The Anglo-Catholics have slowly and painfully followed it [Newman's reception into the Roman Catholic Church], not wanting to but compelled thereto by the arguments he accepted long ago. To them he is the leader whether they will or no. Only the pace at which they will travel is argued over nowadays, only the time when they will arrive. That their movement must follow him is patent to themselves. May the Lord, for the sake of the Elect that be with Him, shorten those days!
>
> (Anon. 1933:538–9)

And in the same issue someone writing under the pseudonym of Jacobin said:

> Anglo-Catholics have travelled far from the position of the Tractarians, and will travel yet further. But the Mother, ever solicitous for them in their wanderings, will never despair of their return:
>
> > et ad Jerusalem
> > a Babylonia
> > post longa regredi
> > tandem exilia
>
> (Jacobin 1933:541)

In the face of the onslaught by Roman Catholics on the Anglican position and in the ensuing apologetic controversies, Anglo-Catholics were weak both in defence and attack.

Not surprisingly Anglo-Catholics chose to defend themselves on the grounds that their form of Catholicism was a more pure and primitive form than that of Roman Catholicism. At least the argument could be upheld by those of them who were not Anglo-Papalists. They attempted to show that Anglo-Catholicism had not embraced later doctrines which were held to be wrong, namely, claims about the doctrine of papal infallibility and the Immaculate Conception of the Blessed Virgin Mary. These points of contention were about all they could muster by way of an offensive. They were seen as the only differences between 'them' and 'us'. 'And don't let us emphasize "them" too much either!' The attitude is evident in the popular book by W. L. Knox, *The Catholic Movement in the Church of England*, published in 1923. Wilfred Knox was never attracted to Rome as was his younger brother, Ronald, but the book as an apologetic for Anglo-Catholicism is very gentle in delineating the differences between Roman Catholicism and Anglo-Catholicism. Nor was he critical of the extremists of his own party, referring to them only in a footnote (Knox 1923:238–9n.1). Another book of a similar kind was that of Humphrey Beevor, *The Anglican Armoury* (1934), which first appeared as a series of articles in the *Church Times*.

If papal claims and the doctrine of infallibility of the pope were the main points of difference in matters of doctrine which separated Anglo-Catholics from Roman Catholics, then it is interesting to note that Anglo-Catholic scholars did not on the whole write academic volumes intended to refute such doctrines. There was no one comparable to George Salmon, Provost of Trinity College, Dublin, whose book *The Infallibility of the Church* (1888) was probably the best of its kind. In its defences, Anglo-Catholicism maintained the validity of Anglican orders and refuted the historical evidence on which Roman Catholics denied the possibility of apostolic succession to the Ecclesia Anglicana. Admittedly, Charles Gore was probably the one scholar who was prepared to consider Roman Catholic claims, in his book of that name (1889a/1905), but his position within Anglo-Catholicism, as has been noted, is somewhat on the borderline. His unswerving loyalty to the Church of England emerges in the sentence: 'Thus, all things considered, we Anglicans thank God that He has put us elsewhere than in the Roman Church, though we would fain give her an ungrudging recognition of her glories' (Gore 1889a/1905:173). But there have been Anglo-Catholics who have written strongly against Roman Catholicism and been responsible for the publication of books by anti-Roman scholars.

In reading Anglo-Catholic literature as a whole over the past fifty or so years, one gets the impression that whatever changes the Church of England proposed at its most authoritative level – be the issues over liturgy, doctrine, church order, or the reunion of the churches – they were wrong. And they were wrong because the Roman Catholic Church had not made them. No marks were given to the Church of England for initiative or originality. Whatever it did it was quite unacceptable (see, for example, E. L. Mascall's letter in *The Times*, 15 November 1978). This observation is impressionistic but it is difficult to find in print some scheme or project which gains the unadulterated praise of Anglo-Catholics. If Anglo-Catholics could admit to any change, it had to come from an outside source (see ch. 6.4).

Lutherans, Calvinists, and Anabaptists have never seen themselves as part of what might be called the Catholic church in the sense that Anglo-Catholics, or even Anglicans at large, have. They have been free, therefore, to attack the Roman Church at whatever point they wished. Unashamedly they have made much of the differences between themselves and the Roman Catholic Church. Basic positions over justification by faith and the doctrine of the mass have been prominent, but Protestants have readily attacked Catholics over the doctrine of the Assumption of the Blessed Virgin Mary, persecutions they have experienced at the hands of Roman Catholics, the practices of missionaries overseas as in the case of Mexico and certain countries of South America, the Index, indulgences, the veneration of relics, papal measures against liberalism, democracy, and modernism, and so on. In contrast, Anglo-Catholics have, with one or two exceptions, never taken the Roman Catholic Church to task on these points. Rather quietly they tended to support the Roman teaching on birth control (see Wilkinson 1988). Perhaps the one exception is Oscar Hardman's *'But I am a Catholic!'* (1958). In it he had no hesitation in condemning the doctrine of purgatory, the Inquisition, relics, and the new dogmas about the Blessed Virgin Mary. He stated that 'the gap between Rome and Canterbury remains as wide as ever it was' (Hardman 1958:134). Nevertheless, such a forthright attack on Roman Catholicism by a convinced Catholic-minded priest of the Church of England did not appear until 1958. So far as we have been able to discern there was nothing comparable to this during the 1930s.

It is interesting to note that the Faith Press, a press totally given to Anglo-Catholic literature, published in the 1930s several books by the renowned medieval historian, C. G. Coulton, of Cambridge, who was also a redoubtable anti-Catholic apologist. Amongst the books was a two-volume work, *Romanism and Truth* (1930–1). It would appear that Anglo-Catholics as a whole did not take his violent attacks too kindly and that his aggressiveness was not welcomed. Coulton was much praised by Sparrow Simpson in a book which came out in 1909. In it Sparrow Simpson tried to show that papal infallibility was a doctrine of recent times and that its acceptance in 1870 as being binding on all Catholics was made in the face of much opposition from Continental theologians. Anglo-Catholics such as Sparrow Simpson, as well as many Anglicans of other churchmanship, supported the notion that Rome, with its tradition of St Peter as its first bishop, had primacy amongst all other bishops, but that this primacy did not imply infallibility. Another leading Anglo-Catholic theologian and historian, N. P. Williams, wrote a pamphlet against the papacy in 1918. The point that is made here is that at the peak of Anglo-Catholicism in the 1930s, and at a time when so many Anglo-Catholics were embracing the Roman faith, Anglo-Catholic scholars did not vigorously attack the Roman Catholic Church, and certainly not in the same way as Roman Catholic writers drove hard at Anglicanism. An Anglican Benedictine has implied that the only real criticism he had of the Roman Catholic Church was its rejection of the validity of Anglican orders, that is, its assertion that Anglican priests were not really priests (Hughes 1961:151).

The reason is quite clear. Anglo-Catholics saw in the Roman Catholic Church, at worst, a church which needed some reform but no more than what we might call today a 'cosmetic change'. The more advanced the Anglo-Catholic, the less was the desired change. Anglo-Papalists wanted none at all. Walter Walsh in 1900 challenged followers of the Oxford movement to state categorically how they differed from Roman Catholics, for some said they did differ when directly challenged. Walsh maintained he was never given an answer (1900:16). In comparing themselves with Roman Catholics, Anglo-Catholics were, and still are, apologetic in speaking about their church. They will say, for instance, that it is not 'quite Catholic'. Their tone is gentlemanly and self-effacing. They do not underline the advantages and superiority of their own position. They have always been severely disadvantaged for they have been fighting rather like a man with one arm tied behind his back. Their main task has been to proclaim and put into practice the Catholicity of the Church of England. How could they then attack the church which professed the same foundation and the same principles? How could they assail a church they wanted to be like? Clearly they yearned to be able to say, and probably did, that 'we (Anglo- and Roman) Catholics are the same – we are all Catholics'. They felt themselves far more in sympathy with Roman Catholics than with Evangelicals or middle-of-the-road Anglicans. That Roman Catholics should reject the affinities and distance themselves from Anglo-Catholics made little or no difference. As we have repeatedly said, Anglo-Catholics, especially Anglo-Papalists, constantly wanted to feel identified with Roman Catholics. Paul Ferris said of the monks of Nashdom, whom he visited about twenty years ago, that they told him they used the Roman missal and that if they 'became Roman Catholics tomorrow [they] would only change one word in the service: the name of the bishop'. And then, in what appears to be a mere playing with words, something bordering on lying, they said: 'we're a perfectly normal part of the Church of England. We're not High' (Ferris 1962:196–7).

There was another reason for silence where there might have been criticism. In the general hope for the reunion of Christendom which began to emerge amongst certain leaders of the churches, Anglo-Catholics from early days prayed for and hoped there would be unity with the Roman Catholic Church. Deep concern for this was voiced in the 1920 Anglo-Catholic congress and it was heightened by the successful initiation of the Malines Conversations, which were held between 1921 and 1925. They were then axed by the intervention of the pope. If one strives for reunion then it is politically undesirable to attack vigorously the very people with whom one wishes to join hands, even if one wishes to do so. On the other hand, Roman Catholics had no hesitation in launching an aggressive policy, for English Catholics had not the slightest interest in participating in a scheme for reunion (see ch. 7.5).

Yet Anglo-Catholics were critical of other religious groups. Their attacks were directed with considerable vehemence against Protestant churches and in later times against what one might call the Evangelical components of the Church of England. In the early days of the Oxford movement the enemies were the latitudinarians and followers of the broad-church party, liberals, and all those who wanted the control of the Church by the State. Although some early Tractarians attacked Protestantism strongly, there was nevertheless a strong respect for Evangelicals, and many of them, such as Newman, had been brought up in that persuasion. It was mainly later and with the growth of Anglo-Catholicism that Protestants and Evangelicals became targets of hostility (see Knox 1933:344ff.; Voll t.1963:29ff.). We have already pointed to an Evangelical streak in certain Anglo-Catholic priests (see ch. 3). Of the opposite sort one might mention one of the earliest and most aggressive critics, W. G. Ward, who saw in Protestantism little more than atheism and the Antichrist (Knox 1933:318). And, when he compared the Church of England with the Roman Catholic Church, 'he presented to England the wrinkles, the deformities, the scanty grey hairs, the toothless gums, the faltering steps of its Mother Church'. By way of contrast he offered 'a highly flattering portrait of the Church which Englishmen had been taught to regard as the Harlot Church' (Knox 1933:321).

But it was not only the Protestant churches of the Continent which Anglo-Catholics wished to distance themselves from as much as possible but Protestant elements in the Church of England. How frequently one reads in the biographies and autobiographies of Anglo-Catholic priests words such as these: 'He had not the smallest affinity to Protestantism' (Rawlinson 1924:xliv). Yet all Anglo-Catholic clergy were Anglican! Fr H. A. Wilson, already mentioned as an organizer of the Anglo-Catholic congresses, wrote of one priest: 'There he learned in its fullness both the Catholic Faith, and its natural and right expression in dignified ceremony'. Then, a few lines further on, he said of the same priest that he was given a living where 'he found his church and parish sunk in the depths of protestantism' (Wilson 1940:20). Apart from 'sunk' and 'depths' being applied to Protestantism in an emotive way, he used an initial capital letter for Catholic but lower case for Protestantism. Arnold Lunn, the convert, called Protestantism 'depressing' and 'dull' (Lunn 1933:46). The saintly Father Andrew, a religious, who never, it appears, was attracted to the Roman Catholic Church, wrote: 'I was, as you know, once a Protestant' (Burne 1948:143). Yet he had been born and nurtured in the Anglican Church! In the church of St Cuthbert's, Kensington, there is a misericord called 'The Brawler'. It consists of the head of John Kensit (1853–1902) (complete with pig's ears), who organized attacks against Anglo-Catholic services in the name of Protestantism (see ch. 2.1).

The Reformation was the *bête noire* of Anglo-Catholics. At the heart of the matter was doctrine. A trusted Anglo-Papalist leader, Dom Anselm Hughes, has written:

> The Catholic . . . knows at once that anything brought in at the Reformation which touches upon doctrine, or tends in unessential matters to favour some Lutheran, Calvinist, Zwinglian, Presbyterian, Anabaptist, or other type of protestantism, is *sui generis* wrong and false, or at least gravely suspect and without a shred of claim upon his loyalty'.
>
> (Hughes 1961:147)

But it is not only a question of doctrine. Everything went wrong at the time of the Reformation and Anglo-Catholics readily marshalled arguments to show the failure, as they saw it, of Protestant religious practice and even pastoral policy. And Protestantism was seen to be the cause of many social evils – the breakup of Christendom, the rise of the secular State, and indeed the root of secularization itself. Some of these political and social criticisms often appeared in the Anglo-Catholic Summer Schools of Sociology, held during the 1930s and after the Second World War (see ch. 5.6). No 'good Catholic' had a good word to say for the Protestant churches. When the Anglican religious order for women, the Society of the Precious Blood, was about to acquire a house which in medieval times had been an Augustinian convent, a sister commented: 'So from the first, the thought of reparation for the sacrilege of 1539 was a dominant one in the Society's acquisition of their new home' (Mary 1968:55). Incidentally, E. A. Knox, bishop of Manchester, deplored the concept of *via media* as the gangplank of the Oxford movement. He did not see the Church of England as being midway between the Roman Catholic Church and Protestantism. For him the true *via media* was Protestantism itself, mediating between the Church of Rome and infidelity (Knox 1933:346). In 1947, at the request of Geoffrey Fisher, archbishop of Canterbury, there appeared the report, *Catholicity*, written by Catholic-minded theologians, which showed a much more generous attitude towards Protestantism and at the same time was critical of contemporary Roman Catholicism (Abbott *et al.* 1947).

Part of the long-standing, generally negative attitude towards Protestantism might be attributed to the English, and especially the Anglican, disease of showing very little interest in church affairs on the Continent, although some Anglo-Catholic scholars knew what was going on amongst Roman Catholic theologians in France and Germany (Voll t.1963:139; also Brilioth 1934:9). But one wonders how many Anglican theologians had any contacts at all with their counterparts in the French Protestant church. And the English clergy knew very little of what was going on in the Roman Catholic Church in, say, France during the nineteenth century. Nor were they aware of what went on behind the scenes in Catholic parish life in Germany or Italy or Spain. Anglo-Catholics were very much armchair Catholic observers. There were, of course, exceptions. Those associated with the Anglo-Catholic Summer Schools of Sociology were well versed in European Catholic thought relating to the social and political ideas of certain theologians and philosophers (see ch. 5.6). Fr Patrick McLaughlin, in the period which immediately followed the Second World War tried to make St Anne's, Soho, an intellectual centre for Christians, mainly of a Catholic outlook, and introduced a number of innovative liturgical changes which came from experiments carried out, particularly, in French

Catholicism. He also welcomed lecturers from the Continent, but his ideas were not immediately taken up and were not in keeping with English culture (see Williamson 1956, chapter 15).

One other aspect of the anti-Protestant attitude of Anglo-Catholics and of certain Tractarians ought to be mentioned. Their presence in the Church of England made relations between that church and the Nonconformist churches not as good as many leaders in both churches wanted. In matters of social reform and education there were chances of co-operation, especially with Evangelicals, but the scene changed when the Catholic revival became established (see Mayor 1967:24). The arrival on the religious scene in the nineteenth century of Anglo-Catholicism sharpened, not diminished, controversies amongst the churches.

10 Conclusion

The popularity of the path which leads from Anglo-Catholicism to Rome can be explained by the fact that Anglo-Catholicism has projected ideals which cannot consistently be put into practice in the Church of England. The movement has encouraged its followers to strive for something which must remain a dream. Thus, a wide gap exists between the ideal and the real, and this for some has bred problems. No one can deny that Anglo-Catholic priests have been able to turn Anglican churches into mirrors of Roman Catholic parish churches. The ambiguity arises in the realization that Anglo-Catholicism is a party and can never be more than that in a church which itself is a *mélange* of Protestant and Catholic ideals and practices. The Anglo-Catholic movement inevitably displays sectarian qualities, not least in creating a religious counter-culture within the Established Church. There is no problem in taking up such a position, save the overriding fact that it is done in the name of Catholicism, which is the very denial of what is meant by the sectarian outlook. Ambiguities are heightened by the close geographical presence of a flourishing manifestation of the ideal. The Anglo-Catholic position has had little to defend itself with against the threatening, but at the same time attractive, religious influence, the beloved Roman Catholic Church. In brief it has been unable to maintain satisfactory boundaries. All social boundaries are upheld by positive and negative sanctions. Lines have to be preserved if the maintenance of a social entity is the object of the exercise. Failure at this point means inevitable weakness in the cohesion of the entity. And within the ideology of a social body there is the need for a strong *raison d'être* and at the same time firm negative attitudes against a potential rival. Groups most successful in maintaining their position are those which have vigorously utilized both approaches and know the meaning of boundaries. Other factors may be important but, unless there exists some process by which a potential rival is belittled or held at a distance, social identity becomes threatened.

Anglo-Catholics needed an adequate apologetic in order to mark themselves off clearly from Roman Catholics. They had to be sure of their boundaries and this they never were. To make Petrine claims about infallibility the main point of difference is to get dangerously near the other party. It is like playing with fire.

Notes

1   Munson offers some interesting statistics about conversions to Rome amongst members of the English Church Union in its early days (Munson 1975:386). Membership in 1901 was 39,000 but only 98 members had become Roman Catholic between 1868 and 1903, that is, just about 3 a year. The figure may not seem very great but it certainly seemed so to Protestant fanatics. Of the 98, 51 were graduates of Oxford, 25 of Cambridge – a ratio of 2:1. At the turn of the century it was reported that there were 33 ex-Roman Catholic priests working in the Church of England.

2   Conversions to Roman Catholicism as a whole is a subject which calls for careful research. Published statistics are not altogether reliable. According to Tony Spencer, who has been one of the few (including more recently M. P. Hornsby-Smith) to have undertaken demographic analyses of the Catholic Church in England, the statistics published about conversions are unreliable just because they do not relate to the age of the converts; some might be for those under the age of 14, as in the case of families which become Roman Catholic. Absolute figures given in Catholic handbooks, therefore, are not to be trusted. Spencer computed figures which he claims are moderately accurate and which show that in 1850 there were about 1,400 conversions; in 1911, 7,700; in 1963, 11,000; in 1972, just under 4,000 (Spencer 1975:102). If one disregards Spencer's words of warning and turns to the official figures, in the heyday of Anglo-Catholicism in the 1920s there were about 10,000–12,000 conversions per annum. Assuming there is the same base of calculation, the number of conversions, now more politely referred to as receptions, was in the 1980s half that of the period just mentioned. (For 1981

and 1982 the number given in the *Catholic Directory* was about 5,700.) From Spencer's adjusted figures, from returns given in handbooks, and from examining the figures given for the Diocese of Hexham and Newcastle (see Archer 1978), it would seem that there has been a dramatic fall in the number of conversions since the 1960s, that is, since the time of Vatican II. One hardly needs to be reminded of the fact that many converts to Catholicism have been received into the Church, not by following the Anglican–Anglo-Catholic path but by moving directly from the Free churches, from Judaism, and from no denominational association whatsoever.

Tony Archer, in a carefully documented study of conversions in recent decades in Newcastle upon Tyne, has shown convincingly that the vast majority of conversions have come through the agency of mixed marriage and friendships (Archer 1978). He found that the most important operating factor was prolonged contact with a Catholic, especially in the home; another factor, closely associated with it, was a basic wish for family solidarity, for the other married partner to become a Catholic, in order, as Archer says, 'to join one's own kind'. The religious quest to find a 'true' religion by someone formerly in another denomination, or to seek a more satisfying form of worship by someone who was a practising member of a church, seemed little in evidence amongst the converts he examined. According to diocesan returns the number who were converted due to 'conviction' was roughly in the order of 10 per cent. Cases examined by Archer cover a very wide social spectrum and include many working-class families. Amongst them concern about doctrine and worship was not prominent. This type of convert was motivated by very different reasons from those which motivated converts from Anglo-Catholicism, who were well versed in theological and ritual matters. Within the total number of Catholic converts the number of those who came via the Anglo-Catholic path was not as great as Anglo-Catholics sometimes imagine.

Chapter 10

Remaining where they are

1 The problem

From what has been said about ambiguities particular to Anglo-Catholicism, an outsider would probably conclude that the only logical outcome for the Catholic-minded Anglican is to dismiss any hesitation he might have and become a Roman Catholic. If the ambiguities are seen to be serious and the dilemmas so numerous that inner tensions arise, a haven has to be sought and that is in the calm waters of Rome. It is not a question of faith or theology: it is one of common sense. Yet the fact of the matter is that thousands, hundreds of thousands (if it is ever possible to talk about numbers in Anglo-Catholicism), in the course of time have kept to their faith and practice right until their dying days. For various reasons they have not taken the Romeward path. So the question arises why Anglo-Catholics have remained where they have, surrounded as they are by ambiguity? These issues are just as important as are those which relate to those who secede. They are questions which inevitably lead us back to the model posited at the beginning of this book (see Introduction).

2 Alternative responses

One of the problems of analysing religious systems in terms of inherent ambiguities is that what is seen to be ambiguity in one person's eyes is not so to another. To someone within a religious system a particular entity, doctrine, or practice may not appear to be an ambiguity in the slightest way whereas, to someone else either in the system or, more often than not, outside it, it is an ambiguity. What is or what is not ambiguous depends on the outlook of the individual, be he participant or observer. There are a number of reasons for this. For the sake of argument let it be assumed that such a difference exists between the observer and the participant. Because of his training and background,

234

because of his logic or rationality, the observer may immediately be aware of ambiguities which are not obvious to the participant. The 'blindness' of the participant may be due to a number of reasons. For one thing perhaps he has spent all his life in the religion and underwent a process of socialization, doubtless as a very young child. He was instructed in such a way that the problem of ambiguity was never apparent to him. Nor did it become apparent to him as he became older. Again, as has been said, religious leaders and theologians have as one of their tasks the elimination or rationalization of ambiguity. Followers generally accept their interpretations. Again, it is possible that the participant may deliberately close his mind to ambiguities within the system. He may be conscious of them but then represses them so that 'he just doesn't want to know about them'. On the other hand he may decide that he can live quite happily with them: they are part of life, whether religious life or life in other dimensions. All life is ambiguous, he may argue. Why make an exception of religion?

3 Remaining for negative reasons

In applying these possibilities to Anglo-Catholicism, one must attempt to see how individuals of that persuasion who remain in the Church of England see the situation. One of the first to do this and to adopt a psychological approach was the French priest, Abbé Martin, who in 1878, wrote an article in *The Contemporary Review* with the title, 'What hinders the Ritualists from becoming Roman Catholics?' In the end it proved to be a polemical study and was answered by Gladstone and the Anglo-Catholic writer, R. F. Littledale (1833–90). As the arguments proceeded some of the earlier remarks by Martin based on socio-psychological factors were forgotten and the issues became historical (Martin 1878a, 1878b; Gladstone 1878; Littledale 1878).

For us, as with Martin, it is necessary to begin with the assumption that the logical development of Anglo-Catholicism is to lead the individual to the Church of Rome. But while that may appear to be the logic of the situation there exist in people's minds good reasons for not taking the 'obvious' step.

There may have been in the past and may still be today apperceptive clergy and laity who fully realize that to move from Anglo-Catholicism to Roman Catholicism is not to have 'the same only better' but to enter the religious life of a group which is far from being the same as the one that has been left. Despite liturgical and doctrinal similarities, the ethos is very different.

235

Those who have failed to see this have suffered the most in remaining in the institution to which they were converted. Some have found the 'cultural shock' too great and have returned to Anglicanism. Penrose Fry, who was a convert Anglican priest, and who remained a Roman Catholic, made this the theme of his book, *The Church Surprising* (1932). And in another book published a year later he went to great pains to show that Anglicanism and Roman Catholicism were two religious systems which were quite different (Fry 1933). This problem of severe change may be more acutely felt by converts coming from Anglo-Catholicism than from, say, Methodism or Anglicanism of a low church kind. The issue turns on expectations. Naïve Anglo-Catholics overlook the difference in ethos because they believe they already adhere to the same doctrines and participate in the same practices as Roman Catholics. They overlook cultural and social differences – different ways of conducting church business – because they believe that doctrine and ritual determine everything. They now have the 'truth'. For them, truth can have no cultural context, or, if it has, it is of no importance. What has been said may not be as applicable today as it was up until the 1960s. The reason quite clearly is that since Vatican II there have been changes in the direction of a more liberal outlook, which has given a greater cultural freedom to Catholic churches in various countries. The effect on Anglo-Catholic converts is not yet clear. Nevertheless it remains true that even today some converts return to their mother church. Others do not need to take the step of trying the ideal for they realize the problems which face them. We now look at some of the issues in a little more detail.

Anglo-Catholic clergy, and indeed Anglican clergy as a whole – perhaps the laity realize it as well – enjoy an enormous amount of liberty in the exercise of their ministry. They are subject to relatively few external constraints: discipline is very largely self-imposed. Maybe, amongst some Roman converts, that liberty is willingly forsaken and the imposition of external ecclesiastical controls welcomed. But for many it is not so and the desire to have intellectual and theological freedom to think and to write remains extremely strong. Such an isssue was of considerable importance to priests of an academic disposition. G. C. Rawlinson, the learned curate of St Barnabas's, Pimlico for thirty-three years, who was much interested in questions of reunion with Rome, wrote in defence of his Anglican position: 'I find also the Church of England more satisfactory because I can live in it a mental life more unhampered' (Rawlinson 1924:183). At a pastoral level, one has in mind unmarried Anglo-Catholic priests, who if they seceded would hope to carry on their priesthood after reordination. They realize they would lose the liberty they enjoyed in the Church of England and that at the same time they would be subject to fairly strong controls imposed by the Roman Catholic Church through the office of the bishop. This applies to two specific areas. The first relates to pastoral work and being one's own master within it and the freedom to arrange services according to one's own predilections. The second relates to homosexuality. By and large the Roman Catholic hierarchy in this country have always acted swiftly and decisively against priests whose sexual lives are known to fall below the moral teaching of the Church. It has its own way of dealing with offenders, which, as we have said, is in striking contrast to the leniency and powerlessness of Anglican bishops (see ch. 8.7). On the whole, also, the Church has allegedly a firm policy of not ordaining those who are known to be homosexuals.

Most of the clergy who become converts have had strong vocations to be priests and pastors and one of their wishes in so many cases is that they may continue to function in such a way in the church to which they have been converted. If they are already married when they are received, reordination is virtually impossible. Admittedly, in very recent times in the United States and in Britain, a select few who are married have been reordained. For those who are widowed there is usually no problem, as in the case of Cardinal Manning. But, for a man who has a firm vocation for the priesthood and would like to carry on with it in the Roman Church, being married presents an obstacle almost impossible to overcome.

For the married Anglo-Catholic priest, probably middle-aged, the practical problems involved in conversion are enormous. First, he has to find an occupation and doubtless has no qualification other than some special training for the priesthood, and perhaps a degree in arts or in theology. He has to find a job that will provide enough money for himself and his family. Further, there is the problem of buying a house with, more than likely, no capital behind him. For all the time that he was in the Anglican Church as an incumbent he will have lived in a tied house, a vicarage or rectory, rent-free. These problems were realized many years ago by the Roman Catholic Church. The Converts' Aid Society was established to help ex-Anglican priests who were married and required financial assistance. It is alleged that Ronald Knox donated £20,000 to the fund from fees and royalties on his books (Fitzgerald 1977:174). Pauline Adams has described in detail the deprivations and sufferings which many converts endured in the nineteenth century (Adams 1977). Today, of course, some of the financial problems facing a convert married priest can be alleviated, perhaps by the social services, perhaps by his wife going out to work. But the fact remains that clergy may not want to fall back on these resources and may feel humiliated by the problems which face them if they are to become Roman Catholics. For some married Anglican priests in their mid-50s or 60s, the great amount of change and effort required as they reach the last few years of pastoral work is probably not worth the candle. They prefer to stay as they are and deal with the problem personally as best they can. This may give rise to cynicism, not least in their attitude towards the Church of England.

Another issue which has certainly affected clergy – those who were aware of it at any rate – was the ritual process through which converts had to go. It certainly pertained in the past: today the rite of passage is less traumatic. The expression 'submission to Rome' epitomizes the process. Before formally embracing the Roman Catholic faith the proselyte must publicly denounce the errors of his past life and, in the case of an ex-Anglican priest or Nonconformist minister, he must consider null and void any work of a spiritual kind that he has attempted to do. It implies declaring that all that went on in the past was wrong, useless, or heretical. This declaration of negation is something which many Anglican clergy have found difficult to accept, for they may have spent many long years working in parishes and felt they were of great assistance to their parishioners. However, they have submitted themselves to it as an act of blind obedience and regarded it as the taking of an unpleasant medicine in order to experience spiritual health. This ritual denunciation Dr Orchard, the ex-Congregational minister, found most disturbing. He was totally unaware that it awaited him when he indicated his wish to be received into the Roman Catholic Church in Rome. He was given some help by an American Jesuit in trying to get around the difficulties but he remained very unhappy about the process (Orchard 1933). It might be said that to others this has not been a stumbling-block. One of the most extreme Anglo-Papalists of recent times, Hugh Ross Williamson, wrote that he 'found relief in the formal utterance demanded and made gladly on my reception: "With a sincere heart and with unfeigned faith, I detest and abjure every error, heresy and sect opposed to the Catholic, Apostolic and Roman Church"' (Williamson 1956:184).

Converts face psychological problems which are often not realized beforehand but which are commented on in some cases by those who go to the end of the road and return to the Church of England on account of them. One such problem arises from the enthusiasm which brings a convert to Rome but which is not shared by those of the congregation the convert joins. He or she may meet no one else but those who have been Catholics all their lives: their religion is just a way of life which they take for granted. It may be a bit of a bore – a convention that is accepted and liked, but nevertheless a convention. The ebullience and hopes of the convert receive the cold shoulder from the old-timer. Further, often much to their surprise, converts are not given the welcome they imagine they will receive. They may undergo a great struggle in eventually deciding to cross the Rubicon. They may feel heroic as a result of the struggle they have been through. Nevertheless, when they have taken the leap they find that they do not get a hero's welcome as they had expected, especially if they become members of an 'ordinary parish'. Some Catholics who have been Catholics all their lives are somewhat suspicious of converts. Further, they have their own particular social groups and habits and do not necessarily welcome others, especially 'strangers', into their midst. And priests who become reordained may not be given the positions of responsiblilty they think their abilities warrant. Witness the treatment of Newman. Anglicans who become converts may well not discover that degree of fellowship they expect from their notion of a church as being a community, a notion which in recent years has been inculcated in the Church of England and which is slowly beginning to emerge in Roman Catholic parish churches.

A knowledge of some or all these and other facts may well deter anyone who is thinking of becoming a Roman Catholic. Let it be said, however, that there is evidence in the other direction, and quite clearly many people who have become Catholic have found enormous happiness and contentment, and also some convert clergy have been given fairly important posts after they have been reordained.

4 Remaining for positive reasons

The existence of ambiguity within a religious system, even when that ambiguity is consciously realized, does not necessarily mean that a person will forsake the system. Despite all the disadvantages, there are people who still find the system highly attractive. We have hinted at some of these for Anglo-Catholicism (see ch. 5.8). An individual weighs up the pros and cons and decides that on the whole the pros outweigh the cons. Rather than enumerate the particular gains to be had by remaining in the Anglo-Catholic camp of the Church of England, we would point to the fact that some people explain their continuing presence in it by referring to bonds of loyalty, and to social and emotional ties which are obviously stronger and more important than its intellectual ambiguities.

What keeps so many Anglicans Anglican is an emotional attachment to the Church of England. There is something deep inside them which creates an affection for the church in which they may have been born and nurtured or to which they have converted, even perhaps drifted into.

Viewed from the outside it has to be admitted that the Church of England is more concerned with religious practice than with dogma, with people than with theology. It is essentially a 'homely' or pastoral church. Evelyn Underhill, daughter of a distinguished barrister, much revered writer and theologian on liturgical and spiritual matters, was, according to her own confession, for most of her life attracted to Roman Catholicism. Nevertheless, she once said that the Church of England was her 'ultimate home' (see Lloyd 1966:247). She justified the fact that she remained in the Anglican Church, not on doctrinal or liturgical grounds, but on pastoral and vocational ones. Dom Bernard Clements, Anglican Benedictine monk and vicar of All Saints', Margaret Street, said he was born very much in and of the Church of England. Eric Abbott, also a Prayer Book Catholic, who was dean of Westminster Abbey in the 1960s and 1970s and had a great affection for the Roman Catholic Church, found that affection was surpassed by his 'love of the Church of England' – words which appeared on the service sheet used at his memorial service. And more recently, Fr Bown, chairman of *Ecclesia*, a bastion of modern Anglo-Papalism, is reported to have said: 'We love the Church of England and . . . we love those thousands of faithful worshippers who gather regularly in the parish churches of our land.' An anonymous writer, calling himself 'An Anglo-Catholic', said in the 1880s:

> [The Church of England] fed me, nourished me, comforted me, tended me in every way, in joy and in sorrow, in sickness and in health . . . shall I leave her and join the ranks of those who though nearest of kin, yet dishonour, defame, and disown her?
>
> (Anglo-Catholic 1881:15)

There is a somewhat moving account in Sabine Baring-Gould's

book on the Catholic revival in the Church of England of an incumbent who obviously loved the Church in which he was ordained and who became a Catholic convert. Some years later he returned to the parish where he had been incumbent and after a period of prayer in the church was seen to be crying (Baring-Gould 1914:322).

Further examples are superfluous. Those which have been given show that intelligent, intellectual Anglicans, priests and lay people, defend their remaining in the Church of England on pastoral and cultural grounds. Priests do not want to desert their congregations, to which they have become attached and for which they show great concern. And, when they say they 'love the Church', they mean of course they love the Church of England in its cultural setting but above all implying that at the heart of the setting there stands what they see as a Catholic ethos. They probably love the architecture of English parish churches and cathedrals; they may be moved by the essential Englishness of the services and their settings, together with the English choral tradition which is to be found in major parish churches and in cathedrals, but which is totally absent in Roman Catholicism and the Free churches. There can surely be few more lovely or pleasing sights, especially on a fine summer's day, than the parish church set in the centre of a small English village: a parish church which has been there since Norman, or even Saxon times and has been the centre around which, for generations, the life of the village has revolved. All this would be lost to the priest if he were to became a Roman Catholic. But, above all, what of the people whom he has so devotedly served? Such a move might bring with it a sense of guilt. Would it not mean denying his English heritage and, more importantly, his vocation? To go to 'the other place' would be to turn away from a church that has been established for 400 years to embrace and become devoted to a church whose 'headquarters' is in another country, where the head of it may have very little sympathy with things English. This is no problem for those who have become Roman Catholic having had no strong Anglican background. Anglo-Catholics may try to create something of a counter-culture within the Church but deep down they still see themselves as very much part of the English scene. Indeed, as we have suggested, Anglo-Catholicism is uniquely English: by that fact its adherents stand or fall. Fr Stanton, a staunch Anglo-Catholic if ever there was one, an 'ideal type' Anglo-Catholic in fact, had a great dislike of Roman Catholicism and felt very sorry for those who were converted to it. He wrote to an undergraduate: 'I think it is deplorable when any young Englishman becomes a papist and associates himself with a system which can never be English or liberal' (Russell 1917:146). Rather strongly he continued: 'It blights his [the convert's] whole life, and the freshness of his character goes, and, as I believe, he does not become a whit better Christian.' Although he confessed he was a papist in the matter of credal belief, he also said he was a thoroughgoing Nonconformist in the matter of church policy and Voll thought that 'his heart beat more warmly for Nonconformity than it did for Rome' (Voll t.1963:96).

There was another kind of appeal. Anglo-Catholicism suited those of a liberal temperament for whom Catholicism was particularly attractive but who at the same time rejected some of the dogmatic and social doctrines of the Church of Rome. Such a figure was the priest and scholar John Neville Figgis (1866–1919). Figgis was originally from 'The Countess of Huntingdon's Connexion' and became a member of the Community of the Resurrection in 1907. His particular interest was in political theory and its relation to Christianity: he was also a very popular preacher. In a little-known book, *Hopes for English Religion* (1919), he openly declared his loyalty to the Anglican Church and Anglo-Catholicism. The 'glorious comprehensiveness' of Anglicanism appealed to him (Figgis 1919:86). Anglo-Catholicism could be supported by a kind of psychological argument with liberal overtones. People's emotional predispositions are highly variable and in religious matters they select a type of Christianity for which they are best suited. Anglo-Catholicism therefore has a legitimate place within the spectrum of Christian manifestations (Figgis 1919:87ff.). Similarly, low church, Evangelical, and broad-church manifestations are also completely acceptable (see section 2 above).

Further, self-satisfaction, consciously realized or not, may be found by remaining in a sectarian ethos. Many Anglo-Catholics past and present, not least the clergy, appear to take pleasure in being in such an ethos. By labelling themselves Catholic, they are able to distance themselves from other Anglicans (see ch. 7). In some ways contrary to the general meaning of the word Catholic, and perhaps unlike Roman Catholics, they take a delight in being different from others, in marking themselves off on account of their particular beliefs and practices (see ch. 7, especially 7.3) Such in-group differentiation gives them pleasure and satisfaction, not least in criticizing run-of-the-mill Anglicans. For example, an Anglo-Catholic priest said to his curate: 'Don't hold your hands like an *Anglican* bishop' (in Williams 1982:121, author's emphasis). Some Anglo-Catholics may realize that to 'cross over' would mean that they would no longer stand in such a sectarian position. Their 'Catholicism' within Roman Catholicism would be part of a total Catholic structure, so that their wish to be different would certainly have to take on a different form from that which they experienced in the Church of England as Anglo-Catholics. Nevertheless, being within a sectarian situation sometimes works the other way around. People get tired of always being in a minority, of always being members of a tiny, 'cranky' group, and this may propel them to move in the direction of a much larger body.

The enjoyment which comes from being in a sectarian position is often associated with personal aggression and the need to have legitimate ways of expressing it against the world outside. Aggression amongst Anglo-Catholic clergy, and in some cases laity, can only be touched on briefly. As we have observed there can be no doubt that, in the attitudes of clergy towards bishops in the late nineteenth century and even today, hostility was much in evidence (see ch. 6.3). This is seen in Mackenzie's trilogy of novels already mentioned (see especially 1923 and 1924). Authoritarian figures in the Church, whether archdeacons or bishops, have been, and perhaps still are, the objects of Anglo-Catholic aggression (see ch. 7.2). The hostility, which is often observed in the form of tasteless gossip, has been used to denigrate bishops who sometimes imagined they were sympathetic towards the Catholic cause but who in the eyes of Anglo-Catholics were clearly not so. Once again, it is argued that if an Anglo-Catholic 'poped', he (almost never she) would lose a legitimate vehicle for the expression of aggression within a religious mode.

5 Remaining for reasons of indifference

A thorough and gradually acquired knowledge of the religious body to which one might be initially attracted may act as a deterrent against converting to it. In anticipating the religious life which will be enjoyed in the 'new' church, an individual may well take into consideration what will have to be embraced and balance it against what will be lost. Of course the concept of 'Roman fever' often means that such rational decisions are irrelevant since no peace can be achieved until the fever has left the patient. A reasonable analysis of the situation is seldom taken into account in such circumstances (see, for example, Benson 1913). A consideration of fears and expectations, some of which have already been mentioned, can be more abstractly represented by saying that to change one's religion is to bid farewell to one set of ambiguities only to take on board another. An individual may decide that one set is preferable to another, one more bearable than another, one less threatening than another. So be it. As a result of such calculations a person may decide to remain in one position or move to another. But the point is that, in ch....ging a religious position, one does not move from hell to heaven, from horror to bliss, from ambiguities galore to rational clarity. In short, as we have repeatedly stated, there is no escape from ambiguity in religion. The point is: which set of ambiguities can one most comfortably live with?

And, faced with that question, many who have experience of various religious systems may feel that a change from one system which is only slightly removed from another is not worth the effort. It is much easier to remain where one is and make the best of it, knowing that no system is perfect; all have their weaknesses and deficiencies. There is more to life than trying to escape from ambiguity. Again, it is probably true to say that in the Church of England at present, because of recent liturgical changes, there are many, irrespective of church party or background, who find much they dislike in the institution, but they are not strongly enough attracted by any other church to change. Using a rather crude push–pull model, which has its origins in radio circuitry, there is ample push but not enough pull.

Some may see this as a cynical reaction: perhaps the reaction of middle, or of old age. Put in a different light it might be said it is an abandonment of the attempt to reduce or eliminate ambiguity. This may create another ambiguity. in bridging the others. Recently an Anglo-Catholic priest wrote: 'As I look back over my life I am fully conscious that I have managed to create my own "Anglican attitude" and hold it against all intrusion of reality' (Stephenson 1972:180). And he went on, 'Perhaps I will manage to continue to live all my life as an Anglican in a fantasy world' (Stephenson 1972:192). In one of Compton Mackenzie's novels, a young Anglo-Catholic priest says: 'I admit my spiritual home is Rome, but I cannot believe that I am not a priest. And so I am just holding on' (Mackenzie 1924:264). Such people have to keep at bay what is seen to be reality by creating rationalizing techniques. It is a position which can be extremely fragile: a single blow, an unexpected event, some unsuspected theological disturbance, and the defences against reality immediately crumble away.

Finally, there is something ambiguous in Anglo-Catholic priests, especially Anglo-Papalists, who by their example lead people towards Roman Catholicism and then get annoyed when they catch Roman fever and take the final step, while the priests themselves remain where they are. There was something of this in Fr Stanton, as we have seen. Fr Ommanney was 'always distressed . . . when anyone he knew made their submission to Rome'. He was said to be no Romanizer, yet he closely followed in the services he conducted the instructions of the Congregation of Sacred Rites of the Vatican (Belton 1936:27). Doubtless he could see the subtleties of his position, which were not clear to those who felt that, having got so far along the Catholic road, they should take the final step.

6 Methodological differences

Finally, something must be said about the general approaches of Anglicans and Roman Catholics to the question of the truth of their religious positions. It was pointed out in the 1870s that there was indeed a significant difference in the attitude of the two religious groups (see Martin 1878a:127ff.). Anglo-Catholics and indeed Anglicans examine Roman Catholicism and the development of the church in an analytical way, looking at various components, for example, bishops, eucharist, the Bible, and so on, quite separately, searching above all for the historical facts relating to them. This is in contrast to Roman Catholics, who look at the system as a whole, and see how each component relates to the other, and therefore look at the entity as a totality without paying too much attention to details. In other words, the Roman Catholic approach looks at the package – the overall structure – and disregards details, which are irrelevant. 'Great institutions, like great buildings, ought to be judged by their broad outlines' (Martin 1878a:134). Strangely enough this is a pragmatic kind of argument which might not be favoured by all Roman Catholic theologians, though it is by apologists. The Roman system as a whole works and has worked well all down the centuries. Therefore it is true! Anglo-Catholics, embedded in Anglicanism, find this kind of approach unsatisfactory. They are much more concerned with what they call historical facts: with the historical development of things, century by century, piece by piece. Gladstone said: 'We think ourselves to be great lovers of historical truth' (1878:430). The English are suspicious of moving beyond facts and making deductions or creating systems. Anglo-Catholics stay where they are, perhaps on account of such a basic outlook. The history they have been taught or acquired for ever remains with them.

Chapter 11

The effects of various options: the position today

1 A general view

It would be absurd to imagine that everyone who has been an Anglo-Catholic has either joined the Church of Rome or has remained a loyal Anglo-Catholic to the end. Some, especially clergy, have in the course of their lives moved away from their early idealistic hopes towards a less Catholic position in adopting something akin to a central churchmanship. They would probably call themselves Catholic or Catholically inclined but would not stand by the ideology to be found at the heart of the movement. It must also be assumed that in the face of internal ambiguities, or perhaps for other reasons, there have been those who have left Anglo-Catholicism and the Church of England altogether and have not established links with another church. They would consider themselves to be amongst the great secular mass typified by an indifference towards institutional religion. How far Anglo-Catholics have helped to swell the ranks of non-practising semi-believers is impossible to know. Only some kind of carefully conducted national poll can provide an answer. The observations of the author would indicate that the proportion of Anglo-Catholics who 'drop out of religion altogether' is not as great on a per capita basis as it is for those of other types of churchmanship.

What has happened in Anglo-Catholicism thus has to be related to the number of those who have left the movement to join another denomination, especially the Roman Catholic Church, and more recently Orthodox Churches, those who have adopted another position within the Church of England, or who have left to join the ranks of 'nothingarianism'. The losses, which of course have to include those who have died as Anglo-Catholics, have to be off-set by recruitment, by those baptized and nurtured as Anglo-Catholics, together with 'converts' to the movement. Clearly, statistics for all these categories are impossible to compute.

Mentioning such possibilities, however, does raise the question which it seems fitting to consider at the conclusion of the book. Is Anglo-Catholicism any longer the force it once was? And, by extension, how has it fared in the period following the Second World War?

There can be no doubt that the movement is but a shadow of its former self – the self of the 1920s and 1930s. It can no longer command the legions which once followed it; it has no outstanding leaders, save perhaps the present bishop of London; its confidence and optimism have gone; the sense of triumph has been eroded; instead of advancing as it saw itself doing in the 1920s it is now fighting, not very successfully, a rearguard action. If life is about battles, this one is over. To some it stands as an essentially Victorian product – to be admired or criticized depending on one's attitude to Victorian virtues and achievements. Either way, its place in contemporary society is clearly not important. Its *passé* appearance is seen in the kind of music it prescribes, the formalism of its services, the dress of its traditional priests, all epitomized by the absence of young families in its congregations. Lest criticism be all too readily heaped on Anglo-Catholicism, let it not be forgotten that many churches and church movements have suffered in much the same way, perhaps to a greater extent. In the period of secularization or alienation which has been in progress for more than a century, Anglo-Catholicism has suffered as much as any of the churches. Just after the Second World War it was said that the movement had ceased to move, or had at best slowed down due to the forces of indifference, materialism, and immorality (Maughan 1947:iii). Apart from these bland concepts, it is true that there has been scarcely a church which has not experienced some kind of shrinkage, be it the Church of England as a whole, Methodism, the Free churches, or, in more recent times, the Roman Catholic Church. But one cannot leave the matter there and put it all down to secularization. Some churches had declined more than others and in different ways. The nature and extent of the changes in different groups needs to be explored.

Rather prophetically the editor of the *Church Times* may have shocked its readers with these words written in 1944. The paper had always been known to support Anglo-Catholicism, though not necessarily rabid Anglo-Papalism.

> For some time the Catholic Movement in the Church of
> England has ceased to move. It has been without a clearly defined
> purpose; it has lacked outstanding leaders; it no longer enlists

the enthusiasm of youth. . . . It might be natural to infer that it has done its work, and that the time has come to sum up its achievement and to write its epitaph.

(quoted in *CT*, 5 February 1988, supplement p. xviii).

To examine these assertions in more detail, one must look first at the internal difficulties which are peculiar to the movement and which have arisen in recent decades. These difficulties have sprung from inherent ambiguities which have been activated by unanticipated historical events. But before these are pointed out one should have some kind of picture of the present state of Anglo-Catholicism, using a crude indicator employed at the beginning of the book, the Anglo-Catholic congresses. How have they fared since the Second World War?

2 The final congresses: the saga ends

After the fifth Anglo-Catholic congress of 1933 it was decided to wait for seven years in order that evangelistic work, which had been planned, could be undertaken in parishes associated with the congress. When that had been completed it was hoped to hold another gathering (ACC 1948). The war intervened and finally a congress was organized by the Church Union in 1948, which coincided with a meeting of Anglican bishops throughout the world held in Lambeth. Compared with the 70,000 which had gathered in 1933, the 11,000 who were present and the 13,000 who enrolled are an indicator of the great change in fortunes of the congresses and most likely of Anglo-Catholicism as a whole over a period of fifteen years. Nevertheless, the organizers were delighted with the response after such an elapse of time and thought it highly successful. Some nostalgically recalled earlier congresses and others were convinced that 'a new start was needed for the active propaganda of the Catholic faith' (ACC 1948:viii).

The old 'cathedral' – the Royal Albert Hall – was not available but the Central Hall, Westminster, was. Here it is salutary to recall how the Methodists at the very beginning of the congresses had refused to accommodate the first one which was planned. Bookings demanded the hiring of the Kingsway Hall as well, another Methodist bastion. The ethos of previous congresses was maintained by having evensong sung in Westminster Abbey where, it was reported, the entire building was full. A similar attendance was reported at the concluding evensong in St Paul's cathedral the following Saturday. As in previous congresses, the cultic shrines of Anglo-Catholicism – the many London churches near the centre, including the most famous of them all, St Alban's, Holborn, which had been almost completely destroyed in the London blitz, and was later restored – had special services with full Anglo-Catholic ceremonial. Attendances were generally high everywhere and in certain cases people had to be turned away. The congress, which had as a theme Catholic evangelization, lasted for a week. All this was very reminiscent of old times, although, as we have just noted, overall figures were down. The most notable difference between this congress and earlier ones, apart from the decline in attendance, was the presence of diocesan bishops, such as those of Newcastle, Ely, London, and Oxford, who all took part at some stage of the congress. But once again, as in previous congresses, attention was given to defence by showing that the major services, at least, were in accordance with the 1662 Prayer Book. On the whole, the lectures were more theologically grounded and less pastorally orientated than they had been at previous congresses. There were many able academics at the meetings immediately after the war, people like Gregory Dix, Michael Ramsey, and Donald Mackinnon, but somehow what they had to say did not click and the congress appeared to lack the social euphoria of previous gatherings.

The impetus generated at the 1948 congress was either not sufficient or of the wrong kind to promote further congresses of the same pattern. In 1958, again coinciding with the meeting of bishops of the Anglican Communion at Lambeth, a Church Union Eucharistic Congress was organized to cover a shorter period of time, and acquired a different name from the previous congresses (see ch. 2.3). Only 1,700 were reported to be at the high mass in the Albert Hall (*CT*, 4 July 1958). Fr Hugh Bishop of the Community of the Resurrection preached at the evensong held in Westminster Abbey in the presence of Princess Margaret and this, it appears, was the first time a royal personage had been present at an Anglo-Catholic congress or its equivalent. Lectures were fewer and perhaps less academic than in 1948. Not very convincingly, it was reported in the *Church Times* that the congress 'is showing that famous spirit of enthusiasm which has marked each congress since 1920; it has characterized every session in the Royal Albert Hall' (*CT*, 4 July 1958).

The next congress was in 1968 when the Church Union convened one in the Royal Festival Hall, covering three days, as in the case of the previous congress. Unlike all other congresses, it had a theme, 'All Things New'. Once again it was graced by the presence of Princess Margaret. The congress held a solemn eucharist according to the new liturgy – new liturgies were then beginning to appear in the Church of England everywhere. The reporter for the *Church Times* noted that, as an example of the changes which were taking place, no priest wore a biretta. A remarkable shift indeed, if one recalls the earlier congresses. The bishop of Peterborough, Cyril Eastaugh, was prominent at the congress and the archbishop of Canterbury, Michael Ramsey, who had lectured at the 1948 congress, was one of the chief speakers. Ecumenism had now entered with a flourish and a Roman Catholic bishop was present (what a reception he would have received had he attended one of the earlier congresses!), in addition to an Orthodox archbishop, and a monk from Taizé, the well-known Protestant relgious community in France. The congress hall was dominated by the great cross which had been used at every Anglo-Catholic congress from 1920 onwards. But this symbol of continuity was placed in a new socio-religious situation in which not only were there radical shifts in modes of worship but also the old symbols and enthusiasms had gone. There were those who still yearned for days gone by and they kept away. In the main they were the Anglo-Papalists who felt that the changes were alien to much that they stood for (*CT*, 10 May 1968). On the whole the congress appears to have met with indifference and, interestingly enough, this time it did not coincide with the Lambeth Conference of that year.

A further ten years and the form had changed even more radically. The venue was no longer London but a provincial university, Loughborough. The 1978 gathering was not an Anglo-Catholic congress or a Church Union congress but a Catholic Renewal conference, prompted very largely by the Jubilee group – a group, started in 1974, dedicated to revive the languishing fortunes of Anglo-Catholicism and its ecclesiastical narrowness (see Leech and Williams 1983:7ff.). The response to the venture was lamentable. The organizers sent out 12,000 letters to parishes, organizations and individuals, asking for financial support and promise of attendance. In the event only 1,000 people were present at the conference, 586 clergy and 423 lay people, and of the latter there were equal proportions of men and women. And only £17,000 was contributed to help finance the conference. It was quite remarkable that one commentator should say 'Anglo-Catholics are recovering their confidence and being renewed' (*CT*, 21 April 1978). Perplexity, indifference, and a failure of nerve seems to have now entered into the heart of the Anglo-Catholic movement and members of the Jubilee Group indicated such a state of affairs (Leech and Williams 1983:9).

This judgement was not reversed when in 1983 festivities were held to mark the 150th anniversary of the founding of the Oxford movement. Clearly such an occasion could not go unheeded by Catholic-minded people and another Loughborough conference was called by the Church Union. In the event only 650 people took part, far fewer than in 1978 and a miniscule number compared with that of fifty years earlier. It gave rise to great dissatisfaction, both at the time and subsequently. Some clergy, Catholic by allegiance, declared their reasons for refusing to go to it. It was evident that amongst other things splits had occurred within the movement. There were two other events that year which might be said to be of interest to Anglo-Catholics. One was a pilgrim eucharist, held in the Parks in Oxford in July, at which the archbishop of Canterbury, Robert Runcie, preached. Organizers had expected 10,000 to turn up on the morning, but according to some estimates there were 6,500 and others put the figure as low as 2,500 (*CT*, 27 July 1983). A little later there was a day's gathering in the Royal Albert Hall in the style of the Anglo-Catholic congresses, where it was reported that 2,000 were present.

Perhaps Anglo-Catholicism and indeed the Oxford movement had now value only for professional historians, for there was also in 1983 a conference held in Keble College, Oxford, which consisted entirely of academic lectures about the movement. These can in no way be compared to the theological and pastoral lectures given at the earlier Anglo-Catholic congresses. The fortunes of the Catholic revival were such that they were now on the dissecting table of professional analysts, who looked back on the past, glanced at the present, and had nothing to say about the future. Yet, given the change of stance to an essentially academic one, it is quite remarkable that so few volumes of this ilk appeared compared with what was published at the centenary in 1933 (see Kent 1987:105). Little else emerged apart from the conference papers, published as *Tradition Renewed* (Rowell 1986), Rowell's book *The Vision Glorious* (1983), *Revolution by Tradition* (Rowell and Cobb 1983), and *Pusey Rediscovered* (Butler 1983). For the same occasion of the 150th anniversary the Jubilee Group produced a series of eighteen essays in a book called *Essays Catholic and Radical* (Leech and Williams 1983). The book was intended to inject new life into a flagging movement and to counteract decay and demoralization. Although the title of the book had obvious parallels with *Essays Catholic and Critical* (Selwyn 1926), which caused a great stir not only in Anglo-Catholic circles but in the Church of England at large, this volume has provoked virtually no interest at all, amongst either 'the faithful' or outsiders. In fact it is very difficult to obtain. A series of books entitled Faith and the Future, and published by Basil Blackwell, was also launched in 1983, which does not appear to have had the success that was hoped for.

In 1988, at the time of the Lambeth Conference, all that could be managed by the Church Union for the Catholic-minded was, apart from a rally for bishops at the shrine of our Lady of Walsingham, a day's 'national Lambeth rally' held at Church House, Westminster. It drew only between 450 and 500 people and was addressed, it would seem, entirely by English bishops and lay people (*CT*, 17 July 1988).

3 Some other indicators

So the congresses were dead and buried and seem never likely to be resurrected. It might be said that their days had to come to an end anyway.

The use of the Anglo-Catholic congresses as an indicator of the fortunes of Anglo-Catholicism is admittedly very crude but it is not without point. In the end what happened in 1978 and 1983 might be said to reflect the current state of affairs in the Anglo-Catholic world. The level of commitment and membership, judged from various observations and statistics relating to parish churches and organizations, shows signs of very serious decline. For example, the Church Union, formerly the English Church Union, which has been the most comprehensive organization of Anglo-Catholicism, had a membership of 39,000 in 1901; but in the 1960s the figure had dropped to about 16,500 (Ferris 1962:187; ch. 4.2). The movement lacks coherence and meaningful goals and at the same time shows signs of exhaustion. The more sceptical would speak of a collapse. Alan Wilkinson, once a committed Anglo-Catholic and potential leader of the movement, wrote an article with the title 'Requiem for Anglo-Catholicism?' (1978b; see also Gunstone 1968:191ff.). More recently Adrian Hastings, in comparing the growing strength of the Evangelicals, has been bold enough to state that in the 1960s the Anglo-Catholic party 'lay devastated' (Hastings 1986:554). Today, about half of all ordinands leaving theological colleges are of Evangelical persuasion. Realizing the implications of this, the Church Union has recently made a call for 'many more' young men who are Anglo-Catholic to offer themselves for ordination (*CT*, 17 July 1988). Generally speaking, there has been no rallying-point, save in the recent and dramatic issue of the ordination of women, which may have injected some new life into the movement, but it certainly has not rallied all Anglo-Catholics.

Apart from extensive sociological research, no better way of assessing the present state of Anglo-Catholicism exists than to visit some of the famous Anglo-Catholic churches in London and its suburbs and in the provinces. The overall impression, judged at least by what one imagined occurred in the past, is one of decline, even pathetic depletion. It is true that some churches continue to flourish, for example, All Saints', Margaret Street (today considered to be just 'high church' by some Anglo-Papalists); St Mary's, Bourne Street; St Stephen's, Gloucester Road; and doubtless there are others. But one can find counter-examples in the famous Anglo-Catholic churches and be convinced that attendances are now nowhere near those of fifty years ago. In this respect one might mention St Alban's, Holborn, with its enormous popularity under Fr Mackonochie and Fr Stanton. About a year ago it had an electoral roll (membership) of 60 and many people on the list came from miles away, as far as Sussex and the south coast. (On a Sunday in 1902 or 1903 total attendances were 865; see Smith 1904:181.) At St Mary's, Somers Town, near Euston station, there were only about 30 people present at a sung mass on a Sunday in April 1986. (On a Sunday in 1902 or 1903 total attendances were 199; see Smith 1904:175.) This church was famous in the 1920s when the the vicar, Fr Basil Jellicoe, created the St Pancras House Improvement Society in a very bad slum area and raised thousands of pounds to build tenement dwellings. Very symbolic is what has happened to St Matthew's, Westminster, during the past decade. The church has been a key church in this book since it was the centre of the Anglo-Catholic congresses. In 1977 it was tragically destroyed by fire and later rebuilt. The new church, which was largely paid for by selling part of the site, seats only about a hundred people, a fraction of the seating capacity of the former church. A friend of the author, who in the early days of the Second World War worshipped regularly at St Cyprian's, Clarence Gate, in north-west London, recently visited the church again on a Sunday and was greatly upset to find the congregation had diminished from a very sizeable gathering as it once was, to a mere handful of people. One imagines, from the state of Anglican churches generally, that this kind of experience could be repeated many times over.

Many of the East End churches, and others connected with slums around London, have, according to most reports, suffered severe losses of membership and in many cases the losses have been so severe as to have brought about the closure of the churches. St Augustine's, Haggerston, and St Columba's, Hoxton, both of them very large and famous Anglo-Catholic churches in their day, lie desolate, if not literally, then ecclesiastically. One is used for a motor-cycle club and the other has been taken over by a black-led church, the Catholic Apostolic Church (see ch. 4.5).

In some cases – in many cases – Anglo-Catholic churches have suffered from demographic changes in the parishes in which they are situated. Changes in inner city populations have affected them radically. Famous Anglo-Catholic churches have, as we have noted, been located in the main either in the centre of cities or in poor areas. With the growth of commerce and business the city parishes have been subject to a continual exodus of people who live in them. Especially in London, but the same applies to other cities, down-town churches, sometimes suddenly, sometimes gradually, find they have no 'natural' population. In the slums and other deprived areas the population changes in the face of social and geographical mobility. Into the vacuum so created come other individuals and ethic groups whose religious background is far from that of Anglo-Catholicism or even the Church of England! From where do the priests draw a congregation? One example of a church so placed is Fr Dolling's famous Italianate church, St Agatha's, Portsmouth, which for many decades has been under threat of demolition, owing to its depopulated position in the city. But there are plenty of other instances where changed demography is not the cause of decline, as in the suburbs of cities. Some Anglo-Catholic clergy saw what was going on before their very eyes and could do little to arrest it. In Sheffield in years gone by Fr Ommanney noted his parishioners moving out to the suburbs with the inevitable weakening of his own popular church (Belton 1936:177–8).

But, as mentioned, it is not always a question of demography. The suburbs are not depopulated. Probably nothing is more tragic for Anglo-Catholics than to see St Alban's, Teddington, a glorious Gothic church in the French style and often referred to as the cathedral of Anglo-Catholicism, now lying desolate, vandalized, and under threat of demolition, although some plan for saving the building itself has just been announced (*CT*, 4 March 1988). On a census Sunday in 1902–3, the church had 1,059 attendances and at an even 'spikier' church in Teddington, St Peter and St Paul, attendances were 909 (Smith 1904:374). In those days Teddington was a dominantly 'Catholic' district.

We have already had occasion to refer to the age structure of Anglo-Catholic congregations today, which augurs ill for the future (see ch. 4.3).There are virtually no Sunday schools or catechism classes for the young. And this means that a minimal number of young people are being recruited. Clubs and societies, especially for the young, are virtually absent, save specifically religious societies such as the Guild of the Servants of the Sanctuary, which today has a membership of 10,000 (*CT*, 8 May 1987). All this is in stark contrast to the early days of Catholicism and to the period of its heyday. With no means of socializing potential adult members, the churches, whether they are of Anglo-Catholic persuasion or not, will continue to have older and older congregations, which, in the end, means dissolution. Recruitment can of course come by adults, young and old, joining the church from outside and this does sometimes happen. But a lack of young people in a church congregation projects the image of living in and for the past.

One might point to other indicators, such as the collapse of various publishing houses, for example the Dacre Press, and that of the Society of SS Peter & Paul, although the Church Literature Association still lives on in a somewhat enfeebled way. There can be no doubt that, in the early days, Anglo-Catholics relied a great deal on their presses in the publication of many pamphlets and tracts which they sold at the back of their churches. In any case, these are bad days for religious presses of any denomination or none.

Probably in the eyes of Anglo-Catholic leaders no place is a better or more revered symbol of their movement at its best than Pusey House, Oxford. It has certainly been the centre of its academic life, not least on account of its library and archives. In 1984, on the occasion of its centenary, an appeal was launched for £1 million to restore the fabric of the chapel, to fund visiting fellowships, and to improve the library, the basis of which was originally Pusey's (*CT*, 19 October 1984). It was the first appeal in a hundred years. So far as is known the target was never met. In place of the hopes expressed at the centenary, Pusey House in fact became St Cross College, a constituent college of the university, which had come into existence after the Second World War and which needed a new site. The chapel and library have remained outside the absolute control of the college, and the principal and librarians now live off the site. Compared with the intentions of the founders of the House, what has happened marks a significant withdrawal and diminution of function and status of its place at the heart of the university which initiated and nurtured the Catholic revival.

Roger Lloyd, who always showed sympathies towards certain

forms of Anglo-Catholicism, concluded his books on the Church of England, written after the Second World War, with no reference to the movement as such or the Catholic wing of the Church of England (Lloyd 1966, the epilogue in 1950; Lloyd was much opposed to Anglo-Catholic extremists). Arguments from silence may be dangerous but it seems legitimate to conclude that looking into the future of the Church he has nothing to say of significance about the Catholic movement. All its achievements lie in the past. It is, as was suggested at the beginning of the chapter, a product of Victorianism and as such it has to be evaluated.

With extraordinary insight there appeared recently in the notices of an Anglo-Catholic church in London: 'Annual Requiem for Catholic Societies of the Church of England. Date to be announced' (Wilkinson 1978b:40).

4 Ambiguities activated: Parish and People movement

Historical factors activate or make poignant ambiguities which heretofore may have been dormant. It is the emergence of these factors which may cause individuals either to change their religious position or else to come to a new understanding of it. Since the Second World War, and more precisely since the late 1960s, a number of events have taken place within the Church of England and society at large which have had direct repercussions on the state of Anglo-Catholicism. Such is their number that only a few of what are considered to be the most important historical factors can be considered here (see Wilkinson 1978b).

Beginning in the late 1930s and gaining momentum in the years which immediately followed the Second World War, there emerged a movement which was centred on the parish communion and later became known as the Parish and People movement. Although its origins can be traced back to the clergy who were either within or on the edge of Anglo-Catholicism, its eventual growth meant a weakening of the very party which had given it birth (for a history of the movement, see Gray 1986; Jagger 1978; Pinnington 1983:118ff.).

The basic ideas behind the movement rested on the Catholic directive that every Sunday members of a parish should attend mass at the local church. Those who founded the movement realized the limited success of Anglo-Catholicism and that if the holy communion service were to take the place of matins as the chief act of worship on a Sunday a less extreme form of ritualization would have to be encouraged. Basic Catholic ideas had to be propagated without arousing hostility or alienation. In Anglo-Catholicism itself there was another problem. It related to the pattern which had grown up where the devout would go to a low mass said on a Sunday morning at, say, 8 a.m., or perhaps earlier. The intention was to receive holy communion in a quiet reverential manner. People would attend the service fasting, a practice which was much stressed by both Anglo-Catholics and Tractarians from the very outset. The devout were urged to return to church later in the morning to attend a sung mass or a high mass, which would be accompanied by full ceremonial, hymns, a sermon, but no communion for the people, because it was assumed that anyone who attended the service would have had breakfast. The role of worshippers at such a service was that of adoration or worship, but nothing more, save being edified by the sermon. Priests felt that it was more important for people to attend mass every Sunday and on days of obligation than just to go to holy communion once or twice a month. Of course, it was often argued by critics of Anglo-Catholicism that such attendance at mass without receiving communion was contrary to the ethos of the Prayer Book. One of the strongest advocates for breaking down the gulf between the two functions of receiving communion and of worship was the Anglo-Catholic theologian, A. G. Hebert (see Hebert 1935 and 1937). Gradually there began to emerge a new ideal that there should be one service in every parish church, that of holy communion, to which people would come to worship and make their communion. It was also realized that the Church had wrongly divided the ministry of the Sacrament from the ministry of the Word and that preaching was also an integral part of eucharistic worship. In addition to a sermon, parish communion advocates wanted to have the service adorned with simple but dignified Catholic ceremonial, if possible with the celebrant wearing vestments, and the service sung, with hymns. Faithful Christian people were expected to come to this one service and it would be the basis of their Sunday duties. Further, it should be held at a time that was suitable to the majority when, for example, mothers and children should also be present. For better or for worse, the hour of 9.00 or 9.30 in the morning was the time which clergy felt was best. Perhaps a light breakfast might be provided in the parish hall after the service in the hope of helping people to accept the Catholic practice of fasting before communion. Having some light refreshment after the service was based on the idea that those who had attended the service should grow together in common fellowship (for the theological foundation of this, see Thornton 1941). Such a gathering could be seen as a meeting of the church in which issues relating to the welfare of the church could be discussed and about which decisions could be made.

On grounds of theology and common sense what the movement advocated seemed very attractive to those living in the decades immediately following the Second World War. Its advantages were obvious to Prayer Book Catholics, who felt that neither sung matins with a sermon nor high mass was a suitable form of worship for most parishes in the Church of England. Hardline Anglo-Catholics could at least rejoice in the fact that the movement was based on the fundamental Catholic premise that 'it is the mass that matters'. It is interesting that these ideas were propagated by one or two individual Anglo-Catholic priests long before the movement took the Church of England virtually by storm. During the last few decades the notion of fasting before communion has became eroded and people have begun to see the popular custom of offering refreshments after the service as a kind of mid-morning coffee rather than a mini-breakfast. The final blow to a strict fast before receiving communion came with the reforms of Vatican II, with the call for frequent communion and above all the fact that mass could now be said in the evenings on weekdays as well as on Sundays.

The great success of the Parish and People movement has meant, among other things, a blurring of the boundaries between the Anglo-Catholic and non-Anglo-Catholic parish churches. People can say: 'We are now all Catholics, for we all know that the eucharist has become our main service.' Little wonder therefore that statistics for receiving communion have remained relatively high despite the falling off of the numbers of those attending church. Another result has been that the notion of 'hearing mass' has tended to disappear, even in Anglo-Papalist circles. A non-communicating mass – usually a high mass, at one time also a children's mass – is now, largely due to the Parish and People movement, almost completely something of the past. The movement has transformed worship Sunday by Sunday so as to satisfy both the Catholic-minded and the more Protestant-minded. Above all, it has to a very large extent broken down many traditional ideas and practices in Anglo-Catholicism in the matter of norms for worship.

5 To compromise or not to compromise over church reunification?

From the early days of Anglo-Catholicism there was a strong desire to bring about a reunion of the churches so as to create that kind of unity which existed in Christendom during the middle ages (see ch. 7.5). It meant a union of Catholic churches to the exclusion of all Protestant bodies. The policy was also strongly advocated by the Oxford Fathers. The Anglo-Papalist, Hugh Ross Williamson, said he wanted the Catholic movement to grow to such a degree as 'to make the Establishment itself seek reconciliation with the Holy See' (Williamson 1956:112). For nearly all Anglo-Catholics any scheme for reunion with non-Catholic bodies turned on the *sine qua non* doctrine of apostolic succession. To abandon such a position would be to de-catholicize the Church of England straight away and there would never be any reunion with Rome. If Protestant churches were prepared to accept such a doctrine, which is the guarantee of the validity of the sacraments, all well and good. If not, there could be no reunion. There were, of course, hopeful ruses for getting around the impasse such as those which emerged in the South India reunion schemes where the bishops were the chief pastors but where the doctrine about them was open to different interpretations. The totally negative attitude adopted by Anglo-Catholics over this and other schemes for reunion which has involved Protestants has in recent decades backfired. Such intransigent attitudes have turned out to be unpopular amongst more moderate Anglo-Catholics, who realized that the preservation of any rigid doctrine over apostolic succession, especially in the light of Vatican II, was in itself no guarantee of *rapprochement*. Anglo-Catholics have moved in various directions as events have overtaken them. The Church of South India was created in 1947. When eventually in 1955 some degree of intercommunion between the Church of England and the Church of South India was sanctioned only a limited number of Anglo-Catholics left the Church of England, including members of the Annunciation group, which had been formed to consider the threat of the oncoming storm (see Williamson 1956:181ff.). Any expectation of a mass exodus never materialized. The intransigence of hard-line Anglo-Catholics, which helped defeat the Anglo-Methodist scheme for reunion in 1972 after many years of preparation, gained them few friends. Indeed, some Anglo-Catholics became disillusioned with the policy of the party and felt that a more open approach should be adopted. They therefore no longer wished to be identified with the movement. Again, in some ways their reactions have coincided with the change in attitude of the Roman Catholic Church since the reforms of Vatican II, where that Church has taken the initiative and entered into negotiations, or at least conversations, with Protestant bodies which have no pretence of having apostolic succession. In this way the Anglo-Catholic position has been bypassed and their servile following of what they held was essentially a Roman Catholic doctrine in the matter of church order has been made to look silly (see ch. 6.2). Further, in negotiations between the churches, the Anglo-Catholics are not going to receive a privileged place within Anglicanism. In no way can it be said that Anglo-Catholics and Anglo-Catholics alone speak for the Church of England. The old dilemma of Anglo-Catholicism being a party within a church rears its head once again. Furthermore, it has been a party that has constantly looked backwards and not forwards and in so doing has had much of its ground cut from beneath its feet (see ch. 6.4).

6 To be Catholic and charismatic?

The Roman Catholic Church was taken by complete surprise when in the United States in the 1960s the phenomenon of speaking with tongues and other forms of charismatic enthusiasm suddenly burst into its very midst. Such exuberant phenomena, once condemned by R. A. Knox in his book, *Enthusiasm* (1950), have been tolerated by church authorities, and perhaps even more than tolerated. Certainly they have not been repressed as they might have been in previous centuries. The charismatic movement as a whole strives to give each person a sense of religious freedom – a freedom from ecclesiastical legalism and to rise above ritual structures, though never to deny them. The speaking with tongues is not a *sine qua non* amongst charismatics in the Roman Catholic Church, but the movement makes much of renewal and unstructured prayer. It is hardly surprising, since the movement raised its head in the Roman Church and was not decapitated, that it should also have appeared within Anglo-Catholicism. Anglo-Catholics themselves now have their own Catholic renewal movement and this has tended to divide those who accept it from those who reject it. The leading Anglo-Catholic priest concerned with the charismatic movement is Canon J. Gunstone (see Gunstone 1982). The movement in the Roman Catholic Church, and also in the Anglican Church as a whole, does not give a special place to occasions of renewal within public services, such as speaking with tongues and intensive group work. These practices have not become part of the Sunday liturgy. This is not the case in Pentecostalist churches. After a sudden appearance amongst Anglo-Catholics, the charismatic movement does not seem to be progressing at a rapid pace. It has more or less found its own level. But within the Church of England as a whole the movement is influential and, what is important to note for Anglo-Catholicism, it tends to break down denominational boundaries. Many charismatic gatherings will involve Evangelicals, Anglo-Catholics, and Anglicans in between, as well as Roman Catholics. Such a mix goes against the grain of traditional Anglo-Catholicism.

7 Divisions over moral teaching and practice

We have already had occasion to mention the great challenge to the morals and values of society made by young people in the late 1960s and early 1970s, which, in particular, was directed towards traditional sexual morality (ch. 8.5). Many clergy appeared to be sympathetic towards the movement, often undergirding aspects of it with theological notions. It was remarkable that some Anglo-Catholic clergy were found in their midst. Among them were those who openly declared their homosexual inclinations and practices. This swing towards a more open morality, in which long-standing sexual taboos were thrown to the winds, split Anglo-Catholics down the middle. It has divided those who wished to support traditional Christian teaching that every act of sexuality outside marriage is to some degree sinful from those who felt that, providing there was a basis of love in a relationship, sexuality could be practised between any two people without moral censure, and irrespective of the sex of those involved. The traditionalists readily found allies in the Evangelicals, who also formally upheld traditional Christian teaching on sexual morality. They also found themselves even more closely drawn to Roman Catholics, who at the official level never wavered from well established moral teaching. Nevertheless, as we have already had occasion to notice, a survey showed that over the question of the sinfulness of homosexual acts, the high church group showed itself to be relatively liberal (see ch. 8.5). But it was clear that they were very divided – about three-quarters taking the traditional moral line, and a quarter opting for the notion that homosexual acts could be moral under certain circumstances (see *Daily Telegraph*, 23 December 1987).

Another point which has proved highly divisive amongst Anglo-Catholics and has caused some to join the Roman Catholic Church is the remarriage of divorced persons in church. The issue was particularly acrimonious in 1983. With the great increase in the level of divorce, even amongst clergy themselves, the number of those who in all good conscience want to be remarried in church and feel themselves to be decent Christian folk has greatly increased. Pressure has therefore built up in the Church of England to allow divorced people to be remarried in church. The hypocrisy of suggesting that such people should be remarried in a Register Office and then have their marriage blessed in church, which is the current practice in the Anglican Church, has now come out into the open. The compromise is the worst, not the best, of all possible worlds. Some Anglo-Catholics have been horrified by the fact that bishops are prepared to allow priests to perform the remarriage of divorced persons in a church. On what grounds clergy should be allowed to do this, whether with the permission of the bishop or with that of some especially appointed committee, has been a matter of considerable controversy and unhappiness. The more liberal Anglo-Catholics are prepared to consider, of course with reluctance, such ceremonies: the more rigorous have strongly opposed the possibility. Hence there is a serious division in the ranks, serious enough to send some people off to join another church.

8 Coping with Vatican II

The Second Vatican Council was convened in 1962 and produced radical reforms, an *aggiornamento*, which was intended to bring the Roman Catholic Church up to date. In practice it has created a great feeling of freedom and openness and introduced measures and ideas which in many cases seem to be borrowed from traditional Protestant churches. This is what might be called the protestantization of the Church – an event which was totally unexpected, at least by those outside the Church. In England it had one very surprising outcome: it placed Anglo-Catholics in an extremely difficult position. As John Gunstone succinctly put it, as a result of Vatican II the compasses of Anglo-Catholics suddenly all went crazy (1968:196). The liturgical practices and cults of the Counter-Reformation, which Anglo-Papalists had so much admired and copied, now became *démodé*, even forbidden, overnight. And without a word of warning what had heretofore been considered sacred and inviolate was suddenly profaned or derided, even forgotten. The rigid structure of the Tridentine mass, which could be found throughout the world, was abandoned, and although Anglo-Papalists may not have copied it word for word (there were isolated cases where they did), that mass was seen to be an ideal which many Anglo-Catholics accepted and indeed attempted to translate into their own terms. Now it has been swept away overnight. In its place is a new structure, with variations, the use of the vernacular, and new musical settings and accompaniments. Above all, there has been a complete U-turn in the acceptance of Protestant ideas and customs, which has changed the mass into a simple and direct, homely and even folksy, gathering. Ever since Anglo-Catholicism emerged, an evening communion service was 'Protestant', unthinkable, and never to be found in churches of the Catholic revival. Yet today evening masses with communion freely distributed is found pretty well universally in Anglo-Catholic churches. There has been one reason for the change – the change in the Roman Catholic Church itelf. Similarly, Protestants are no longer seen to be heretics but separated brethren, who are not to be ridiculed (as Anglo-Catholics have been so successful in doing) but to be understood through the medium of dialogue.

Because Anglo-Catholics were far removed from what was going on in the Vatican they had no time to make a measured response to the lightning changes which were enacted – lightning at least by ecclesiastical standards. What were their reactions? When the pope relaxed the rules over fasting on Fridays, it is said that Fr Keet of St Clement's, Cambridge, wrote on the notice-board outside the church, 'We no longer pray for the Pope.' The story highlights the excruciatingly difficult position in which Anglo-Catholics found themselves. If, on the one hand, they continued to use the old forms, the Counter-Reformation cults and usages, the piety, the vestments, the distance the clergy separated themselves from their people, their anti-Protestantism, they would be accused of being reactionary, rigid, and failing to accept what Roman Catholics – at least the vast majority of them – saw as changes, not only of an authoritative kind, but desirable and indeed necessary for the renewed life of the Church. However, if Anglo-Catholics continued along the path which they had so uncritically chosen, they could at least claim a certain integrity, based on the notion that these rituals and forms had an intrinsic value and were related to some coherent principle. They stood by that principle. If, on the other hand, they readily accepted the changes of Vatican II, and without any hesitation abandoned old rituals and cultic forms in order to adopt the new, then it was apparent to all and sundry that this was but further evidence of the fact that Anglo-Catholics automatically followed whatever Rome directed. When the pope says jump, Anglo-Catholics jump and jump higher than anyone else! As a result of Vatican II they were in fact trapped in a catch-22 situation. Whichever way they turned they would be open to criticism. Were they to be like the Latin Mass Society, or the followers of Lefebvre in France, and be held up to ridicule as being backward-looking, rigid, reactionary, failing to move with the times? Anglo-Catholics once derided Tractarians as being antiquarian, now the tables might well be turned on them. But, if they decided to go along with the changes that Vatican II demanded, out would go, in all probability, incense, statues, rosaries, chasubles, birettas, kneeling, exposition, benediction, plainsong, high mass, and so on. The altar would have to be moved into the centre of the church so that the priest faced the people, lay people would take a much greater part in the service, wearing, not ecclesiastical garments, but their ordinary clothes, and they would be encouraged to give the peace to one another in the middle of the service. If Anglo-Catholics had the courage to take this path, they would once again be ridiculed as slavish imitators of all the Roman Church did. They were lackeys with no reason to be lackeys. How many Anglo-Catholic churches have taken one path or followed the other is impossible to assess. Those who favoured the Vatican changes were probably in a slight majority. But the situation was made even more complex by changes which were taking place within the Church of England itself.

As we have said, during the 1960s the Established Church at its most authoritative level decided to embark on a number of liturgical changes to the 1662 Prayer Book, which after a series of experiments led to the acceptance of the Alternative Service Book (ASB) of 1980. The changes which were eventually accepted were in many respects in keeping with those carried out by Vatican II. Nevertheless, they tended to divide hardline Anglo-Catholics. There were those who were delighted by what had transpired in so far as the new service book had incorporated a large number of Catholic ideas and practices, although by no means all of them. In this way it could be seen as a triumph for the Catholic wing in the Church. On the other hand, the more cautious preferred the 1662 Prayer Book as they felt that the changes in the ASB were in some respects Protestant, others wanted to keep the old Prayer Book on grounds of language, and others perhaps thought that changes did little good anyway. In most cases all these Anglo-Catholics rejected the changes of Vatican II. Another group decided to act more or less 'lawfully' and to follow the forms and variations set out in the ASB, although they continued to hold public services, such as benediction and exposition of the Blessed Sacrament, which were not found in the ASB. A third group, nearly all Anglo-Papalist, preferred the changes of Vatican II with some alterations, but these were quite minor (see ch. 6.3). The point is that the advent of Vatican II and the ASB created many groups and diversities amongst Anglo-Catholics, which, although it may not have produced much tension, has certainly undermined a sense of common purpose.

The overall result of the changes is that the church-goer can now experience a bewildering number of combinations for the mass based on parts of the 1662 Prayer Book, and, with their many variations, the ASB and the new Roman rite. Since Anglicans are not subject to the controls operating in the Roman Catholic Church, anything seems possible. Old types of vestments and furnishings are all combined with the new. Old word forms mingle with modern language. Nowhere in the Christian world can such variety be found as in Anglicanism, and nowhere in Anglicanism than amongst the Catholically inclined. All this is done, not in the name of individualism or Protestantism, but in the name of Catholicism!

9 A new threat: the ordination of women

It is a strange and ironic turn of events that the recent growing pressure to ordain women as priests in the Church of England has given to Anglo-Catholics a new impetus and that they have found themselves in alliance with those who could not in any way be called Anglo-Catholic, namely, certain Evangelicals. Set against this fact, however, is the threat that at the same time the issue has divided Anglo-Catholics between the more moderate and the more extreme. Anglo-Papalists and others fear, perhaps quite rightly, that the ordination of women will radically erode and finally eliminate any claim that the Church of England, or any church within the Anglican Communion, has for its Catholic character and heritage. No issue has emerged in the Church of England in recent decades which has been as divisive as the ordination of women. It threatens to split the Church of England and perhaps the Anglican Communion. The growing demand that women should be ordained as priests has certainly polarized the situation by producing cohesion where before there was none, and division where there was thought to be unity. Something of the dilemma is to be seen in the attitude of the *Church Times*, which has traditionally stood very close to the Catholic revival and still does so, and it is still very much a clerical paper. When the first woman, Miss Florence Li Timi Oi, was ordained during the Second World War in 1944 by the bishop of

Hong Kong, the editor of the newspaper at the time, the Rev G. L. Prestige, had no hesitation in labelling the bishop who had carried out the ordination as a 'bishop in insurrection who had found the wrong solution' (see *CT*, 3 February 1984). When the fortieth anniversary celebration of the event took place in Westminster Abbey, considerable coverage was given to it in the same *Church Times* and the editor, now a layman, received communion at the hands of the same ordained woman who had been virtually condemned by the earlier editor. Small wonder then that traditional Anglo-Catholics have felt betrayed by the newspaper which has been for so many years an influential mouthpiece of their movement. The dissatisfied have no alternative newspaper that can in any way rival the circulation and following of the *Church Times*. Needless to say a series of letters was subsequently printed in the newspaper condemning the service in Westminster Abbey.

This is no place to enter into the theological, sociological, and psychological arguments which might be put forward by those who would oppose the ordination of women. Perhaps the most widely accepted argument against such ordination is basically a pragmatic one and turns on the divisive effect that the ordination of women is likely to have within the Church of England itself and perhaps also on a worsening of relations between that church and the Church of Rome. It is a plea for holding back until the time is ripe and until loyal members of the Church of England show a greater willingness to accept women priests. In the early months of 1987 procedures were adopted by the General Synod of the Church of England to ordain women as deacons, which by most people is seen to be a first step along an inevitable path. Some Anglo-Papalists, not least those in the society called Ecclesia, hold that the ordination of women in the Church of England might mean the end of the efficacy of the sacraments (see *CT*, 11 September 1987). Most Anglo-Catholics are convinced that steps to ordain women to the priesthood will automatically bring to an end any hope for the reunification of Anglican and Roman Catholic churches. Letters from the pope to the archbishop of Canterbury published at the beginning of July 1986 would appear to confirm their worst fears. The possibility of a continuing Anglican Church consisting of those Anglo-Catholics and Anglo-Papalists and perhaps others who feel that Catholic order and sacraments will be jeopardized by the ordination of women has in fact itself divided Anglo-Catholics. Ecclesia, which supports a continuing Anglican church, has found itself being vigorously attacked by those whose support it thought it could rely on (see *CT*, 14 August 1987 for hostility centred on a sermon). The division, even amongst Anglo-Papalists, is all the more serious as some radical, open-minded Anglo-Catholics, rightly or wrongly, believe that in the end the Roman Catholic Church will come to accept the ordination of women. Certainly there is a very strong move within that church for such a change and certain liberal Roman Catholics have praised the Church of England for the steps it is now taking towards the ordination of women to the priesthood and inevitably the episcopacy. Nevertheless, high-church and Anglo-Catholic clergy are not unanimous in their objection to the ordination of women. A recent poll showed that about 30 per cent did not follow the 'anti' line (*Daily Telegraph* 23 December 1987).

10 Conclusion

The historical events discussed here have undermined the Anglo-Catholic party because they have been issues of division, which in most cases have cut clean across the old Catholic–Protestant lines on which Anglo-Catholicism was built. Using warfare terminology one might say that the movement has been outflanked and taken completely by surprise from behind. Neither the events themselves nor the responses had been predictable. What gave Anglo-Catholics a considerable degree of cohesion – a fairly unified system of belief, ritual, and ethics – and, at the same time, hope and enthusiasm, was that they were as a party dedicated to the catholicization of the Church of England. What had to be done was fairly clear-cut. Platitudinously one may say that times change – *autre temps, autre mœurs*. The old cliché that 'only in Catholicism is there hope', which had been so much the cry of Anglo-Catholic apologists before the war now seemed to make little sense within the parochialism of the movement. Changing religious and social ideas seemed to make all that Anglo-Catholicism stood for irrelevant. It is interesting that, in recent times, when Anglo-Catholicism was attacked intellectually, no theologian, scarcely anyone in fact, has come to its rescue. Wilkinson's article of 1978, 'Requiem for Anglo-Catholicism?', seemed to make no heckles rise. None had the stomach or heart to reply – all assurance as to what Catholicism is about, or wants to achieve, seems to have vanished. The 1930s, as we have shown, was totally different, with the publication of a great deal of fairly learned polemic. Anglo-Catholicism was worth fighting for.

Critics who had half their hearts in the Anglo-Catholic camp felt that, with its encrusted ideology, it was finished, at least as a party. The past must not be confused with the future. The achievements of bygone decades have indeed been incredible, although they were not without their seeds of destruction. To be sure they have not got reservation of the Sacrament in every church, but did they think they ever would (see ch. 2.7)? In many respects it might be argued that Anglo-Catholics have been remarkably successful. They have got what they wanted. They have been victorious in changing the texture of the Church of England, they are allowed to worship as they want to, they no longer have to fear bishops, courts, or mob violence. So one might conclude as an outsider that that is that: it all resides in the past. The present demands that one looks elsewhere: to other societies, other groups, other movements, which do not necessarily deny the basic tenets and practices of Anglo-Catholicism and at the same time seem to be concerned with more important issues. Above all, a mere slavish copying of the Roman Catholic Church, not least in the light of the tricks that it played at Vatican II, is to be shunned. Imitation gains little respect.

Thus the movement has given something to the Church of England, which has become part of it. It has deposited itself and transformed the Church, making it indeed comprehensive, though perhaps in a way not everyone has liked. But it has, as it were, left itself there. It has not developed or moved on. And so, almost in contradiction to the Roman Catholic Church, it now seems to present a kind of fossilization, which it is unable to bring to life because of its internal ambiguities which have been high-lighted in a changing and hostile world. Anglo-Catholics have for a long time played for safety above everything else. Thinking Anglicans, many of them much drawn to things Catholic, who might have been potential members of the movement in the 1920s and 1930s, have found that as time has proceeded it has not provided the modified aspirations with which they wished to be identified. To them it seemed that the same drum was being eternally beaten, no matter whether the audience heard it or not. To be sure one might point to the Christian imperative to preach the Gospel in season and out of season, to the many or to the few. That is the demand of the Gospel; it is also the demand of the church. To the more thinking clergy and laity, however, the imperative of the Gospel is not to be equated with an acclaimed imperative encased in a particular cultural form, which must one day give way to other forms as culture itself changes. The Gospel is not to be contained in a fossilized crust. Fossils have value only for museums.

But one must be careful about subjective evaluations of how some people see Anglo-Catholicism at the present time. The movement is by no means finished. It would be absurd, as we have indicated in the previous chapter, to suggest that, despite its abundance of ambiguities, people do not still cling to it. It may be that it is just a shadow of its former self but it is certainly not without followers. As we have suggested Anglo-Catholic clergy number about 2,000 and constitute a large proportion of younger clergy (ch. 4.2). Worshippers in their churches may also represent about a fifth or more of those who attend Anglican services on a Sunday. At the present time in the General Synod of the Church of England, they have a very powerful clerical lobby, well organized on account of the threat to them of the ordination of women.

The future of Anglo-Catholicism no one can predict. Much will depend on the emergence of events and on their interpretation. Its present weakened state may be reversed and a traditional Catholic form of Anglicanism grow; or it may become smaller still and increasingly sectarian. Most observers would opt for the second possibility. It is impossible to predict the future of religious institutions, not least because all religions display ambiguity. Traditional Anglo-Catholics ought to know this better than most.

Bibliography
(including abbreviations)

(t. signifies the date of the English translation. Where two dates are given, as in 1955/1964, the first date refers to the original edition, the second to a later edition. In references the page number which follows the second relates to that edition.)

Abbott, E. *et al.* (1947) *Catholicity*, London: Dacre Press.

ACC (1920) *Report of the Anglo-Catholic Congress, London, 1920*, London: Society for Promoting Christian Knowledge.

ACC (1923) *Report of the Anglo-Catholic Congress, London, 1923*, London: Society of SS Peter & Paul.

ACC (1927) *Report of the Anglo-Catholic Congress, London, 1927*, London: Society of SS Peter & Paul.

ACC (1930) *Report of the Anglo-Catholic Congress, London, 1930*, London: Church Literature Association.

ACC (1933) *Report of the Oxford Movement Centenary Congress, London, 1933*, London: Church Literature Association.

ACC (1948) *Report of the Sixth Anglo-Catholic Congress, London, 1948*, London: Dacre Press.

ACPC (1921) *Report of the First Anglo-Catholic Priests' Convention, 1921*, London: Society of SS Peter & Paul.

Adams, P.A. (1977) 'Converts to the Roman Catholic Church in England *c.* 1830–1870', unpublished D.Phil. thesis, University of Oxford.

Adderley, J. (1916) *In Slums and Society. Reminiscences of Old Friends*, London: Fisher Unwin.

Allier, R. (1925) *La Psychologie de la conversion chez les peuples non-civilisés*, 2 vols, Paris: Payot.

Almedingen, E.M. (1945) *Dom Bernard Clements. A Portrait*, London: Bodley Head.

Anderson-Morshead, A.E.M. and Blood, A.G. (3 vols. 1897, 1957, 1962) *The History of the Universities' Mission to Central Africa*, London: Universities' Mission to Central Africa.

'Anglo-Catholic' (n.d. 1881?) *A Reply to an Invitation 'Come and Join Us'*, London: Masters.

Anon. (1933) 'Editorial notes', *Blackfriars* (July):536–40.

Anson, P.F. (1955/1964) *The Call of the Cloister*, London: Society for Promoting Christian Knowledge.

Anson, P.F. (1960/1965) *Fashions in Church Furnishings 1840-1940*, London: Faith Press.

Archer, A. (1978) 'A sociological study of religious conversions, with special reference to conversion to Roman Catholicism in the area of Newcastle upon Tyne', unpublished MA thesis, University of Newcastle upon Tyne.

Archer, A. (1986) *The Two Catholic Churches. A Study in Oppresssion*, London: Student Christian Movement.

Baring-Gould, S. (1914) *The Church Revival. Thoughts Thereon and Reminiscences*, London: Methuen.

Beevor, H. (1934) *The Anglican Armoury*, London: Centenary Press.

Belton, F.G. (1936) *Ommanney of Sheffield*, London: Centenary Press.

Benson, R.H. (1913) *Confessions of a Convert*, London: Longman, Green.

Bernanos, G. (t.1937) *The Diary of a Country Priest*, London: Boriswood.

Biot, F. (t.1963) *The Rise of Protestant Monasticism*, Baltimore and Dublin: Helicon.

Bocock, R.J. (1973) 'Anglo-Catholic socialism: a study of a protest movement in a church', *Social Compass*, 20(1):31–48.

Booth, C. (1902) *Life and Labour of the People in London*, series 3, 17 vols, London: Macmillan.

Borlase, G.W. (1930) 'V.S.S. Coles', in J.F. Briscoe (ed.) *V.S.S. Coles, Letters, Papers, Addresses, Hymns and Verses, with a Memoir*, London: Mowbray.

Bowen, W.E. (1904) *Ritualism in the English Church*, London: Nisbet.

Brilioth, Y. (1934) *Three Lectures on Evangelicalism and the Oxford Movement*, London: Oxford University Press.

Briscoe, J.F. (ed.) (1930) *V.S.S. Coles, Letters, Papers, Addresses, Hymns and Verses, with a Memoir*, London: Mowbray.

Brown, H.M. (1980) *The Catholic Revival in Cornish Anglicanism*, privately published.

Burne, K.E. (1948) *The Life and Letters of Father Andrew S.D.C.*, London: Mowbray.

Butler P. (ed.) (1983) *Pusey Rediscovered*, London: Society for Promoting Christian Knowledge.

Calder-Marshall, A. (1962) *The Enthusiast: an Enquiry into the Life, Beliefs and Character of the Rev. Joseph Leycester Lyne alias, Fr. Ignatius O.S.B., Abbot of Elm Hill, Norwich, and Llanthony, Wales*, London: Faber & Faber.

Carpenter, S.C. (1949) *Winnington-Ingram*, London: Hodder & Stoughton.

Cecil, Lord H. *et al.* (1934) *Anglo-Catholicism Today*, London: Allen.

Chadwick, O. (1970) *The Victorian Church*, Part II, London: A. & C. Black.

Chadwick, O. (1983) *Newman*, Oxford: Oxford University Press.

Chapman, R. (1961) *Father Faber*, London: Burns & Oates.

Church Association (1900) *The Disruption of the Church of England by*

More than 9000 Clergymen who are Helping the Romeward Movement in the National Church, London: Church Association

Church Association (1902) 2nd edn of Church Association (1900).

Church Association (1903) 3rd edn of Church Association (1900).

Church Association (1908) 4th edn of Church Association (1900).

Clarke, C.P.S. (1932) *The Oxford Movement and Afterwards*, London: Mowbray.

Clarke, W.K.L. (1912) *Facing the Facts or an Englishman's Religion*, London: Nisbet.

Coulton, C.G. (1930–1) *Romanism and Truth*, 2 vols, London: Faith Press.

Cross, F.L. (1943) *Darwell Stone*, London: Dacre Press.

Crowther, M.A. (1970) *Church Embattled: Religious Controversy in Mid-Victorian England*, Newton Abbott: David & Charles.

CT, Church Times.

Currie, R. *et al.* (1977) *Churches and Churchgoers*, Oxford: Clarendon Press.

Dark, S. (1937) *Mackay of All Saints*, London: Centenary Press.

Dearmer, P. (1899) *The Parson's Handbook*, London: Oxford University Press.

Denis, Fr, SSF (1964) *Father Algy*, London: Hodder & Stoughton.

Dolling, R.R. (1896) *Ten Years in a Portsmouth Slum*, London: Swan Sonnenschein.

Donovan, M. (1933) *After the Tractarians*, London: Philip Alan.

Donovan, M. (1935) *The Faith of a Catholic. A Manual of Christian Instruction*, London: Faith Press.

Driberg, T. (1977) *Ruling Passions*, London: Cape.

Eaton, J.W. and Weil, R.J. (1955) *Culture and Mental Disorders*, Glencoe, Ill.: Free Press.

Ellsworth, L.E. (1982) *Charles Lowder*, London: Darton, Longman, & Todd.

Embry, J. (1931) *The Catholic Movement and the Society of the Holy Cross*, London: Faith Press.

English Church Union (1931) *The English Church Union Church Guide for Tourists and Others*, London: Mowbray.

Faber, G. (1933) *Oxford Apostles*, London: Faber & Faber.

Fairbairn, A.M. (1899) *Catholicism: Roman and Anglican*, London: Hodder & Stoughton.

Ferris, P. (1962) *The Church of England*, London: Gollancz.

Figgis, J.N. (1919) *Hopes for English Religion*, London: Longman.

Fitzgerald, P. (1977), *The Knox Brothers*, London: Macmillan.

Ford, C.S. and Beach F.A. (1952) *Patterns of Sexual Behaviour*, London: Eyre & Spottiswoode.

Fry, T.P. (1932) *The Church Surprising*, London: Cassell.

Fry, T.P. (1933) *Conversions to the Catholic Church*, London: Burns, Oates, & Washburn.

Fry, T.P. (1938) *The Making of a Layman*, London: Cassell.

Gallup (1986) *Gallup Survey of Church of England Clergymen*, London: General Synod of the Church of England.

Gladstone, W.E. (1878) 'The sixteenth century arraigned before the nineteenth. A study of the Reformation', *The Contemporary Review* 33:425–57.

Gore, C. (1889a/1905) *Roman Catholic Claims*, London: Longman, Green.

Gore, C. (ed.) (1889b) *Lux Mundi*, London: Murray.

Gorman, W.G. (1884) *Converts to Rome*, London: Swan Sonnenschein.

Gorman, W.G. (1899) *Converts to Rome, Since the Tractarian Movement to May 1899*, London: Swan Sonnenschein.

Gorman, W.G. (1910) *Converts to Rome*, London: Sands.

Gray, D. (1986) *Earth and Altar*, Norwich: Canterbury Press.

Gunstone, J. (1968) 'Catholics in the Church of England', in J. Wilkinson (ed.) *Catholic Anglicans Today*, London: Darton, Longman, & Todd.

Gunstone, J. (1982) *Pentecostal Anglicans*, London: Mowbray.

Hardman, O. (1958) *'But I am a Catholic!'*, London: Society for Promoting Christian Knowledge.

Harris, S.M. *et al.* (1933) Nine pamphlets, *The Church of England and the Holy See*. The Oxford Movement Centenary Tractates, London: Council for Promoting Catholic Unity/Talbot.

Harris, S.M. (1934) *The First Ten Years: the Witness of the Early Tractarians*, second series of *Tractates*, London: Council for Promoting Catholic Unity/Talbot.

Hastings, A. (1986) *A History of English Christianity 1920–1985*, London: Collins.

Hebert, A.G. (1935) *Liturgy and Society*, London: Faber & Faber.

Hebert, A.G. (ed.) (1937) *Parish Communion*, London: Society for Promoting Christian Knowledge.

Heeney, B. (1969) *Mission to the Middle Classes*, London: Society for Promoting Christian Knowledge.

Heitland, L. (ed.) (1903) *Ritualism in Town and Country*, London: Murray.

Hennock, E.P. (1981) 'The Anglo-Catholics and church extension in Victorian Brighton', in M.J. Kitch (ed.) *Studies in Sussex Church History*, Brighton: Leopard's Heart Press.

Henson, H.H. (1898) *Cui Bono?* London: Skeffington.

Higton, T. *et al.* (1987) *Sexuality and the Church*, Hawkwell, Essex: Action for Biblical Witness.

Hill, M. (1971) 'Religion and pornography', *Penthouse* 6(1):62–4.

Hilliard, D. (1982) 'Unenglish and unmanly: Anglo-Catholicism and homosexuality', *Victorian Studies*, 25(2):181–210.

Hughes, Dom Anselm (1961) *Rivers of the Flood*, London: Faith Press.

Humphreys, L. (1972) *Out of the Closets: the Sociology of Homosexual Liberation*, Englewood Cliffs, NJ: Prentice-Hall.

Ingram, K. (1936) *Basil Jellicoe*, London: Centenary Press.

Jacobin (1933) 'Observations', *Blackfriars* (July):540–4.

Jagger, P. (1978) *A History of the Parish and People Movement*, Leighton Buzzard: Faith Press.

Jones, P.d'A. (1968) *The Christian Socialist Revival 1877–1914*, Princeton, NJ: Princeton University Press.

Kaye-Smith, S. (1925) *Anglo-Catholicism*, London: Chapman & Hall.

Keast, H. (n.d. 1983?) *The Catholic Revival in Cornwall 1833–1983*, Stratton: Catholic Advisory Council for Cornwall.

Keast, H. (1984), *Our Lady in England*, Helston: Helston Printers for the Society of Mary.

Kelway, C. (1914) *The Story of the Catholic Revival*, London: Cope & Fenwick.

Kemp, E. (1954) *N.P. Williams*, London: Society for Promoting Christian Knowledge.

Kent, J. (1978) *Holding the Fort. Studies in Victorian Revivalism*, London: Epworth Press.

Kent, J. (1987) *The Unacceptable Face. The Modern Church in the Eyes of the Historian*, London: Student Christian Movement.

Kinsey, A., Pomeroy, W.B., and Martin, C.E. (1948) *Sexual Behavior in the Human Male*, Philadelphia and London: Saunders.

Kirk, K.E. (1937) *The Story of the Woodward Schools*, London: Hodder & Stoughton.

Knox, E.A. (1933) *The Tractarian Movement 1833–45*, London and New York: Putnam.

Knox, R.A. (1918) *A Spiritual Aeneid*, London: Burns Oates.

Knox, R.A. (1950) *Enthusiasm*, Oxford: Clarendon Press.

Knox, W.L. (1923) *The Catholic Movement in the Church of England*, London: Philip Alan.

Lacey T.A. (1926) *The Anglo-Catholic Faith*, London: Methuen.

Leech, K. and Williams R. (eds) (1983) *Essays Catholic and Radical*, London: Bowerdean.

Legg, J.W. (1914) *English Church Life from the Restoration to the Tractarian Movement*, London: Longman, Green.

Leslie, S. (1933) *The Oxford Movement 1833–1933*, London: Burns, Oates, & Washburn.

Littledale, R.F. (1878) 'Why Ritualists do not become Roman Catholics: a reply to the Abbé Martin', *Contemporary Review*, 33(Nov.):792.

Lloyd, R. (1946, 1950) *The Church of England in the Twentieth Century*, 2 vols, London, New York, and Toronto: Longman, Green.

Lloyd, R. (1966) *The Church of England 1900–1965*, London: Student Christian Movement.

Lowther Clarke, W.K., see Clarke, W.K.L.

Lunn, A. (1933) *Now I See*, London: Sheed & Ward.

Lunn, B. and Haselock, J. (1983) *Henry Joy Fynes-Clinton (1875–1959)*, London: Church Literature Association pamphlet.

Lyon, D. (1983) 'Arthur Penty's post-industrial Utopia', *World Future Society Bulletin* Jan./Feb.:7–14.

Mackenzie, C. (1922) *The Altar Steps*, London: Cassell.

Mackenzie, C. (1923) *The Parson's Progress*, London: Cassell.

Mackenzie, C. (1924) *The Heavenly Ladder*, London: Cassell.

Mackenzie, K.D. (1931) *Anglo-Catholic Ideals*, London: Student Christian Movement.

McLeod, H. (1974) *Class and Religion in the Late Victorian City*, London: Croom Helm.

Martin, Abbé (1878a) 'What hinders the Ritualists from becoming Roman Catholics?' *Contemporary Review* 33(Aug.):113–36.

Martin, Abbé (1878b) 'What hinders Ritualists from becoming Roman Catholics. A rejoinder', *Contemporary Review* 34(Dec.):77–107.

Mary, Sr Felicity SPB. (1968) *Mother Millicent of the Will of God*, Stoke-on-Trent: Webberley.

Mascall, E.L. (1959) *Pi in the High*, London. 1984 edition, Worthing: Churchman Publishing.

Maughan, H.H. (1916) *The Leslie Dialogues*, London: Cope & Fenwick.

Maughan, H.H. (1922) *Some Brighton Churches*, London: Faith Press.

Maughan, H.H. (1947) *Seven Churches*, Hove: Coelian Press.

Mauss, M. (1935) 'Les Techniques du corps', *Journal de psychologie normal et pathologique* 32:271–93. (English translation by B. Brewster (1973) 'Techniques of the body', *Economy and Society* 2(1):70–88.)

May, J.L. (1933) *The Oxford Movement*, London: Bodley Head.

Maynard-Smith, H. (1926) *Frank, Bishop of Zanzibar*, London: Society for Promoting Christian Knowledge.

Mayor, S. (1967) *Churches and the Labour Movement*, London: Independent Press.

Morgan, E.R. (ed.) (1928) *Essays Catholic and Missionary*, London: Society for Promoting Christian Knowledge.

Morse-Boycott, D. (n.d. 1947?) *They Shine Like Stars*, London: Skeffington.

Mudie Smith, R., see Smith, R.M.

Munson, J.E.B. (1975) 'The Oxford movement by the end of the nineteenth century: the Anglo-Catholic clergy', *Church History* 44:382–95.

Musgrove, F. (1977) *Margins of the Mind*, London: Methuen.

Nias, J. (1961) *Flame from an Oxford Cloister*, London: Faith Press.

ODCC, Oxford Dictionary of the Christian Church.

Oraison, M. (t.1977) *The Homosexual Question*, London: Search Press.

Orchard, W.E. (1933) *From Faith to Faith*, London: Putnam.

Orens, J. (1983) 'Priesthood and prophecy: the development of Anglo-Catholic socialism', in K. Leech and R. Williams (eds) *Essays Catholic and Radical*, London: Bowerdean, pp. 158–80.

Paul, L. (1964) *The Deployment and Payment of the Clergy*, London: Church Information Office.

Penhale, F. (1986) *Catholics in Crisis*, Oxford: Mowbray.

Pickering, W.S.F. (1967) 'The 1851 religious census: a useless experiment?' *British Journal of Sociology* 18(4):382–407.

Pickering, W.S.F. (1972) 'Abraham Hume (1814–1884). A forgotten pioneer in religious sociology', *Archives de sociologie des religions* 33:33–48.

Pickering, W.S.F. (1977) 'Hutterites and problems of persistence and social control in religious communities', *Archives de sciences sociales des religions* 44(1):75–92.

Pickering, W.S.F. (1980) 'Theodicy and social theory', in D. Martin, J.O. Mills and W.S.F. Pickering (eds) *Sociology and Theology*, Brighton: Harvester.

Pickering, W.S.F. (1981) 'The development of the diocese of Newcastle', in W.S.F. Pickering (ed.) *A Social History of the Diocese of Newcastle 1882–1982*, Stocksfield and London: Oriel Press.

Pickering, W.S.F. (1984) *Durkheim's Sociology of Religion: Themes and Theories*, London, Boston, Melbourne and Henley: Routledge & Kegan Paul.

Pickering, W.S.F. (1986) 'Mission et conversion dans l'anglo-catholicisme: buts, concepts et résultats', in C. d'Haussy (ed.), *Evangelisation et missions en Grande Bretagne*, Paris: Didier-Erudition.

Pickering, W.S.F. (1987) 'The one and the many', *New Blackfriars* 68(2) (Feb.):56–72.

Pickering, W.S.F. (1988a) 'The development and functions of religious institutes in the Anglican Communion' (forthcoming).

Pickering, W.S.F. (1988b) 'Sociology of Anglicanism', in S.W. Sykes and J.E. Booty (eds), *The Study of Anglicanism*, London and Philadelphia: Society for Promoting Christian Knowledge and Fortress.

Pinnington, J. (1983) 'Rubric and spirit: a diagnostic reading of Tractarian worship', in K. Leech and R. Williams (eds) *Essays Catholic and Radical*, London: Bowerdean, pp. 94–130.

Plummer, K. (1975) *Sexual Stigma*, London and Boston: Routledge & Kegan Paul.

Poynter, J.W. (1932) 'The Church of England as seen by a former Roman Catholic', *The Modern Churchman* 22(Dec.):501–10.

Purcell, W. (1957) *Onward Christian Soldier*, London: Longman, Green.

Pym, B. (1952) *Excellent Women*, London: Cape.

Rawlinson, G.C. (1924) *An Anglo-Catholic's Thoughts on Religion*, London: Longman, Green.

Reynolds, M. (1965) *Martyr to Ritualism: Father Mackonochie of St. Alban's, Holborn*, London: Faber & Faber.

Roberts, G.B. (1895) *The History of the English Church Union 1859–1894*, London: Church Printing Company.

Rowell, G. (1983) *The Vision Glorious*, Oxford: Oxford University Press.

Rowell G. (ed.) (1986) *Tradition Renewed: the Oxford Movement Conference Papers*, London: Darton, Longman, & Todd.

Rowell, G. and Cobb, P. (eds) (1983) *Revolution by Tradition*, Cambridge: James Clarke.

Royal Commission on Ecclesiastical Discipline (RCED) (1906) *Report*, London: HMSO.

Russell, G.W.E. (1902) *The Household of Faith, Portraits and Essays*, London: Hodder & Stoughton.

Russell, G.W.E. (1913) *St. Alban, the Martyr, a History of Fifty Years*, London: George Allen.

Russell, G.W.E. (1917) *Arthur Stanton. A Memoir*, London: Longman, Green.

Salmon, G. (1888) *The Infallibility of the Church*, London: Murray.

Selwyn, E.G. (ed.) (1926) *Essays Catholic and Critical*, London: Society for Promoting Christian Knowledge.

Simpson, W.J.S. (1909) *Roman Catholic Opposition to Papal Infallibility*, London: Murray.

Simpson, W.J.S. (1932) *The History of the Anglo-Catholic Revival from 1845*, London: Allen & Unwin.

Slesser, H. (1952) *The Anglican Dilemma*, London: Hutchinson.

Smith, R.M. (ed.) (1904) *The Religious Life of London*, London: Hodder & Stoughton.

SOED, Shorter Oxford English Dictionary.

Sparrow Simpson, W.J., see Simpson, W.J.S.

Spencer, A.E.C.W. (1975) 'Demography of Catholicism', *The Month* (April II):100–5.

Stephenson, C. (1972) *Merrily on High*, London: Darton, Longman, & Todd.

Stephenson, G. (1936) *Edward Stuart Talbot 1844–1934*, London: Society for Promoting Christian Knowledge.

Stevens, T.P. (1943) *Father Adderley*, London: Werner Laurie.

Stewart, H.L. (1929) *A Century of Anglo-Catholicism*, London and Toronto: Dent.

Stone, D. (1926) *The Faith of an English Catholic*, London: Longman, Green.

Stone, D. (1928) *The Prayer Book Measure and the Deposited Book*, London: Longman, Green.

Sutcliffe, T. (1973) 'Husbands of Christ', *Spectator*, 5 May, p. 553.

Symonds, J.A. (1984) *The Memoirs of John Addington Symonds*, London: Hutchinson.

Thornton, L.S. (1941) *The Common Life in the Body of Christ*, London: Dacre Press.

Troeltsch, E. (t.1931) *The Social Teaching of the Christian Churches*, London: Allen & Unwin.

Trott, S. (1983) *Charles Fuge Lowder*, London: Church Literature Association.

Vidler, A.R. (1977) *Scenes from a Clerical Life*, London: Collins.

Voll, D. (t.1963) *Catholic Evangelicalism*, London: Faith Press.

Walke, B. (1935) *Twenty Years at St. Hilary*, London: Methuen.

Walsh, W. (1897) *The Secret History of the Oxford Movement*, London: Swan Sonnenschein.

Walsh, W. (1900) *The Ritualists, Their Romanizing Objects and Work*, London: Nisbet.

Wand, J.W.C. (ed.) (1948) *The Anglican Communion. A Survey*, London: Oxford University Press.

Waugh, E. (1945) *Brideshead Revisited*, London: Chapman & Hall.
Waugh, E. (1959) *Ronald Knox*, London: Chapman & Hall.
Webb, C.C.J. (1928) *Religious Thought in the Oxford Movement*, London: Society for Promoting Christian Knowledge.
Weber, M. (t.1930) *The Protestant Ethic and the Spirit of Capitalism*, London: Allen & Unwin.
Webling, A.F. (1931) *Something Beyond. A Life Story*, Cambridge: Cambridge University Press.
Weeks, J. (1977) *Coming Out*, London: Quartet.
Westwood, G. (1960) *A Minority. A Report on the Life of the Male Homosexual in Great Britain*, London: Longman.
Wilkinson, A. (1978a) *The Church of England and the First World War*, London: Society for Promoting Christian Knowledge.
Wilkinson, A. (1978b) 'Requiem for Anglo-Catholicism?' *Theology* 81:40–5.
Wilkinson, A. (1988) 'Three sexual issues', *Theology* 91:122–31.
Wilkinson, J. (ed.) (1968) *Catholic Anglicans Today*, London: Darton, Longman, & Todd.
Williams, H. (1982) *Some Day I'll Find You*, London: Beazley.
Williams, N.P. and Harris, C. (eds) (1933) *Northern Catholicism*, London: Society for Promoting Christian Knowledge.
Williamson, H. Ross (1956) *The Walled Garden*, London: Michael Joseph.
Williamson, J. (1963) *Father Joe*, New York and Nashville: Abingdon Press.
Wilson, A.N. (1978) *Unguarded Hours*, London: Secker & Warburg.
Wilson, H.A. (1940) *Received with Thanks*, London and Oxford: Mowbray.
Yates, W.N. (1975) *The Oxford Movement and Parish Life*, Borthwick Papers No. 48, York: University of York.
Yates, W.N. (1983) '"Bells and Smells"; London, Brighton and South Coast Religion reconsidered', *Southern History* 5:122–52.

Name index

Subject index

Alcuin Club 91
Alternative Service Book *see*
  Prayer Book
ambiguity, in general 1–12, 141,
  234, 256
Anglican, Anglican Church *see*
  Church of England
Anglo-Catholic: clergy in general
  98, 114–16, *see also* slums;
  congresses 29, 48–64, 96–8,
  248–52; devotional literature 39,
  see also Anglo-Catholic
  spirituality; humour 169;
  language 165–9; praise of
  Roman Catholicism 27–31,
  223–31; schools and colleges
  134–5; social and political theory
  132–4; spirituality 39, 127–9, *see
  also* Mary; theologians 12, 124;
  worship 15–17, 34, 125–9,
  256–8, 262–5
Anglo-Catholicism: its
  achievements 2, 88–137, 212,
  reasons for 135–7; aims 10–11,
  24–31, 41; a British
  phenomenon 222; a clerical
  movement 97; conservative
  156–60; decline of 64, 246–56, in
  churches and attendances 252–6;
  defined and outlined 15–40;
  demography, class and
  geographical distributions
  95–117, *see also* slums;
  dissenting attitudes 169–76, *see
  also* clergy marginality; doctrinal
  emphasis 121–5; evangelical

streak 65–87; future 267–9;
  history 1–2, 41–4, 118–19,
  246–67, *see also* Anglo-Catholic
  congresses; its nature 15–40
  (especially 22–4, 31–4);
  sectarian 163–83; statistics
  88–95; tensions within 34–9,
  256–69; and the working class
  117, *see also* Anglo-Catholicism,
  demography; slums
Anglo-Papalism 120, 144, 178–9,
  250; defined 28–40; examples of
  155; *see also* Anglo-Catholicism
Association for Promoting the
  Unity of Christendom 178, 180

bishops, problems with 57–9, 91,
  120, 212, 237; ambiguities over
  148–56
branch theory 145–7
Brotherhood of the Ascension 86

Caroline divines 11, 18–19
Catholic, ambiguity over word
  142–6, 166
Catholic League 24, 30
change, ambiguity over 156–60
charismatic movement 260
Church Association 43, 89–94
Church congresses 49–50
Church of England: adhesion to it
  234–45; its Catholic nature,
  comprehensiveness 119–20,
  146–7, 231, 242; cynicism about
  it 243–5; its essential
  Englishness 171; losses to

284